Aesthetics and the Art of Living in the Zagros Mountains of Iran

Aesthetics and the Art of Living in the Zagros Mountains of Iran

Erika Friedl

EDINBURGH
University Press

Edinburgh University Press is one of the leading university presses in the UK. We publish academic books and journals in our selected subject areas across the humanities and social sciences, combining cutting-edge scholarship with high editorial and production values to produce academic works of lasting importance. For more information visit our website: edinburghuniversitypress.com

© Erika Friedl, 2024, 2026

Edinburgh University Press Ltd
13 Infirmary Street
Edinburgh EH1 1LT

First published in hardback by Edinburgh University Press 2024

Typeset in 11/15 EB Garamond by
Cheshire Typesetting Ltd, Cuddington, Cheshire,
printed and bound by CPI Group UK Ltd,
Croydon, CR0 4YY

A CIP record for this book is available from the British Library

ISBN 978 1 3995 3673 8 (hardback)
ISBN 978 1 3995 3674 5 (paperback)
ISBN 978 1 3995 3675 2 (webready PDF)
ISBN 978 1 3995 3676 9 (epub)

The right of Erika Friedl to be identified as author of this work has been asserted in accordance with the Copyright, Designs and Patents Act 1988 and the Copyright and Related Rights Regulations 2003 (SI No. 2498).

Contents

Note on Language and Transliteration   vii
Map of Kohgiluye-and-Boir Ahmad   viii
Preface: Earthquakes, Demonstrations, 'Tribe'   ix

Introduction: Purpose, Place, Residence, Methodology   1
    Purpose   1
    The Place   1
    Our Residence   10
    Assumptions and Methodology   12

1   Art and Aesthetics   18
    Art in the Mountains   18
    Local Aesthetics   28

2   The Senses are Friends   36
    Introduction: Senses, Knowledge and Progress   36
    Sight and Eye   39
    Hearing and Ear   47
    Smell and Taste   53
    Touch-Feeling   62

3   Aesthetics of God's Order   67
    Introduction: Necessity, Benefits, Contradictions   67
    Beauty   68
    Work   78
    Time   88

4	The Flair of Kith and Kin	104
	Introduction: People need People	104
	Kin Group Aesthetics	105
	Small Group Aesthetics: Comfort and Discontent	107
	Kin Terms: Structure, Behaviour, Emotions	109
	The Ambient of Marriage: Necessity and Emotions	118
	Inheritance: Tradition, Ethics and Modernity	131
5	The Aesthetics of Needs	139
	Introduction: The Logic of Life	139
	Animals	140
	Humans	144
	Character and Personality	153
6	Reason, Logic and the Good Life	163
	Introduction: What Ought to Be and What Is	163
	Reason and Intellect	163
	Common Sense	167
	Truths and Lies	171
	Vernacular Logic	174
7	Useful Religion (*din*)	186
	Introduction: Local Islam and Canonical Authority	186
	Religion is Good	187
	God Must Exist	189
	Why Things Happen	191
	Saints who Listen	194
	Islam as Guidance	197
8	Shapes of Things to Come	203
	Introduction: Choices and Consequences	203
	Education and Emigration	204
	Birth Rate and Work	205
	Marriage and Singles	206
	Religion	210
Notes		213
Bibliography		233
Index		252

Note on Language and Transliteration

Local people in the province of Kohgiluye-and-Boir Ahmad in southwest Iran speak dialects of Luri, an unwritten Persian language. In public schools they learn Farsi, the official lingua franca language of Iran, and thus many people are bilingual now. Neither language has a term for aesthetics. Art has no Luri term, and people who talk about art now use Farsi *honar* and *fani*, both related to crafts (and also to mystery). I am quite aware that in this book I am using concepts alien to the culture I am describing, and I see this as a problem for ethnography in general: we try to cover local people's ways of speaking, feeling and acting with our own concepts. Science is hegemonic.

Local people as well as Farsi-speakers find it difficult to write or read Luri in Farsi script, which is based on Arabic, and therefore many prefer to use the Latin alphabet (*'inglisi'*) when they want to write Luri words. In the text I limit quotes to key concepts and phrases, writing them with slightly modified letters: *ā* is close to the vowel in English 'law'; *i* is as in 'big'; *ou* as in 'low'; *u* as in 'good'; *gh* is a soft guttural sound between 'g' and 'r'; *z* as in 'haze'; *č* as in 'child'; *kh* as in Scottish 'loch'.

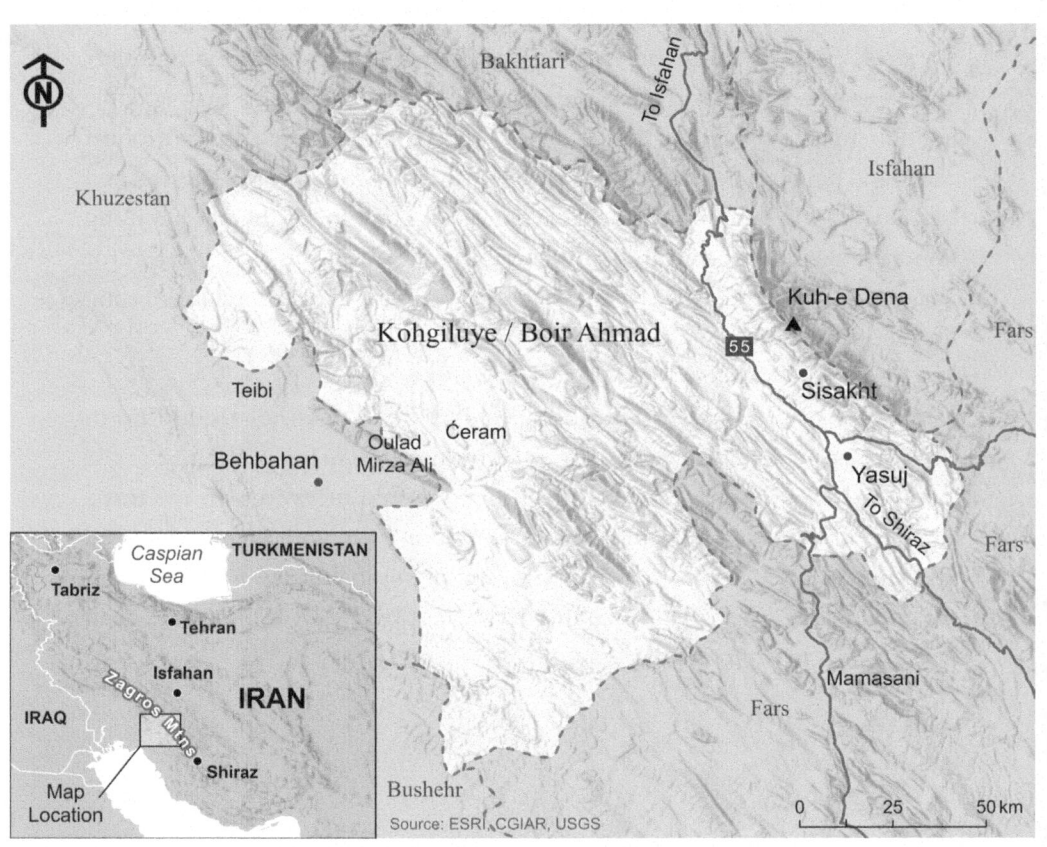

Map of Kohgiluye-and-Boir Ahmad

Preface: Earthquakes, Demonstrations, 'Tribe'

Earthquakes

On 17 February 2021, a 5.6 magnitude earthquake shook the small town of Sisakht high up in the Zagros mountains of Iran. Nobody was killed but some people were injured, several more decided to leave, and those who stayed had to brave snow and cold in the damaged houses.

However, despite devastation, tears and derailed livelihoods, the spirit of the place is alive, people say. Soon after the shock, a local merchant joked that by destroying the old houses God was forcing people to build a better town; a neighbour of ours, the moment she stopped sobbing, said, 'Now I finally will get a proper bathroom'; a local family's expatriate children discussed on the telephone with their parents and siblings in town plans for rebuilding the house; and a farmer declared that God obviously had not wanted people to die, which meant that everybody had to say thanks and get to work. Two years later, 'everybody' was, indeed, working hard to build new houses, to 'modernise their lives', as they say, paying for it with loans and by selling fields for development. The town is alive and growing.

Demonstrations

The 'Women, Freedom, Life' demonstrations shaking cities in Iran in 2022/23 were less intense in the hinterland but they were disruptive there, too. In town the unrest resulted in arrests and the punishment of protesters by security forces. These events deeply upset local people who assume that authoritarian measures are necessary for orderly life, yet chafe against authoritarian relationships in the family and with the government. People insist that they are a lot more concerned with their economic difficulties than with the government's 'useless rules'. Young women show disregard by doffing scarves and mantles, 'just like city-women', as one reported – until the next governmental crackdown in the form of the 'Hejab-law' in 2023 changed this mode of defiance again. Civil disobedience has become a popular choice in dealing with authorities.

'Tribe'

There used to be several tribal areas in the province (and elsewhere in Iran) with their own names, ethnic identities, languages, leadership and political histories. They consisted of patrilineally organised groups and sub-groups (*tāife*) headed by autocratic khans and sub-tribal chiefs. In terms of identity and politics in Kohgiluye-and-Boir Ahmad, tribal affiliation has lost its importance and has been replaced by people's ethnic and linguistic assignation ('Lur' in our case) in the multi-ethnic modern state, but the traditional tribal names are still known and used to place people and to refer to land ownership even where chiefs no longer wield political power. I use 'tribe' in historical contexts and when local people make a point of their former tribal identity.

I thank Professor Tapper and my editor, Emma Stone, for discussing the issue with me. For a recent use of 'tribal', see Hole and Amanolahi-Baharvand 2021 ('Baharvand' is the name of a 'tribal' unit in Lurestan from where Professor Amanolahi-Baharvand hails).

Introduction:
Purpose, Place, Residence, Methodology

Purpose

The main theme for the book, lifeways and aesthetics, is based on the observation that quality of life plays out within the aesthetic parameters of day-to-day happenings.[1] Based on data and insights gained during my several years of living as an anthropologist in a Lur 'tribal' province in Iran between 1964 and 2015, the text provides a cultural backdrop to these happenings in an ethnography of aesthetics, that is, of local assumptions about the art of living, of choices and habits people have relied on and created over half a century. With this focus I wish to contribute to the understanding of the lifeways of people at the margins of comfort and development in Iran beyond psychology or a particular social science theory. In paying close attention to people's commentaries on their own culture, on reflections on their lives and those of others, my observations and insights contribute to ethnographic knowledge on the culture-as-lived level where people's emotions, hopes and wants reflect, re-work and transcend socio-political and economic conditions of the day.

The Place

History and Memory

Archaeologists and historians suggest, and people vaguely remember, that in the eighteenth century transhumant agro-pastoral groups were moving across the southeastern flanks and hills of the high Zagros range in southwestern Iran, in what is now the province of Kohgiluye-and-Boir Ahmad with over 700,000 inhabitants. These were mostly kin-based groups, variously called 'tribes, nomads, tent dwellers' – *tāife, ashāyer, ćadorneshin* in Persian – or else simply '*Lur*', an ethnic and linguistic entity.[2] Most used to live in black goat-hair tents which are easy to transport, in brush-and-reed huts quickly built when needed, and in small stone-and-mud houses where they stayed in various locations on their migrations through the seasons. Steep mountain slopes and valleys were covered with light oak forests and provided game and edible wild plants that augmented agricultural products. However, these landscapes were difficult to transverse and arable only with intense labour, and eight generations later people talk about these difficulties.[3]

Many conditions in the karstic landscape that had marked life throughout the millennia, such as good sources of water, strong seasonal differences and native edible flora remain today. The earliest inhabitants were hunter-gatherers following migrating herds of game such as gazelles and wild sheep and goats through the different ecological zones. Until the mid-twentieth century, hunting partridges and ungulates, and gathering plants and fruits remained important sources of food for local people. (Koelz 1983, describes the area's lush environment around 1945.) These animals and the hunter's rifle remain tropes for masculine strength and beauty to this day, although hardly anybody has a gun or is allowed to hunt now. There is evidence that agro-pastoral use of the ecological niches with herd animals and early agriculture (mainly pulses, barley and millet) had co-existed with hunting in the Zagros mountains since the pre-pottery Neolithic period. The seasonal migratory lifeways put limits on transported goods, encouraged ways to minimise costs in time and energy, and fostered the opportunistic use of local raw material, be it convenient stones casually knapped for tools, caves for shelter or anything edible. We observed vestiges of these skills in the 1960s.

Beyond these general circumstances, little is known about past populations in the area. Oral histories, place names and sparse written notes point to mostly Persian inhabitants who spoke variants of Luri, a Persian language (in contrast to neighbouring Turkish and Arabic groups). Archaeologists and local people assume that no single ethnic group developed in place in the area but that different units were moving around there. Homo itinerans, the 'wandering human' (Monsutti 2020), fits the pattern of dislocations, emigrations and migrations of small-scale population movements in the Zagros area. The most recent sets of transhumant pastoralists consisted of patrilineally organised, small groups including immigrants from as far away as the Gulf areas to the southwest and the central Zagros region to the northwest. The groups were mostly named after their founders (*Oulad Mirza Ali*, 'Descendants of Mirza Ali') or a location (*Tinada*, 'Mulberry Place'; *Sisakhti*) and most of these names are used to this day.

In Boir Ahmad there are archaeological remains of villages along a river, of a silver mine in the northwestern part of the province and of Sasanian settlements. The Safavid dynasty (1502–1736) maintained some control and influence over feuding local tribal groups and secured a trade route from the Persian Gulf to cities on the Iranian Plateau through what today is called Kohgiluye-and-Boir Ahmad. Customs and ideas from refined Persian urban cultures dribbled in from the outside, followed by a slowly rising stream of features of modernity since the 1920s and a flood of intense Shia Islamic ideologies and practices of the Islamic government since the 1980s (for the history of the region, see R. Loeffler 1989; Friedl and R. Loeffler 2013).

For as long as people can remember, a paramount tribal chief, a khan, kept some order among unruly local sub-tribal, patrilineal kin groups in the area and represented them vis-à-vis outsiders and the central government, which off and on tried to take control of the 'wild tribesmen in the mountains', as they were called in Iran. For centuries, the kaleidoscopic pattern of coming and going of tough, fierce people gave the area the reputation of a wild, inaccessible and dangerous hinterland marked by rivers, rocks and reckless robbers, and to this day people there are a bit proud of this aesthetic facet in their identity. Even the famously dauntless British explorers skirted the area in the nineteenth century. Anecdotes from that time (Schulze-Holthus 1944)[4] as well as contemporary ones speak to this self-image. Here is my summary of the one about 'Shirali' (literally, 'Lion-Ali'):

> Young, strong Shirali, a fine sword in his belt, had to take a bag with gold to a khan of Boir Ahmad. In the woods near Sisakht he met a man who offered him protection against robbers, and they walked on together. When they rested at an oak tree, the robber asked to see the beautiful sword, and as soon as he had it, he threatened Shirali and demanded the bag. Shirali handed it over and said, 'The khan will call me a coward when I tell him how I lost

the gold. You have to cut off my hand so that he will believe that I put up a fight.' He put his arm on the trunk of the tree, but when the robber swung the sword Shirali quickly dropped the arm, the sharp sword was stuck in the tree, and he jumped the robber and strangled him with his bare hands.

Most people had a hard-scrabble existence at best, though, and in addition suffered much strife and fighting as chiefs vied for power and territory and casualties prompted blood revenge killings. By all accounts, including those in songs and proverbs, life was difficult and people rarely were comfortable. The harsh conditions selected for an aesthetic of violence, for robust, aggressive men valorising war and guns, and for markedly androcentric values and behaviour that appear in song lyrics to this day in a mixture of denial, disapproval and pride.[5] Without exception, people in what now is the town of Sisakht take themselves to be better, more progress-oriented and cultured than the 'wild thieves and robbers' elsewhere in the province, and, given their schools, orchards and eager acceptance of new skills and opportunities, they have a point. Yet people also talk of their own raiding expeditions in the past, of skirmishes with other groups, and of hostilities and fights among neighbours. This is neither beautiful nor good, they say, but difficult to avoid, given how flawed human nature is especially among Lurs, and how poor they were.[6]

The Town of Sisakht

Around 1880 the transhumant people in a semi-permanent hamlet situated to the southeast of craggy Dena Mountain in the eastern Zagros range were running out of water, land and game. Blocked in to the south, west and east by settlements and other transhumant tribal groups, they choose to extend their habitable zone north into their summer pastures on the rock-strew high plain called 'Sisakht' at the foot of the snow-laden flanks of the mountain range. (The local explanation for the name is 'Thirty-in-difficulties', referring to a story of thirty brave men who perished there in the deep snow.) The place gave the inhabitants the name: Sisakhti. Present-day Sisakhtis claim that the area had been no-man's land with remnants of ancient water channels, ruins, graves and re-wilded grapes and fruit trees that some long-gone people had left behind. They planted walnut and apricot trees to mark property claims, and poplars along water channels. An open-air cult place, remembered as a 'shrine' (Imamzadeh or *pir*) until a generation ago, was located at a small spring near an ancient east–west road crossing the plateau. In 2006, officials at the Provincial Antiquities Service agreed with Donald Whitcomb of the University of Chicago who earlier had identified remnants of a Sasanian town there on satellite photographs. *Ćagei*, the name of an ancient hamlet on the plain, means 'Cowpit' and local people explain it with their memory of a 'very old' ritual of cattle sacrifice that fits Langer's 2004 descriptions of Zoroastrian rituals.

Camel caravans of the neighbouring Turkish-speaking Qashqa'i still transport salt to markets from a salt mine high above Sisakht. People recall that several times in the past Qashqa'i herders had tried unsuccessfully to take over pastures around Sisakht, and that the new settlers furthermore had fought and driven away intruders and small clusters of an earlier Lur tribal group, the Nuï. This violent part of Sisakht's history is clouded by embarrassment, denial and filtered memories.[7] History as told by the conquerors is rarely fair to the conquered, an amateur historian in Sisakht said, and locally it remains an ethical and aesthetic problem: to this day, the southernmost part of the plain, the old Nuï area, is said to be a vaguely dangerous, jinn-plagued, 'bad' place, and people avoid it.

The early experiment in making a living where snow and wild animals endangered people and their sheep and goats, and recurrent droughts threatened survival, was successful.[8] The village attracted and lost people from its very beginning. Newcomers came in search of land; local men with too little land to survive left, as did those who fled inter-tribal and intra-family violence. More recently, local people have left for jobs and education, and others come to town from small villages in the province for the same reason.

The new settlers used every niche in the rocky environment for fields of barley, wheat, legumes and, later, poppies,[9] for pastures, for gathering edible plants and for hunting (with bows and arrows, later with guns) the abundant game allowed as food in Islam and also any animals that posed a threat. Within fifty years they had killed nearly all the wildlife, their herds had degraded the brittle pastures, and they had burned the surrounding woods for firewood and for clearing fields. (In the absence of saws and power tools, burning trees at the roots and then smashing them were used to clear fields and get wood.) 'People are like locusts,' said a local teacher in 2015 about the denuded hills.

When Mohammed Reza Shah disarmed the tribes in the mid-1960s, little was left of the local fauna besides wild boars, hyenas and other animals prohibited by Islamic food laws.

In 2008, the area became the Dena Protected Area. Hunting was licensed and felled native trees such as oaks and plantains have to be replaced with 'useful' fruit trees. By then, most people were burning gas instead of wood and pursued non-agricultural occupations, which helped flora and wildlife. Poaching became a problem, though: game counts as especially savoury food, and restaurant chefs in big cities pay good money for it. The aesthetic value of nature has shifted from providing a livelihood to relaxation and enjoyment for local people as well as urban tourists. People expect that this trend will continue after the recent disruptions caused by the earthquake, Covid-19 and political upheavals.

Politics

It was taken for granted that the 'chief', the leader (called *khan* and *kadkhodā*)[10] of the small group, represented the new settlement in dealings with neighbours, other tribal groups, the paramount khan and government officials. In the 1920s, Sisakht's famous chief Qobād Nikeqbāl reportedly rode on horseback 'a thousand kilometres' to Tehran to petition Reza Shah for a government teacher because in Sisakht the only way to acquire literacy was in occasional Quran classes for boys. Public, secular education meant 'good progress' in Sisakht already then. (The link is weaker in other provincial towns but strong throughout Iran; see *Iran Digest* 2022.) For his services people supported him with food and labour. Some of his heirs, though, demanded ever more services in a power-and-privilege spiral of taxation, and adopted despotic aspirations and conspicuous displays of wealth and status such as fortified dwellings, gardens, horses, women and other aesthetic hallmarks of power.[11]

The Sisakhtis soon protested, arguing that they were tribesmen (*ashāyer*) not peasants, and that the chiefs had no title to the communal land. However, for the shah's authorities 'tribal' transhumant Lurs were peasants working for a landlord, and the misery of subsistence farming and inter-tribal warring continued until the Land Reform (1962–79), when a government supporter assassinated the rebellious paramount khan of Boir Ahmad in 1963. This weakened all chiefs, and eventually local men could buy titles to their land.

The deals impoverished the former tribal chiefs, but soon the fields no longer afforded a liveable income for many Sisakht residents either because of the rapidly increasing population and the traditional inheritance law that accords all brothers equal shares of their father's land. By the 1970s, for most families fields had become too small to feed them. But by then other means of making a living in Iran's modernising, oil-driven economy had become available, and the enterprising and progress-oriented people of Sisakht used them.

Development and 'Progress' (pishraft)

The earliest houses were built of stone and mud-bricks with flat dirt roofs, and grouped around courtyards. (People remember the entrance to houses via a ladder through a hole in the roof of some dwellings 'in the earliest days'.) The village was well-administered and well-defended and attracted newcomers from the greater area. By 2015, having integrated surrounding hamlets it had grown to a small town of over 6,000 people, and had become the county seat of newly formed Dena County. It has an agricultural college, several schools, a bank, a public health clinic and private physicians, pharmacies, a beauty parlour and a barber shop, craftsmen (including a seamstress), a jewellery shop and two 'women's stores' run by women, restaurants, a lively bazaar, two mosques and a government-sponsored public hall, several apartment buildings, modern houses with indoor plumbing, a few old mud-brick houses in the old courtyards, several big, sleek 'Gulf-style' villas in gardens, tourists, and two coffee shops for young men. The 'best' villas belong to prosperous professionals from Sisakht living in cities and turning land in their ancestors' famed place into a vacation paradise in the tradition of adapting urban aesthetics to enhance their own prestige.[12] Their '*shik*' admired lifestyles became models for the emerging local middle class.

Following the earthquake in 2021, the government's development plans for rebuilding the town reportedly necessitated the razing of a third of the town's damaged houses and a collapsed hotel that a government agency had just built on public land for tourists from the Gulf. Two years later the town is 'one big construction project', as a visitor reported. Socio-economic developments, real estate speculation and house building drive up the price of land. By about 2005 only a couple of families lived off agriculture, and small orchards providing income in addition to salaries and wages are being sold for development. This is declared to be a pity and a necessity. The sales provide some income but people also rely on loans, support from the government and from charities 'to make it', as they say. High unemployment, inflation and corruption make life difficult, and several decades of untenably high lifestyle ambitions leave people frustrated, unhappy and angry (R. Loeffler 2011).[13] Of the few options people have for explaining the ever-widening, worrisome split between the wealthy and everybody else, the most popular is what most describe as the ideologically rigid and economically inept revolutionary government. It has made many people 'poor, unhappy and ugly', a banker in Sisakht declared in 2019, and a popular saying reminds mullahs 'to look after souls, not the economy'.[14]

As difficulties mount and memories of earlier toil and hardships recede, nostalgia colours the past, but despite worries, debts and many shortcomings Sisakht is a good place, people say. Coping with the lack of good jobs and rising inflation in everything from food to building material, Sisakht's people are reconstituting their lives, expanding the town, and between grumblings and complaints show cautious optimism: 'We'll see what happens' ('*tā binim će iābu*'), and 'We'll see what God wants' ('*tā binim khodā će ikhā*'), and 'We have to agree to it and will deal with it' ('*basi besāsim*')[15] are much-used final words in talks about the future. They amount to philosophical statements, implying that 'whatever we meet, we shall cope'.

Local Religion

How and when Shia Islam came to the area nobody knows for sure. The present inhabitants claim they have 'always' been good Muslims, adhering to Islam's tenets that tradition and occasional interactions with preachers made important. These tenets are said to provide the cornerstone of ethics to this day, they are quintessential aesthetic features (Ammerman 2021: 122–58, discusses religious aesthetics in general). Several settlements in Boir Ahmad have a sizeable population of Seyeds, that is, purported patrilineal descendants of the Prophet Muhammad. Literate men among them offered Quran lessons in the past and performed lifecycle rituals while travelling throughout the area, collecting gifts and religious taxes. Itinerant dervishes who disseminated religious wisdom and wrote amulets received alms from local people, and theatre performers spread legends among paying spectators. 'Religion always was connected to money,' observed a local amateur historian. Sufi lore was popular.[16] People say that they received most of their religious knowledge from those informal sources and from their own traditions. A lively cult of dead saints flourished around shrines dating back to pre-Islamic times. 'Saints' in this context include buried Seyeds as well as charismatic men and some women and pre-Islamic deities, all known for their purported efficacy in helping people who petition them properly.[17]

Within living memory people placed their rituals, philosophical tenets, aesthetic principles and family traditions within Islam: 'good' or 'bad', useful or out of tune with local habits – everything was Islam. The choices local people see for dealing with everyday existential and transcendental matters are rooted in pre-Islamic cosmologies and ethics on the one hand, and in quite different but equally well-rooted canons of Islam on the other, all tempered by scepticism based on people's own, experience-based knowledge of how things work: trial-and-error-based examination (*emtehān*) trumps doctrine. 'Good' and 'bad', the most-used frame for aesthetic judgements, are deeply rooted in experience. Locally, *din* (religion) is comprehensive, but Islamic authorities insist on firm boundaries around the 'correct' Islam, and thus differences between orthodoxy and heterodoxy become amplified. Orthodox puritan theology provides only one choice for piety.

The local life philosophy includes pre-Islamic notions of a world where strong and valiant people can control evil, dark forces and can choose to make the world a good place, a pre-cursor to paradise. 'Paradise starts in this world', people often say when discussing somebody's well-deserved success. This is in contrast to the equally important Abrahamic tradition that presents the world as a tough, often painful place that needs redemption from a saviour. Until then evil, darkness and ignorance make it hard for people to follow the order to be 'good', and death is a day of reckoning, the moment when a person's moral weight will determine punishment and reward in the afterlife (Hutter 1993). Local vernacular philosophies include both views, allowing people to choose from both sides as they see fit. The habitual use of the wide umbrella term 'Islam' for all their moral and ethical tenets is an easy choice.

Furthermore, neo-Islamic ideas (Wright 2015) are merging with local sensibilities in the rural middle class. Doubts about Iran's post-revolutionary Shia Islam is provoked by disillusionment with the Islamic government's brand of

Shia doctrines, its economic inefficiency and heavy-handed puritanism, as a recent survey of Iranians' attitudes as well as the anti-government demonstrations suggest.[18] But despite the Islamic leadership's many shortcomings and an increase of epistemological scepticism by local doubters and agnostics, being a Shia Muslim continues to be a matter of identity and is generally declared to be good, beautiful and reasonable by critics, doubters and the pious. The popular choice to explain the glaring difference one can see between 'good' Islam and the not-so-good behaviours and customs of individual Muslims is to take bad behaviour as a function of people's own personal shortcomings rather than as a shortcoming of Islam. Critics, though, deplore a high rate of unrest among Muslims generally and conclude from discussions of news on the media that 'Muslims are quarrelsome (*gelavis*).' Despite the problems, believers, critics and doubters alike take *din* to be a sturdy aesthetic frame enclosing local philosophies, traditions and Islamic doctrines. It is a powerful, popular concept.

Accounts of rural life in Iran tend to overlook signs of people's personal beliefs and rituals: scholars take 'religion' to be official Islam.[19] In Sisakht, the Islamic government's intended disruptions of local pieties did not bring about a widespread quest for theological knowledge such as is reported from other areas where missionaries changed people's lives profoundly (Robbins 2019). Rather, globalisation of ideas and lifestyles together with governmental missionary efforts are modifying local rituals and religious routines towards urban aesthetics and patterns, which local people are wont to call 'progressive': modern religious buildings and activities have aesthetic merits because they are 'modern and beautiful'. However, the same people also comment on culture loss. Like hegemonic movements generally, 'government Islam' standardises religious life and devalues traditional practices, aesthetics and philosophies; it creates differences between orthodox and heterodox beliefs and practices that earlier did not exist in Sisakht.[20]

Our Residence

Reinhold Loeffler, '*aghāye* (Mr) Hans', and I, '*khānom*' (Madam) or '*khānom* Hans' first came to Sisakht as anthropologists with a toddler daughter in 1965, just after bloody fights between khans and the shah's soldiers had ended in the province. It was difficult to get permission to visit the troubled area then and in the subsequent fourteen visits (for me, the last in 2015), and we deeply thank many friends, colleagues and government administrators for their assistance in obtaining permits and for facilitating our independence and research integrity.[21] We ascribe our success to their help and to our two patient and supportive daughters whose language facility, interests and local engagements became invaluable for us in Sisakht; to our polite tenacity, tireless lobbying in Tehran, openness about our work, a naïve lack of fear, much talking and good luck. Still, it was time-consuming to work around bureaucratic difficulties. For generous shelter, a congenial atmosphere and encouragement during difficult times we thank our families and friends in Europe as well as the Austrian Cultural Institute and the German, British and American Archaeological Institutes in Tehran. Special thanks for help with questions go to my colleagues and friends Dr Hana Azizi, Nushāferin Boir Ahmedi, Dr Mary Hegland, Elaine Jayne, Dr Max Klimburg, Dr Agnes Korn, Ela Mehr and Golrokh Pakpaz. Our most heartfelt gratitude goes to our hosts and neighbours in Boir Ahmad who accepted us with understanding, interest, support and generosity. Men and women alike were curious about us and the world 'out there': 'What have you seen, what have you heard?' is a standard, jovial greeting for visiting travellers. We heard it often – to be a conduit for information and change is an unavoidable feature of fieldwork.[22] Despite our different looks and behaviour we were accepted as part of the local landscape to the extent that in 2006, after a prayer session at the local girls' high school Hans had photographed, the girls threw governmental school modesty in the wind and swamped him for autographs. Considering how difficult and limiting ethnographic fieldwork can be in Iran beyond getting permits and access, I greatly appreciate the relative ease with which we and our two children could live and work in Boir Ahmad.[23]

In terms of comfort, the early visits were difficult for lack of amenities such as water, electricity, roads and food. Dealing with cramped quarters, infections, parasites and slow travel over cumbersome and dangerous tracks was the price we paid for having free access everywhere in the province with our own transport and without supervision. Various secret police informers assembled thick folders about us. These supported us before and after the Revolution of 1979, and the governors and the police mostly treated us as bona fide academics. For us, Sisakht and the people in the hills and hollows of wider Boir Ahmad were congenial, and with few exceptions were our staunch supporters when occasionally authorities were overbearing.

Our link with Sisakht was known throughout the province and made us 'familiar strangers' nearly everywhere. It diffused sticky situations. When Hans and a daughter in a remote valley met some unexpectedly unfriendly men, Hans kept talking, and after they realised our connection to Sisakht they decided that we 'belonged' rather than being friendless strangers, and the encounter ended on good terms. (Later we heard that they were robbers who allegedly had stripped a geologist working in the mountains a few months earlier. True or false, the story illustrates our position.) Another memory involves a new young policeman in the provincial capital who sternly sent me back to Sisakht to fetch my forgotten car papers. Returning three hours later I found him the butt of jokes at the police station for having asked 'Mrs Hans' about identity papers. A third example for such support regards the high-status widow of a local former chief who vouched for us when a hostile police officer, an outsider, balked at accepting the permits we had brought with us from Tehran.

We paid for our needs and for services (but never for information) like any other outsider, but our tangible thanks for the hospitality and support we received in Iran are our publications. Local people keep reminding us to this day that our fifty-year-long cooperation, the looking and listening and mutual curiosity about 'everything', and the books and articles that came of it got them 'on the map and into books' and make them feel appreciated. Several of our publications were translated in Iran and circulate there.[24]

Assumptions and Methodology

Assumptions

The ability for aesthetic appreciation is pre-human and pan-human.[25] We can safely assume it for all cultures, expressed in diverse local forms and criteria for evaluation of appearances and experiences. Yet precious few archaeological and ethnographic sources in the Zagros area document local people's aesthetic leanings. Power and its corollary, wealth, appear as aesthetic markers in rock reliefs of past empires in the area, but local contemporary transhumant farmers have little in common with these bygone times, arts and mores. While busloads of tourists now visit the Parthian relief at Tang-e Servak in southeast Boir Ahmad, for example, local people pay little attention to 'this old king'.[26] Royal traditions influenced the aspirations and lifeways of some powerful, wealthy local khans of the past, yet little is known about how hard-working, poor ordinary people appraise the ambient of their habits or aesthetic aspects of their surroundings and possessions, and even less is known about what they thought of their personal experiences and moral considerations. Matters such as beauty or wellbeing or good conduct are rarely documented in ethnographies,[27] and we know little about people's feelings and everyday routines, or how tastes change under the influence of enlightenment ideas in the 'epistemic domination of modernity' (Ahmad 2021; 2022).

Yet much can be inferred about the manifold aspects of aesthetics of an unassuming, small-scale, transhumant rural group of people in the Persian mountains when one focuses on everyday quiet practices and people's comments, using a phenomenological, experience-driven outlook.[28] Interest in 'practice' in the social sciences became popular with Bourdieu 1977; 1990. By the time McGuire's influential work on 'lived religion' appeared, that is, on religion as practiced (McGuire 2008; also called 'religion from inside'; Plichta 2023), people's suppositions behind their beliefs were acknowledged by social scientists, but most scholars working in Muslim areas nevertheless continue to take laws and rituals of a generalised Islam or those proclaimed by local religious authorities as the defining elements in Muslims' lives. Jeldtoft (2011: 1134) warns of reifying Muslims as being 'all about Islam' when the focus of inquiry is on 'institutionalized forms of Islam'.[29]

While living in Sisakht on and off for years, I got to know many people and their different ways of looking at things. This made working with broad terms such as 'tribal culture' impractical and led me to look carefully at the various ways lives are lived and experienced, and at people's philosophical tenets that endure in their habits and language, in oral literature, and in values and criteria for judging behaviour. Unlike one-time fieldwork that produces a fairly realistic ethnographic present in publications, the great variety in the ways that people make sense of their lives and the changes I witnessed over the years were a methodological and linguistic challenge because terms such as 'traditional' and 'modern' were losing substance.

The widespread assumption of anthropologists, including myself, that to notice creativity one ought to look for unique art creations, worked to my disadvantage because I realised late that focusing on aesthetics rather than on artistic creativity brings a wealth of insights into what moves people, and serves well when applied to mundane issues of everyday life. Caring about tastes, ethics, emotions and criteria for 'beauty' was not 'in' during our professional heydays, and after a short period of ethno-scientific interest in such matters (such as Heider 2011) it is not now a pressing subject either. Neither are semiotics, ethics and life philosophies popular issues now, although they form the bases for theories of culture and for people's identity.[30] Reading my fieldnotes spanning fifty years, I nevertheless found a wealth of information on topics ranging from the art of keeping chickens or sawing a board to the art of reading the Quran, of children building tiny mud-forts, of people telling funny stories, of being a good grandmother or uncle, of expressing feelings.[31] Vernacular aesthetics permeates local life and is a key to understanding how people see themselves and approach the world.

Methodology

Luckily, many local people took to my preferred methodology of paying attention to small things that leads to such insights. They talked about their concerns du jour to me and among themselves in my presence, and about their experiences and opinions with only little input from me by way of questions or suggestions. I avoid questionnaires with their built-in biases, thematic preferences and the danger of overfitting, and rely instead on long-standing personal rapport with local ways of life that affords insights into people's options for living and into the reasons for making their choices.[32]

Translators were not available. I learned Luri and vernacular Farsi well enough to keep up with conversations and to honour the insight that words acquire various meanings while being used in daily interactions, especially those pertaining to ethics and value judgements. For clarification of issues I gratefully accepted – and keep accepting – help from friends and neighbours in town. My partners became my teachers, and I thank them deeply for their patience. Although I associated mostly with women, men talked to me freely, too, especially younger ones who have known me since they were children. People's willingness to talk about what moved them, and their trust in my discretion were key to my overall success with this projective methodology. Names in this text are generic, and details given about particular people are vague on purpose. Direct quotes and anecdotal examples express choices available in town and are backed by many similar incidents. My husband concentrated on different issues and used a different style of fieldwork. I am gratefully using here what I learned from his insights and from the notes and memories of our children (A. Loeffler 2008; R. Loeffler and K. Loeffler 2022).

Research methodology and focus were based on several assumptions:

- Writing ethnography is writing history. Anything we observe and hear is gone while it happens. This makes the construction of a 'culture' possible only in broad strokes that level diversity and change. I am painfully aware of this problem, having intermittently been coping with variety and changes in this place over a span of half a century. My occasional switch in the text between past and present tense reflects the pickle I am in, but people's own sense of change helps: people talk about what was and no longer is pertinent; what was and still is around and how it may be in the future, and I try to capture this flow, sometimes ignoring good grammar.
- Every culture provides choices for beliefs and behaviours. The many available choices rarely point to just one compelling decision. People pick and choose from a range of habits and ideas they consider appropriate, common-sensical or fitting their circumstances. Even people who oppose or despise certain options or hold a minority opinion recognise other options as possible; they understand them and select even 'bad' ones if need be. Rather than inventing a common local culture, I watch for the choices, for personal opinions, for comments on habits and customs, for judgements.[33]
- In the communities we met in the Zagros mountains permanent art creations are rare. Yet, as human aesthetic universals, imagination, appreciation ideas, skills, colours, talk, and judging good and bad, well and uncomfortable, joy and pain form many aesthetic frames and scales for evaluation of most aspects of life. Criteria such as good/bad, proper/improper, useful/not useful, beautiful/ugly apply to cooking food and dealing with authority, to evaluating behaviour, sights, sounds, taste and feelings as well as to ploughing a field and constructing poems and religious tenets. Thus, even in small groups with few resources and little artistic activity, variegated choices for thinking and acting have aesthetic markers, and many of those are tied to ethics and to local philosophies of life.
- People express their aesthetic leanings in language (including poetry, storytelling, humour and body language), in talking with each other about their

surroundings, about what makes them feel good or bad; in their songs and anecdotes, comments and asides, and in how they react to their own and others' looks and behaviours. People 'read' each other and I 'read' and appreciate the wide view these observations afford for recognising local ways of experiencing the world, time and tradition.[34] In order to keep local people's voices alive and to illustrate my observations, occasionally I quote their comments, jokes and short anecdotes as well as local professionals' opinions.

- Certain circumstances (see Anderson 1990) encourage particular forms of creative expression and aesthetic criteria in social groups, which are shared, copied and developed further. Most are based on the five senses, traditional skills, available material and time. The institutions of a modernising state encourage individuation and secularisation. These offer new identities and aesthetics in many features of local existence: choices for skills, behaviours and ideas grow fast with outside contacts.[35] What used to be a small, partly settled transhumant group in the Zagros mountains three generations ago is now a town open to many possibilities for living, and 'tribe' has become a minor option among several others for perceiving identity.

- Ethnographic fieldwork being an interdependent endeavour, the anthropologist's personality inevitably affects people's opinions and behaviour, as do personal histories and the socio-political conditions of the day. They constitute 'ethnographic realism' (Narotzky 2007). Locally I am known as a quiet, private, discrete person who listens well but is not especially entertaining (in contrast to my husband, whose bon mots are remembered to this day). Mostly I interact with people as a foreign visitor who likes to hear what they have to say about any topic they choose, occasionally asking questions that encourage them to teach me and to elaborate on their opinions and experiences. I consider it futile to try to be 'one of them', and this was appreciated in town and helped me to learn and observe openly.[36] My kind of humour fits the local tendency to quick self-deprecation, and some of my mistakes and mild jokes endured and established me as an 'understanding' person. To prove a hostess right who assured her guests that I really liked the simple rice/lentil dish she served, I ate so much that she turned it into a funny story of me bursting that never died. People also found me a bit innocent in this dangerous world and tried to take care of me occasionally with advice and offers of assistance. Once on a long evening drive from Shiraz back up the mountains to Sisakht a gendarme stopped me just at the provincial border and was beside himself finding me driving alone at night. I had to promise him to keep the car doors locked and to phone his station upon my safe arrival in Sisakht, which he clearly doubted. And several friends insisted on feeding me with their own food 'to get me back on my feet sooner' when I was a patient in the district hospital. The assumptions behind these anecdotes together with my status as a sympathetic academic foreigner marked my persona and influenced my projective research methodology in every encounter.

1

Art and Aesthetics

Art in the Mountains

Art as we know it is hard to find in 'low-culture' Boir Ahmad, even if we concentrate on the term's core features of representation, symbolic meaning and decoration. The term has a high-culture and historically circumscribed origin and use, and the connections between art appreciation and Enlightenment values make the term an ill-fit for so-called traditional, non-Western creative expressions as well as as for 'popular' art.[1]

Limitations of 'Art'

Three limitations are relevant here. The first lies in the history of the concept 'art'. As an European Enlightenment project, art was meant to establish a natural foundation for morality and to help people transcend their selfish inclinations.[2] The promotion of ethics is hardly a professional goal for scientists, though (Grote 2017), and the scientific push towards 'objectivity' leads to neglecting the experiences and personal feelings of the creator, user and observer of creative work. Arguably, attention to the subjectivity of people (Bourdieu 1977: 42), to their habituated tastes and practices is better suited for the appreciation of people's creative efforts. In the daily business of living, the practices also include various non-scientific ways of knowing, judging and reasoning. Dismissing these on principle as unscientific is unhelpful for understanding people and points to unexplored assumptions in echo chambers, be they of scholars or theologians or art critics.[3]

A second relevant culture–historical burden is in 'high' Art's many symbolic uses especially of death and decay. In Boir Ahmad, old, worn things have no practical and thus no symbolic and aesthetic value. A cracked teapot, a broken shovel, a split bread-board are carefully mended so as to be made usable again, but they are not an illustration of the resilience of the human spirit or the fleeting existence of earthly goods: the mended things are flawed now and their days are numbered. (For contrast see the Japanese aesthetic in turning repairs into philosophical–aesthetic statements by accentuating mended cracks with gold or colourful glues, or to see perfection as dull (Kemske 2021).) Locally, ruins are places abandoned by humans and thus likely hang-outs for dangerous jinn rather than a poetic commentary on the transience of life, and wilted flowers are simply fodder for a goat. Only recently, in fleeting moments of hindsight, has the pastoral–nomadic life taken on a beautiful tinge of nostalgia especially in the families of former chiefs. But even in watercolour paintings by a few anonymous, untrained artists in the 1970s, 'beauty' lies in the detailed, realistic depiction of customs and skills that make a well-ordered transhumant life pleasing to watch: everything works and everybody knows what to do and how to do it; it is representational.[4]

The third limit in the use of 'art' in our case is in Islamic Art generally. It is linked to religion as well as to Muslim Middle Eastern 'high' culture, which is so different from pastoral life that Burckhardt (2009: 7) was moved to state about the earliest Muslims that 'Nascent Islam knew no art in the proper sense', given the 'stark simplicity' of the nomadic life with its concentration on 'vital needs' (see also Anderson 1990). This was applicable to Boir Ahmad until the mid-twentieth century. Indeed, the only few sketches I have ever seen by local men (only men), were of bovids, the emblematic herding and game animals, and of partridges, an equally emblematic game bird for hunters. Islam's aniconic bent discourages realistic depictions of humans, animals and perspective: landscapes in Persian miniatures have no shadows, perspective or three-dimensionality. Furthermore, Persian/Muslim aesthetics favour the art of calligraphy and architecture, both irrelevant for illiterate, transhumant farmers, and makes the appreciation of Persian miniatures quite complicated and controversial for them (see Burckhardt 2009: 29–42).[5] Finally, since the eighteenth century Middle Eastern art has suffered – or benefited, depending on the commercial and political interests of the speaker – from Western interests in 'Oriental Art'. Persian rugs in Europe, for example, soon reflected European tastes which the manufacturers in Persia recognised and accommodated.[6]

Local creativity cannot be found in such durable intentional art endeavours, but is in evidence in oral creations that have permanence in people's memories and are kept alive by being performed again and again in stories and anecdotes, jokes, poking fun at others and oneself, proverbs, clever comebacks, homespun poems, and in a vast amount of tales and songs floating in people's minds. This wealth of poetry has been shrinking since radio, television and the Internet have provided endless new stories but the appreciation of oral performances of any kind has endured.[7]

As far as Boir Ahmad is concerned, such art discussions are mostly of academic interest. Hardly anybody in Boir Ahmad made – or makes – visual art for the sake of art, neither for themselves nor for tourists. The few local drawings feature animals that are aesthetic motifs by being good food; recently, a local man made a few sketches of antelopes and of men with guns in traditional garb, motivated by nostalgia for a beautiful, vanished life, as he said. Local bazaars offer the choice for people to buy domestic decorations such as prints of Japanese and Alpine landscapes, and some people import mosaics from urban workshops depicting nature scenes to adorn their walls. Photography and video recordings ignore religious prohibitions against the representation of people and stay in the aesthetic realism mode, whether the object be a beautiful bride or a famous mullah, a meadow in bloom or a young man leaning nonchalantly against a car to impress his fiancée. Propaganda for government leaders and the Iran–Iraq War furthermore allowed 'revolutionary art' with human figures and symbolic content in posters, photographs and murals.[8]

Changes in grave-art, too, illustrate ideological and political influences on aesthetics. Until the 1970s, depictions of horses, goats and partridges and of hunters with rifles appeared on local grave stones as indicators of a man's social standing (Demant-Mortensen 2010 also documented them in Lurestan Province). A few parallel engraved lines standing for a loom identified the grave as a woman's (these were the oldest fully symbolic lines I have seen there). When progress ideas became popular this status-marking grave-art disappeared, and since the Revolution of 1979 grave-art favours calligraphic Quran verses engraved on stones and cement covers, but also photographs and other decorations especially on graves of fallen soldiers. Such depictions vacate the taboo on human representation in post-revolutionary, political aesthetics.

Indeed, the more elaborate and expensive grave decorations are, the more beautiful they are declared to be.

Creativity and Crafts

Although anthropologists acknowledge creativity as a human universal in all cultures and as favoured by evolution (Anderson 1990, 1992; Brown 1991; Dutton 2010), manifestations of creativity pose problems for them: 'art' is a cultural, commercial and academic category that is difficult to apply cross-culturally and backward in time. We are not routinely trained to look for art in places where the commonly applied criteria for artistic creations are absent: 'folk art' belongs to folklore, to the fringes of the social sciences, while tools and useful material objects, no matter how well-crafted, pleasing and popular, are treated as 'materialities' in museums. To my great regret and consternation I do not have a photograph of a woman making the only traditional local toy for little girls, a stick-doll. And even if these items get squeezed into 'art', as in 'Non-western art' or 'Art in Small-Scale Societies' (Anderson 1988), the terms are loaded with increasingly problematic burdens of 'othering'.[9]

Yet the etymological roots of 'art' link it to crafts and to skills applied to usable things, a link that lives on in the 'Arts and Crafts' movement and in 'applied art' and 'artisan' (Blakeslee 2006). This helps anthropologists a little because it allows them to put well-turned artefacts of any kind into the art bin without qualms as long as their aesthetic qualities are widely appreciated locally and appeal to some people outside. Furthermore, symbolic importance and a viewer's imagination may transfigure any commonplace thing into 'art' (Danto 1984). Thus, while the Sisakht village council bulldozed the 'dirty' garbage dump to hide it from the visiting governor, at the same time Leddy 2011 managed to turn a junkyard into an aesthetic adventure.

European artists in the early twentieth century derived creative impulses from the strange 'primitive art' outside Europe.[10] The many superb illustrations in Fraser's 1962 book show that by the mid-twentieth century the art world was attuned to 'exotic beauty' just as this beauty was on the verge of mass appeal and commercialisation in the West. Fraser, however, included information on what the spectacular objects and their decorations represent, mean and are used for beyond 'beauty', thus widening the objects' aesthetic significance. In his classic *The Traditional Arts and Crafts of Persia*, Wulff

1966, united the two aesthetic aspects of form and meanings explicitly. Derek 2013, added to them the emotions and aesthetic pleasures that objects elicit in people who see and use them.

The wealth of skills, motifs, colours and symbols we see in the material culture of many non-western societies is unthinkable in austere Boir Ahmad. There, people draw no firm boundaries between mere objects (mostly unadorned at that) and those that aspire to be beautiful, as long as they are of use. Favourite, pleasing things simply are 'good' (*khub*), the single most important quality term in the local vocabulary: they are good to use, good to have, good to look at. These are the important criteria. In 2004, a young man who had 'learned to like old things', as he said, pressed into my hand a well-carved, well-used wooden slider for keeping tent ropes taut because his grandfather had sold the tent planes and now 'this beautiful thing' would end in the fireplace unless I took it to a museum (I did). His – and others' – opinion about conservation in museums is in sharp contrast to the growing sentiment among scholars in the West against such collections (see, for example, www.decolonizingmuseums.com). For local people, museums, especially those in Europe, count as safe places for preserving artefacts with historical value. A physician from Sisakht took his family all the way to Austria to see the collection of traditional Boir Ahmad artefacts we had deposited at the World Museum in Vienna,[11] saying, 'Nowhere in Iran would I be able to find our own history; nobody there cares.'

Meanwhile a small museum has opened in the provincial capital, concentrating on 'big, good' things such as rugs and tents. A farmer in Sisakht who found a Bronze Age arrowhead in his field called it a 'useless old thing' to be thrown away, while on the Internet such arrowheads are for sale as 'Lurestan art'. A cache of faded blueish beads a plough unearthed in a local field was discarded by the farmer's womenfolk because unlike 'good' beads used to ward off jinn and the evil eye, these blue beads had lost most of their colour and thus most of their apotropaic power, usefulness and aesthetic value. An exquisite flask that a worker at a building site in the river valley south of Sisakht found in 2002 – likely of Sasanian origin – for him was a money maker: 'The Arabs in Kuwait buy such things and put them in their houses and then say they are their own history', he said, grinning and shaking his head. The local culture is pre-ceramic, and shards of coarse ceramic vessels that appear in ploughed fields in many locations in Boir Ahmad are thrown away; a rare intact bowl will be put to good use by the finder as a salt container, for example. And a huge ceramic grain vessel, unearthed at an unknown site in Boir Ahmad and standing near a road for many years, had by 2014 disappeared 'into a rich man's collection in the Gulf', according to a local man.

Although the inhabitants of the province are Persian by identity, language and religion, their creative expressions are not at all comparable with those of 'high' Persian culture, and they have difficulties relating to urban Persian art.[12] When we first visited, five generations back, few people could read or write and even fewer could 'read' a traditional Persian mosaic or illustrations in children's school books. This has changed but not to the point that people will now paint illustrations for books or make colourful tile pictures. My attempt to administer a short, modified Rorschach Test (Zulliger 1969) in the village in 1981 was short-lived because of people's inability to 'see' anything at all in the panels. They were not representational and thus the drawings were meaningless. At most they elicited scant, tentative comments on minute details. The big picture, which individuals would have had to construct in their minds from the inkblots was beyond their imagination: the blotches were 'nothing', they said, confusing and unattractive, and they asked me politely what in the world they were supposed to be.

Tools, Things and Skills

Transhumant–pastoral people with a long history of living near the edge of basic subsistence may be expected to have few creative productions that involve special materials, tools and technology.[13] In traditional Boir Ahmad there was no paper, thus no drawing, painting or calligraphy, the cherished art in Iran and among Muslims (Blair 2006; Burckhardt 2009). Tools of stone and wood and a few metal tools were handy for carving use-items such as boards, cradles, spindles, looms, spoons and bowls, and for an occasional rough stick-doll for a little girl or a slingshot for a boy, but not much else. The only mud objects were bricks made by men and small chicken coops made by women. The tools themselves got their aesthetic significance by being used. Women's jewellery was limited, too: small gold-coloured coins along the front edge of women's caps were called 'pretty' and bought in the bazaar (they were copied from Safavid gold coins linking beauty with wealth and status). Likewise 'for beauty' were gold-coloured nose-beads and ornaments made of coloured glass seed-beads on the front of women's caps and on safety pins holding the head scarf in place under the chin. These ornaments had few variations and were treated as part of a 'good' costume.

Until about two decades ago women were stringing beads of various shapes and materials (such as minerals, shells, bone, wolves' teeth, ceramic, metal) to wear as necklaces that were 'pretty' but valued mostly as apotropaic and protective devices and for furnishing medication for animals (for example, scrapings off the so-called donkey-stone, when added to a sick donkey's drinking water was said to stop its diarrhoea). The beads were a woman's adornment, protection and personal pharmacy, but beads and also scripture-based amulets around the neck have gone 'out of fashion', as a woman said when I missed her bead necklace in 2015. Also gone are wolves' teeth and iron bangles hung on cradles to ward off jinn. 'No more wolves, no more jinn!' said a young mother with a shrug and a twinkle in her eyes while tying a blue-bead ornament onto a cradle, counting on the bead's power to ward the evil eye off cradle and baby. Women also liked the clanging of iron bangles made by the local blacksmith and by gypsies – the metallic sound was said to ward off jinn.

As status symbols for women beads and bangles have been replaced by jewellery made of high-carat gold, which is said to have 'good' power. It emphasises social as well as gender difference: Islam forbids men from wearing gold, while on women gold is beautiful and 'good' and also demonstrates the economic power of the man who paid for it. The first woman in town who wore a gold bangle was a teacher from the former khan family who converted part of her salary to gold, starting a fashion trend. By now gold jewellery visibly divides rich and poor and fits comfortably into the aesthetics of religion, modernity and social class. The fact that I do not wear jewellery flummoxed people – in their eyes it did not fit my status and made me vaguely vulnerable. All uses of jewellery were important in the aesthetics of wellbeing by offering control over purported extra-human powers and health, and by improving beauty and status. All but those made of bones and teeth of animals were imported and traded; shells have come to Boir Ahmad from the Persian Gulf since antiquity.[14] Locally the use of beads has declined, but blue beads and amulets remain popular throughout Iran. Doostdar 2019, describes items meant to further healing, love, wealth and enemy destruction for sale in the bazaars in Tehran.

In a crisis or 'just to be sure', women in traditional houses in Sisakht continue to burn wild rue seeds (*dinesht*) and to string ornaments of the seeds for wall hangings to guard against malevolent powers; blue beads, said to deflect the evil eye, are bought in the bazaar; some men and women in a nearby village write amulets meant to protect young children, but also 'black' amulets meant to harm clients' adversaries such as a co-wife. Apotropaic items can be bought at shrines, from gypsies and from some 'wise' women. Whether they already have their power while hanging in a store is a matter of opinion. A popular choice is to say that yes, the power is inherent in the bead and the amulet, but it is activated by 'doing something with it' such as wearing it: one has to focus its power by using it. Fashionable gold pendants with Quranic inscriptions, called '*allah*', add the power of gold to the power of the mighty word, as a neighbour told me: gold is 'good' and Quran verses are 'good' and their beauty around the neck is 'good', too, and thus together the pendants are 'very good'. Like many 'very good' things, though, they are expensive.

Coarsely knotted rugs, another artisan mainstay of visible comfort and pleasure, were made by women on horizontal looms with yarn from sheep fleece and goat hair spun by them on drop spindles. Using traditional, geometric patterns and 'Turkish' knots, women could complete a coarse rug within days if they had help with their other chores. These rugs were judged mainly by their use value. The bazaar agreed: traders priced the few pieces men sold in town by wool-weight, not by aesthetic appeal or the women's labour. So-called *gabbeh*, fashionable in Europe for several decades were based on these simple rugs for home use, knotted with mostly undyed wool yarns. Local weavers neither had reliable access to markets nor could keep up with the changing tastes of rug buyers to make a business of them. Tents of woven black goat-hair which can be put up and taken down quickly do not inspire architectural elaboration, and neither do huts of stones, reeds and branches. A 'good' tent is dense and tautly stretched to keep out rain; a 'good' branch hut in summer is stable and affords shade but also lets cooling wind through; and a 'good' stone hut is sturdy, built by men who know how to deal with gravity and planes when stacking undressed field stones (see Feilberg 1952: 113, for a photograph of such a stone wall). Quick assembly, durability and keeping out the elements make for the aesthetic success of these dwellings, and this is enhanced by their promise of hospitality and rest: seeing a group of black tents or some huts in the vast expanse of a landscape lifts any traveller's spirits.

In small, semi-nomadic groups that measure wealth and status by the size of herds and by the amount of available food, there is little variety in families' belongings. A successful herder may have a bigger tent with more rugs and cushions and more tea glasses and sugar for guests than a poor neighbour. Such a tent household was called 'better' and more attractive than one that was small, tattered and bare, but the difference was small. Khans' dwellings were larger than anybody else's and thereby demonstrated high social and political status. A few important khans lived in forts or urban-style palaces surrounded by gardens. The last paramount Boir Ahmad khan's residence in southern Boir Ahmad was a Safavid stone-built castle vacated by the last khan of the Nuï, an earlier Lur tribe in the area. Ordinary people had few choices for turning economic success into social prestige through status goods – 'even our Khan is sitting on the floor', we were told, 'but on two rugs and two thick cushions'.

Inside tents and dwellings, along the back or as a divider between kitchen and living area, flat-weave blankets with geometric patterns covered a pile of stacked household goods. Dried seeds of wild rue and dried rose buds turned into something useful, good and nice when strung into flat ornaments and hung on tent poles against purported negative influences such as from jinn. By the mid-twentieth century women were stitching flowers with multicoloured floss on the covers of seat cushions, learning skills and patterns 'from each other'. This was as close to decorative arts as one could find. Felt mats, colourful flat-woven blankets (*kelim*) and knotted rugs were spread where needed to sit and sleep on, and flat-weave and knotted bags of many sizes held everything from toiletries to wheat and flour. The geometric patterns on these traditional felts and fabrics, mostly in indigo blue and madder red, were traditional and sparse rather than new, inspired creations. When families settled, woven tent-planes disappeared, and when cheap carpeting became available, weaving petered out. By about 2012, no woman was weaving in Sisakht. It was no longer necessary to make rugs and bags, and weaving now was said to be an ill-paid drudgery connected to poverty rather than a chic handicraft for tourists as in other areas.[15]

Weight and durability of goods set narrow limits to what could be taken along on migrations because everything people owned was transported on their own backs and on donkeys and mules (horses were a luxury of wealthy khans). For these reasons people had few metal (mostly copper) cooking pots, no ceramic vessels and few baskets. The only ubiquitous glass items were small tea glasses (*estekan*),[16] glass ('seed') beads, small window panes in a few houses, and women's small mirrors. A few water pipes had a glass container. Hides of sheep and goats traditionally provided bags holding water and fat. It is fair to say that until the 1960s the material culture was pre-wheel and pre-ceramic – 'pre-pottery Neolithic', a local history student called his grandfather's old house in 2006 – with some metal items such as copper cooking pots, trays and cans for water, iron shafts for drop spindles, all made by blacksmiths or bought in urban bazaars, and iron/steel knives, shears and needles.

In the 1960s, melamine plates, metal forks, plastic toilet-water cans and aluminium bowls and pots were added, all from urban bazaars. Their aesthetic value came from being handy and cheap. Later, more cheap plastic items flooded the place and, easily broken and discarded, became an eyesore in public spaces because the usual clean-up devices, such as children picking up things to play with, chickens and dogs eating refuse and people burning garbage, were overwhelmed. Complaints about dirt (*kessāfat*) and stink (*bu bey*) were ubiquitous, and people did not know how to handle the nuisance. This made the indoor–outdoor difference a matter of aesthetics: order and cleanliness inside versus disorder and refuse outside. 'Street dirt' furthermore intersected with health concerns, and eventually garbage dumps outside town, cesspools and banning herd animals from town brought a modicum of appreciated cleanliness. The surrounds, though, frequented by tourists who discard 'all their junk' en route, are declared to be really dirty, and the littering urbanites are readily labelled 'wild, without culture'.

Local people found well-done things pleasing, but the main aesthetic value came from the items' usefulness and, increasingly as time went on, from monetary value: expensive stuff is better than cheap stuff, and things are even better if one buys or sells them at a good price. Personal creativity continues to find outlets in everyday chores and skills, limited by utility and the need to make do. Creativity under these circumstances is less about producing novelties than about re-thinking, re-designing routines and honing and adapting skills. Locally there is no word for art or artist separate from craft and craftsman. Many mundane creations are still impermanent, such as a well-shaped flat bread, a song, a witty story, a seed-bead ornament on a girl's cap easily broken and beads scattered. People who were 'good' at the respective skills were appreciated – critical appreciation of local technical expertise is basic in discussions of aesthetics (Dutton 2010), be it a well-kept garden, a new skirt or a smooth handle for a knife. Although a transhumant lifestyle sets material limits, people have criteria and words for 'beauty' and its opposites and use them often; they have words to evaluate appearances and behaviour, and words and gestures to express their feelings about them; they assign meanings to things and they have a sense and words for aesthetic experiences. The most popular, most used word-pair for a verdict on anything is good/bad (*khub/bey, bad*), with 'very' (*mahli, kheili*) in front if needed for emphasis.

Local Aesthetics

Aesthetics belongs to the branch of philosophy that deals with the nature, appreciation and effects of beauty, pleasure, comfort, taste and wellbeing. It privileges personal experience, the insider's views, practice and habituated skills, is expressed most directly in language,[17] and thus is well suited for anthropologists to use when dealing with 'art' issues in societies that are too far from the scholars' own boundaries of aesthetics to fit their comfort and familiar ambient.[18] Because the term is broadly defined I can avoid trouble when I use it to make sense of the toned-down world local people experience and talk about. The political side of aesthetics, that is, its use as a tool to manipulate people or to distinguish social rank and power in order to separate the 'in'-people from the 'others', rich from poor, refined from boorish that Bourdieu 1984 eloquently and critically described for French Society, is in evidence in traditional Boir Ahmad, too: food habits, women's dress, weddings, men's weapons, all have this separating effect, but it reached the level of class distinctions only after the 1970s and still is not a pressing issue locally.

The narrow aesthetic range of the ubiquitous Persian 'blue bead' (*mohre kyelun*) in Boir Ahmad is a good example for this feature of aesthetics. The small, turquoise/blue, roundish or disk-like, perforated ceramic object was traditionally hung on women's necklaces and on cradles, and pinned on infants' shirts against the evil eye, which is widely assumed to be a harmful effect of some people's gaze. The purported apotropaic qualities in colour, form and use combine into an aesthetic with few choices: the blue bead is mostly an apotropaic device. It does not show wealth, for example. Although it also has the aesthetic value of being pretty, in traditional Sisakht one would not buy or use it just for its beauty.

Thus, when a student described her professor's 'odd' (*ajib*) curtains in Tehran that were adorned with blue beads all over, her family in Sisakht was at a loss: nobody needed that many evil-eye beads, they argued; it was a witty nonsense. Obviously, for them beads on curtains were not within the aesthetic range of blue beads. The professor, of rural ancestry herself but schooled in urban middle-class tastes, had styled a powerful use-object into domestic decorative art, a choice acceptable in her urban socio-cultural circle but not in Sisakht. The beads had switched meaning.

Indeed, there are few overarching cultural rules and practices that fit and oblige everybody at any given time. Rather, people choose from various possibilities for creating and judging aesthetic qualities, and may change their opinions and behaviours within a matrix of often widely divergent options and life conditions.[19] Artists famously create beyond the aesthetic middle range their clients feel comfortable with, thereby creating and exploring aesthetic choices of the future.[20]

Without locating creative expressions in their own cultural meanings, discussions of non-western items and practices in Western art terms amount to a kind of orientalism (Netton 2013) as they aim to make 'the exotic' understandable and thus usable for the Western observer. In contrast to 'art', 'aesthetics' has few culture-bound prejudices and is a generous concept that can cover any expression of feelings, be it in words or body language – a smile, a frown, a shoulder shrug, all are worth many words. Wittgenstein 1967, who declared aesthetics to be a key to understanding any culture, emphasised the importance of 'kinesthetic feelings' shown in body language which expresses feelings and opinions on what is good and not-good, right and wrong, beautiful and ugly, pleasurable and painful. In Sisakht, judged by local people's non-verbal reactions, a gentle, cool evening breeze in summer is a powerful aesthetic experience, as are the looks and fragrance of a rose, the feelings one may have when playing with a baby, while praying or visiting a grave, making perfect furrows in a field or appreciating a good deed, a generosity, a kind word, a joke. People do not create breezes and roses and do not talk much about good deeds but their bodily reactions show that they appreciate them as pleasant or as a fleeting fascination that gives them pause during mundane routines. They are good (*khub*) or pleasant (*khosh*), pretty (*malus*) or even beautiful (*qashang*), clean (*pāk, tamiz*), new (*nou*) or else the opposites: not-good (*nakhube-*), bad (*bad*), uncomfortable (*na khosh, na rāhat*), ugly (*zesht*), old, broken (*pir, kharab*) or even painful (*dard dāre*).

Opposites to 'good' delineate aesthetic boundaries: talking about a boy with a somewhat lop-sided face, his cousin complained that when talking to him, 'one doesn't know where to look, poor boy!' Pruning his roses, a neighbour said that without the whiffs off the outhouse his rose bush would be less attractive; and a young man stretched his shoulders with a grin when his aunt approvingly compared him with his rough, unfriendly brother. Bad, unlovely, unpleasant, dangerous qualities define aesthetics just as do good, beautiful, pleasant ones, and both produce visible and audible signs.

In addition to the choices for preferences and avoidances that a culture provides within habits, traditions and expectations, people create new ones, such as in styles of clothing or food. The many aesthetic domains, from religion to smells, have their own dynamic and ranking systems, which frequently overlap, enhance or cancel each other. For example, a local host's and guest's social competence forms an aesthetic domain: it is easy for hosts and guests to honour or slight each other by (mis)timing arrival, by (in)appropriate attire, an (un)timely gift, the words used in greetings, the performance of polite self-effacement (*ta'arof*). Meanings of kin terms, too, can be manipulated. A toddler who feels his or her pleading cries for mummy (*dādi*) are ignored, may switch to a shrill *dā*! (mother!) to get attention. At a wedding luncheon the hostess welcomed a female relative, an esteemed teacher, with the authority-heavy term for father's sister (*āme*) and a bow of her head. This looked and sounded very polite and proper but offended the guest. 'Why does my cousin call me an "old aunt?"' she said with puckered brows, 'I am hardly older than she is!'

Criteria for aesthetic qualities are primarily connected to the senses but also reach into thoughts: a good memory makes one smile, a bad one frown or cry; thoughts about a beloved relative 'warm the heart', a good joke 'lightens the heart'; images of the promised comforts of the other world, the excitement of travel, auntie's kindness, crying at a grave, the solace felt in trusting God or a saint – all are 'good'. When a lovelorn young man felt neglected by the saint he had petitioned to make a girl's father accept his marriage proposal, he dismissed the saint with a defiant toss of his head: 'If this miser won't help me, there are other saints I can go to', he said.

Changing Options in Local Aesthetics

As a judgement, 'beautiful' and its opposites are subjective: beautiful is what the judge values. But the main criteria for good and bad are known, understood and shared in the community, they are open choices that need no explanation. The criteria for judgement and for aesthetic frames thus are consensual and, given that change is inevitable, they shift. This makes the construction of an ethnographic present for aesthetic norms and principles problematic (Friedl 2020). I will demonstrate the difficulties inherent in changing aesthetic choices in three cases: the appreciation of rugs, of women's attire, and of nature.

Rugs (*qali*)
Rugs are called 'good' based on the thickness of the pile (the higher and softer, the better); on signs of age and wear (decay diminishes softness and durability); on the straightness of lines in the geometric patterns which depend on the competence of the weaver (a sloppily tightened warp makes wrinkles in the fabric and distorts the pattern); and how well the yarn is dyed (pastel colours used to be counted as poorly dyed and thus not beautiful. Mouri et al. 2014, analyse dyes from an archaeological site). Everybody knows these criteria – 'good' just sums them up. In addition, the simple, geometric patterns are different in different tribal groups because young women learn them from their older women relatives. They become identity markers. A neighbour in Sisakht not only identified at a glance the rug we had bought in the south of the province as 'from the Oulad Mirza Ali' but also knew the sad story of the six-year-old son of the weaver who, playing with his father's gun, had accidentally shot and killed his mother at the loom.

When imported machine-made floor coverings became readily available, around 2000, people quickly adopted them as a good choice. They liked them better than their own hand-loomed ones for the same traditional reasons: they were new, soft, warm and had well-defined patterns and colours that did not fade. They were also cheap and lessened women's work duties. Identity woven into the traditional rugs in patterns specific to different groups was an aesthetic criterion, too, but its loss to the anonymous machine-made rugs was an issue only with a few people. The floor of a khan's house we visited in southern Boir Ahmad at that time was covered with new wall-to-wall machine-made carpeting. The khan explained that he had all his 'good' rugs, hand-loomed by his own people, safely stacked away as testimony to tribal history and as an investment. He figured that given the ongoing demise of the art of rug-making, his cache would likely become collectors' items. Local rug aesthetics for him turned historic and financial. For a local neighbour it became entirely a matter of money. He said he would rather buy land now than hoard rugs – in a few years it would bring a better profit than 'rags for the floor'.

Women's attire (*lebās mahalli*; *lebās ashāyer*, local clothes; 'tribal' clothes)
When we first arrived, in 1965, without exception women wore one to three long, colourful cotton skirts, one above the other, each between 4 m and 10 m wide and correspondingly heavy; a similarly colourful long shirt with side-slits and long sleeves; a dark red or dark blue velvet jacket; a velvet cap decorated in front with seed beads and coins, and this topped with a scarf held in place under the chin with a safety pin adorned with beads, and a folded-up large, silky, dark-coloured kerchief wound around the head. Everything but the kerchief was hand-sewn by women, often in cooperative arrangements that combined the pleasures of 'good work' and hanging out with other women. This attire was colourful and pleasant to look at but ill-adapted to cold, snow and hard physical work, and women remarked on this down-side of beauty. The improving economy allowed them to add more substantial jackets – less beautiful but 'good' on the comfort scale. When man-made fabrics became *shik*, the clothes became lighter and cheaper, and women now added more, and wider, skirts. In the 1970s, women were considered most beautiful and well-off when they wore so many wide, long skirts one above the other at festive occasions that the sheer weight and momentum allowed them only small, slow steps.

By 2006, women had added the new choice of rural Iranian women's generic attire, calling it 'appropriate' and 'good' because, they variously said, it conformed to norms of religious modesty, had urban–modern ties, was more comfortable and practical to wear and much cheaper than their own Lur outfits. But the new drab, grey/black uniformity of trousers, skirt and blouse, cardigan and grey-black headscarf and veil was also called ugly when compared with the colourful traditional costumes. For weddings, tribal fashions continued, especially among people who could afford fancy ones. Indeed, women in the former tribal elites affirm their status by creating neo-traditional outfits with expensive, novel fabrics for skirts, shirt and headgear in a monochrome trend towards pastel colours with sparkling highlights and made by local seamstresses. Such costumes are loaded with nostalgic memories of a pastoral 'free life', wedding music and local nobility, pointedly in contrast to the prevailing 'black and drab' government-defined modesty. They appeared on television and are adopted outside the so-called tribal areas in towns and cities for little girls at parties as 'beautiful Persian' novelties.

Thus, culture change produced shifts in the criteria for good/bad, beautiful/ugly in choices for women's clothing on the aesthetic scales of Lur identity, traditional tribal social hierarchy, political leanings, cash economy with unequal access to resources, urban longing for a romanticised pastoral life and 'nature', technology, and the sewing machine. 'Tradition' is thereby outed as a rubbery invention used mostly by local elites, and aesthetic considerations as depending on increasingly commingled circumstances. This is not confined to Iran: members of the upper classes elsewhere also like to preserve signs and customs that continue to accord them privileges of power and influence.[21] A young woman in a former khan's family in southern Kohgiluye, whose household had moved to a new bungalow below the big abandoned castle, had this comment: 'We like to live comfortably but also want to see our big, old fort, and we learn in school to curse the Americans but I am wearing American *blujinns*, and when we have a wedding I wear a fine Lur costume, and I speak Farsi in the city and Luri with everybody else.' She knew how to manipulate the different strands of aesthetics in 'these modern times'.

Nature (*tabiat*)
The surrounding environment furnishes a third example for changing options in aesthetics. As long as people were living off the land in the mountains, 'nature' meant hard work to make it useful. It meant potential danger from snow and cold, from wild animals, from outlaws hiding in the rocks and woods, and from purported extra-human powers in various forms. When people talk about nature and all things natural they firmly link the appreciation

(or avoidance) of their surroundings to physical experiences. While during one of our early visits my husband and a young friend were walking in the woods, the young man became more anxious the farther they ventured – he was afraid of wild boars, he said, and, indeed, at one point a boar chased them both up a tree. 'It's dangerous out there,' the young man summed up the adventure. Nature was good when controlled by human order established in fields and settlements.

There was no romantic element in this orderly nature. When on a sunny winter day in 1971 an elderly neighbour and I on a walk to the next village came upon a – for me – stunning vista of snow and light that made me stop in admiration, he found my reaction laughable. Why I should be overcome by the view of snowy fields was beyond him. As hamlets grew in size, and fear of outside dangers diminished, nature lightened: it became pleasant with orchards in bloom and outings at brooks and springs, and 'healthy' with natural foods that favourably contrasted to 'artificial' foods such as sweets, 'factory eggs' and dubious cooking oil. The traditional chore of collecting acorns which in the past was necessary so as not to die of hunger in the winter, now became a pleasant exercise. By the year 2000, a narrow road led up to a high pasture for picnics, and weekend travellers were taking selfies on ski slopes and at the 'very, very beautiful' waterfall in the next town. Nature had become familiar.

These examples suggest that experiences and aesthetic appreciation largely depend on the biological five senses. Aesthetic experiences have a spiritual side, too, and on principle are linked to ethics, but to make sense of things, to discern and deal with happenings in everyday life above all requires 'the head and the limbs ('Are you deaf, don't you have hands and feet and a brain?' is a routine scolding for clumsy children). Routines based on memories and habits, on 'how we do it here and now', aid the senses. However, reliable as they may be, they facilitate easy access only to whatever happens inside a narrow horizon around oneself. Without added colours and images, without tools to measure, weigh and see better, without access to outsiders, to money and 'stuff', the cognitive field expands only slowly and 'what one can know is very little', as a local teacher said. Physicians advise men whose wives are ailing and in low spirits to take them on a journey, and for this same reason of 'opening one's spirit' television programmes of nature as well as pilgrimages to far-flung shrines have become exceedingly popular.[22]

During rapid culture change over the last three generations people came to link aesthetic preferences to urban fashions, but intentional art remains rare in town. A local professional photographer is making a good living documenting weddings. His work is appreciated for the likeness, beauty and propriety of those pictured and, in videos, for recording the lavish demonstrations of status in dress and decorations of the families involved. The recordings are frequently shown in full to guests as a backdrop to socialising. It is an imported art, as are Gulf-style villas in lush gardens, Persian-style mosaics from urban workshops adorning some hallways, tiled mosques, white bridal gowns, plastic flowers in plastic vases, and Japanese prints of blossoms and mountains on some indoor walls. All are imported from the city. Public art in form of sculptures (vetted by religious authorities) and illustrations in children's books elicit little comment; a few billboards depict landscapes together with calligraphic information. As of 2023, there was no artist in residence in town, and likes and dislikes continue to start with everybody's basic sensibilities.

2

The Senses are Friends[1]

Introduction: Senses, Knowledge and Progress

It is taken as an undeniable fact (rather than a mere 'belief') that the five senses make life on Earth possible. Beyond this insight there is the popular choice to take the senses as important features in God's design people have to be grateful for. However, this assumed fact is paired with the observation-based opinion that the senses easily lead people to violate God's order of gratitude, modesty and peaceful management of affairs. In a popular religious image two inquiring angels will question every dead person explicitly about sins committed by each of the senses before letting the soul into the other world. Believers in a kind of afterlife that preserves the pleasurable traits of earthly life and omits the hurtful, unpleasant ones, assume a continuation of good sensual experiences after death at least until the Day of Judgement. Preachers encourage this view, although they also insist that as 'pure souls' dead people lose all earthly senses when they move to the other world, and that only unredeemable sinners tormented in hell will continue to feel pain. In moments of critical introspection people argue that these competing ideas and proclamations are confusing and dismiss them with remarks such as, 'We will know soon enough how it really is', and 'Nobody fully understands God's Will'. For pious believers, the senses are God's gift to people and animals for living a good life right in this world; for everybody else they mostly allow one to get along and ahead.

A popular option has people point out that they understand their surroundings by using their God-given senses plus reasoning. It is a truism. Eyes, ears, voice, taste and feeling with one's skin form the basis of any aesthetic domain and for any aesthetic experience. 'They are our friends', said a mother, and for an elderly farmer they were 'our servants'. People decode sensory inputs, but like all decoding it is done on the basis of preconceptions. The most important was – and for most local people remains – the stalwart assumption that God as creator and manipulator of the universe and of order on Earth gave people senses and reasoning power to manage their lives; that, furthermore, the (sensual) experiences of the forebears, condensed into 'customs' (*adab o rosum*) now help people to carry on; and that questions leading beyond the horizon of the sense-able, such as what makes the sun come up and go down, why good people are poor and suffering and scoundrels are rich and healthy, are concerns for curious thinkers but are of little consequence for conducting and appreciating life. Pious people can always choose to say that whatever is not immediately sense-able and understandable belongs to the realm of God, not of people.

Reliance on their own, presumably God-willed, experiences kept only a few people closed to new ideas, that is, ignorant of their own ignorance when dealing with ideas different from their own.[2] Rather, in Sisakht new (in)sights and experiences are welcome: 'Tell us what you saw, what you know!' is a popular, informal greeting for a visitor. Stories on radio, television and the Internet are declared likely to be 'lies', but nevertheless to provide an appreciated link to 'the world out there'. Progress (*pishraft*) and the ever-receding alluring goal of a better life are by far the most popular choices for people's uses of their senses and mind, with knowledge as the vehicle to reach a good place. There is general understanding that creating knowledge (*dānesh*) needs curiosity, good sense and senses, effort and the kind of sharp mind (*tizhush*) that lets some people use their skills more effectively than others when given the chance. The chance, though, often hinges on money. The look of a young woman with an unusually big nose was such an embarrassing hardship for everybody – 'I have no idea why God did this', said her aunt – that her brothers pooled their resources to pay for cosmetic surgery in the city. At our next visit she had a 'California nose', was pretty and married, and the aunt blessed the surgeon and the nephews who had paid for it.

There is consensus based on observations and experiences, people say, that human beings' sense-abilities are not created equal, and that differences in sense-perception and other traits between men and women, old and young, slow and energetic, leaders and followers may create problems in a community. The pious choice to handle inequality to everybody's benefit is to praise

God's order which assigns specific duties and behaviours to people of different backgrounds, standing and abilities. An elderly weaver suggested a karma idea, entirely based on experience: about my ('odd') spectacles she remarked that they helped my eyes to read books and to study, while her ('ugly') leathery fingers turned tough yarn into good rugs in a dusty courtyard. 'This makes our lives very different', she said, 'but we both benefit from each other's work.' A man who handled his domestic affairs noisily, quashed criticism with, 'I am doing my duty. A house without a master (*arbāb*) who has good eyes and ears will fall apart.' Such arguments make inequality acceptable and reasonable, but they anger critics who claim that inequality is a political issue.

The more pragmatic, preferred choice is to declare differences in the workings of the senses to be a matter of inheritance and chance, and to insist that all senses can be honed somewhat to create better outcomes. Beyond God's design, thus, sense-abilities and personal engagement are part of the aesthetics of knowledge and lifestyle. Thinking this way is declared to be an obvious fact rather than just a choice. A teacher with a house full of bright, ambitious children said that the best proof of his own good intelligence was that he had married a bright, alert, capable woman so as to make sure his children could make good progress in school. Musing the opposite condition, an illiterate grandmother said of her grandson's wife that she was 'beautiful, so good to look at, but a bit simple-minded (*sāde*), and we'll see what her children will be like'.

The popular assumption that sensual experiences are linked to health and physical wellbeing promotes skills for manipulating them. Thus, an unappealing facial feature that causes depression can be re-arranged surgically; dance moves make the body feel good regardless of the mullahs' modesty requirements; a whiff of perfume makes a man pay attention; a 'sweet tongue' is persuasive; a festive spread of well-prepared food elicits signs of wellbeing 'just by looking at the dishes', guests say. Most foods are placed on a scale from healthy to unhealthy. A meal of rice with butterfat and a piece of game or mutton is universally declared to give more strength than any other food one can think of, such as dishes made with maize, for example, while potatoes are called 'cold' (in the Galenic health system) and blamed for joint pains. Indeed, it is a truism that ailments may be caused, avoided or cured by what one eats. Rich people are expected to be healthier and better looking than poor people because they can afford good food: wealth, health and good looks are an aesthetic cluster.

Colours, too, are said to have an impact on one's feelings: to get 'white, chalky-looking' drugs from the doctor may cause disappointment because white means weak (*zaïf*), while red pills are seen as potent – they have power (*qouve*) inherent in the colour. Looking at 'a flock' of black-veiled women in the street easily creates a depressive mood even for those who tend to take black clothes to be a pinnacle of modesty in the street and of elegance as presented in foreign movies. A bazaar merchant was shaking his head while commenting on the backs of three women passing by: 'Very proper it is, the black veil, but sad, too.'

Sight (*bini*) and Eye (*tië*)

Of all abilities, people name sight as most important for making it in life as well as for discerning beauty and its opposites. Blindness and poor eyesight are taken to be hardships sent by God, as were diseases such as measles that cause them but can now be prevented by (God-sent) doctors. Poor eyesight in old people is called 'dim light' and is accepted as an inevitable part of aging and thus of God's order, but it can be improved with access to money and eye-doctors. Occasionally, pious people seem to be a bit baffled by the various relationships among God's order, God's Will, science and the wherewithal needed to access God-sent modern methods for changing bad health conditions and thereby averting potentially severe social consequences.

'Dim, weak eyes' can now be improved with (expensive) corrective lenses and surgery in the city, but having to admit to bad eyesight and to the need for wearing glasses is considered an embarrassing imperfection, a taint (*eib*) with aesthetic consequences especially for women.[3] Young men name glasses in the same breath as 'ugly, arrogant, misshapen' when they list young women's off-putting features, but young women may see glasses in men also as 'not good', as pretentious or else as a bodily weakness like a limp. Thus, a health-enhancing gadget can be both 'good' on the aesthetic scale of health and 'ugly' on the aesthetic scale of gender propriety with assumptions that support unequal male–female relations critics call 'very bad'.[4] The unpleasant appearance is an aggravation for those who have to look at it, and avoiding the offence is an aggravation for oneself by forcing one to cope without seeing well. When the hostess briefly left the room where I was visiting, her new daughter-in-law pressed some needles and twine in my lap and said, 'Quickly, please thread the needles for me . . .' in order to help her hide her bad astigmatism from the in-laws.

Eyes need light to see, and darkness and light are heavy with symbolic meaning. Light–day encompasses life and its pleasures, warmth and truth, and darkness stands for cold, danger, malevolent powers, untruth and the grave. God, as pure light and goodness, is called the apex of all beauty in Sisakht and by Muslim believers in general. This is debatable only for doubters and agnostics, and these keep quiet.

The dark–light dichotomy contains both an appraisal of death as darkness and not-seeing, and a popular truism about the human condition: God sees everything, always, while people see only a little bit and only for a short while. God is light and truth, always, but people, mortal as they are and with dim eyes and dim understanding, are surrounded by darkness, and in the end are left in darkness, as mourners like to point out. The dark grave is a frightening prospect even for people who, under different circumstances, emphatically insist that death means that the immaterial soul is leaving a lifeless, buried corpse right away. 'Dark! Damp! Alone! The worms!' said a mourner right after a funeral. The night sky can be acknowledged as a manifestation of God's order but rarely figures as an uplifting aesthetic experience. A falling star is a death omen, and the weak night-light makes one easily feel surrounded by dangers, human and non-human, people say. As providers of light, sun, moon and stars are appreciated and their beauty is alluded to in women's names (such as *Aftāb*, Sunshine; *Setāre*, Star; *Māhrokh*, Moonface). After the town got electricity, in the 1980s, the new powerful light encouraged a feeling of safety: 'Turn on the light!' fearful youngsters heard when hesitating to use a bathroom unaccompanied, and robbery became more difficult. 'It was a really dark night, but if our sheep pen would have a lamp above the door, the thieves couldn't have taken the animals,' said a sorry householder.

Sight pleasures are ubiquitous, ranging from features in nature and beauty in people (especially in the young and in women) to anything colourful. They make people glad and, therefore, it is ethically meritorious to provide visual beauty such as flowers in a garden, and to hide unpleasant sights such as a woman's grey hair. Yet, no matter how pleasant a beautiful object is, politeness and common sense discourage staring at it or commenting on it loudly lest the evil eye harm the object and blemish the gazer's reputation. This is part of well-established social etiquette. New houses in colourful gardens are walled in partly because this is a general Persian practice, a defence against thieves, but also to prevent jealousy (*hamćeshmi*) and purported dangers from people's admiring gaze. 'Beauty pulls desire', is a popular warning, and 'Beauty is difficult to handle from beginning to end,' said a young woman half-jokingly: 'First you have to spend time and money on it – hair and face and clothes and handbag and all – and then you have to guard it against jealousy and the evil eye and to hide it so as to avoid gossip, and then you have to hope that the right man will see your beauty nevertheless and marry you.'[5] She then gave her friends and me an hilarious performance of how to toss one's head a little and shake the shoulders and fuss with one's headscarf and veil to give a certain man a quick glance of one's face without making anybody else aware of this flirt. 'But good girls don't do this,' she assured me, and this made the good girls around us shake with giggles even more.

*Colour (*rang*)*[6]

The most eye-catching pleasure is colour, particularly in a local landscape where dun, grey and green dominate. People exhibit colour hunger when they see saturated pigments. In older people's moments of nostalgia that make past hardships fade, beauty and the gathering of edible plants merge in recollections of colourful dots in the earth-monotone landscape, when young women in bright clothes were collecting wild spinach and artichokes, mint, onions and rhubarb in the spring. 'I see the girls out on the hill picking wild rhubarb, and Uncle Ali's daughter Goli in the red skirt is one of them,' goes a song. Although skirts and shirts were soon tattered and torn, their colours were permanent in the sense that as soon as a garment was worn beyond repair it was replaced by a new one in bright flower patterns. The colours in costumes furthermore supported order by expressing gender and age (men did not wear colourful clothes and older women wore dark colours) as well as social status (in the number of skirts and in new fashions in colours and patterns of fabrics). The first local women teachers copied tribal fashion trends from the Qashqa'i students in the tribal teacher training school in Shiraz: they taught the poor Boir Ahmad girl classmates tribal chic.[7] At home the new young teachers expressed their professional, salaried status with these new fashions and stood out in any women's group by the tulle fabric of their short veils, their jewellery and their voluminous bright skirts ending in black pleats.

In terms of stages of the evolution of colour terms, until recently the local colour terminology represented a stage III system,[8] with five abstract terms for colours: *se* for dark/black; *sepid, safid* for light/white; *sorkh, qermez* for red, including brown and violet; *souz*, green, including most blues (the 'Grue' range typical for this stage); and *zard*, yellow plus pastel hues mostly in the 'red' range. People perceived most colours as different from each other, but linguistically placed them into the five categories or identified them with an object, such as 'tree-bark' or 'sky-colour', 'henna' or 'orange'. When once I inquired explicitly about the name of the colour of a showy, bright yellow thistle, my companion said it was 'nothing, just a thistle, donkey-fodder'. This reflects the customary association of the word 'colour' (*rang*) with colouring–dyeing of yarn: nobody had dyed the thistle – the colour was just the thistle. Brown (*bur*) was used only for naturally brown fleece and hair; in women's hair light-brown became a popular hair-dye, high on the scale of beauty. In other contexts it also included purple (*benoush*) because in yarn-dyeing it was achieved with red dye on brown sheep's wool. Dyeing was difficult at best; yellow dye, the most difficult, was rarely used in rugs – and always was tricky, often resulting in faded tints. Light red was called 'half-dyed' (*nimrang*) and taken to be a sign of lack of skill or of bad luck with a batch of dye. Other light hues were subsumed under white or yellow: pink likely is called yellow to this day, and light grey is 'nothing' or 'earth' (*khākī*) or 'white'.

This is the basic linguistic structure with terms that may account for confusion when talking about colours. The aesthetic qualities of the local basic colour terms are a different matter, though.

White and Black

The oldest category, 'light/dark', has acquired the most symbolic connotations, with white weighing in on the 'good' side with 'light' (*nur*) for God, the sun and 'enlighten' (*roshan*), and also for wisdom, as in asking a 'white beard' (*rish safid*) for advice. It is synonymous with beautiful in unblemished, light skin and, via 'clean' (*tamiz*), also extends to character: for a young person to be called *tamiz* is high praise for a good reputation. There is a link to death, though, in the white shroud and also in clothes: a pure white garment is considered to be somewhat frightening. For several years, a young local woman, unusually self-confident, outspoken and proud of being a little different, insisted on wearing only white tribal clothes. This vexed everybody. When challenged, she manipulated two aesthetic realms: she knew that her outfits were startling, she said, 'not good for the people', but also insisted that to dress in white was 'the only way to stay clean because any speck of dirt shows on a white skirt, and doesn't God demand cleanliness?' White bridal attire is a recent, expensive fashion and has no symbolic significance aside from conforming to urban–global fashion aesthetics.

'Dark/black' (*se*) has negative connotations, such as in dark ('ugly') skin, old age ('granny is old and dark') and when alluding to swindle: 'making somebody black' (*se kardan*) means to betray the person. Death and the grave are dark, as is mourning attire, and black-clad women conforming to post-revolutionary street aesthetics elicit comments such as, 'The women are invisible', thereby affirming that black, indeed, is a cryptic, camouflage colouration. In, 'The streets are filled with black crows,' the death connotation is doubled because crows may be taken to be harbingers of death. Dark hues of green, red and blue/violet are considered 'good' for elderly women's clothes, while bright hues indicate youth and are praised in songs. Men's clothes range 'from dark to earth-coloured and back', a young man complained, and nobody sings about them.

*Bright Red (*sorkh*)*

The first colour named in the 'dark' range, red, is the preferred colour, well defined and with mostly positive meanings: life (blood is dangerously powerful, ritually polluting and its loss brings death); henna-red for hair and for painting hands is linked to health and good fortune; 'red-and-white' (*sorkh o safid*) stands for health and beautiful skin; red lips and cheeks are a beauty feature and indicate youth and health, but lipstick and red clothes in public make a woman 'too sexy' for morality police. 'Red rider' (*sorkhan suvār*) stands for a beautiful, brave young man on a horse, and wild red tulips stand for spring and new life. Onions and other foods taste better when 'made red' (*sorkh kardan*), that is, roasted brown. Traditionally a good, powerful colour, red has moved into the 'immodest, sexy' realm in the Islamic Republic's aesthetics of public life.

*Green (*souz*)*

Green shades indicate growth and life: *souz kardan*, 'to make green', means to sprout, to grow, even if the plant is not green, and in this context the opposite of green is 'dry' as in 'lifeless', such as hay or an old, wrinkled, 'dried up' person. 'Your place was green' means that you were missed as a guest because the grass where you would have been sitting is not matted down. Most important, green is the Prophet's colour and one ought not to dishonour it by standing on it, as a weaver explained the near-absence of green in weavings. For this reason and because green dye is difficult to make it was rarely used in rugs, but in women's tribal costumes and in stitcheries of blossoms and leaves it is a popular colour, 'good to look at'.

Blue

Blue is rare in nature. Most blue is in the sky, the *asamun*, and thus light blue is called *asamuni*, but it is not a preferred colour for anything. Saturated shades of blue are subsumed under the term for green, *souz*, except when they are the tint of a particular thing such as the apotropaic 'blue bead' (*mohre kyelun*, made of turquois-blue glazed ceramic), or the dark indigo-blue (*sirmei*) used in rugs, in blue jeans and in fabrics fit for elderly women. Asked what colours were good for old women, a young woman pulled a face: 'No colour – just black and dark blue for old grannies.'

*Yellow (*zard*)*

Used to describe skin, it stands for being weak and sick, as with anaemia and jaundice (*zardiun*), and in 'he turned yellow and died'. It is the least 'good', popular colour, a thistle-colour, but pink, too, may be called *zard*, and is deemed attractive in women's clothes.

When more colourful objects in the bazaar appeared and industrial dyes became available, people added bright orange (*naranj*) and dark purple (*benoush*) to the traditional 'good' palette. There is some confusion and a marked generational and gender difference in the choices and uses of colour terms. Older people and men stick to the traditional dye terms when in doubt about the 'right' words to use.

Dyes and Weaving

Dying and weaving greatly influenced the naming and appreciation of colours. The most eye-catching, colourful and durable things made locally were flat-weave items (*gelim*), and rugs (*qali*) and bags of many sizes knotted with dyed wool yarn, all spun and woven by women.[9] Black goat-hair was used for tent planes and, spun together with sheep's wool, for the warp of most rugs. The rugs combined the touch pleasures of softness and warmth with the eye pleasures of colour and geometric order, and merged tiring yarn work with the satisfaction of accomplishment. 'Ha, that's it, done now!' said a weaver, smiling, shaking her head, stretching her shoulders and supporting her back while getting up from the loom, where she had knotted an urgently needed rug of undyed yarn within a day. Traditional dyes were based on plants, mostly indigo-blues and madder-reds. In the mid-twentieth century commercial dyes became dominant, and the quality became unreliable because few women and only a few itinerant dyers followed instructions for dying or knew how to do it correctly in order to make the dye colourfast. Fading is 'not good' but as long as the rug is warm and soft hardly anybody is bothered by it.

Local designs used only a few geometric motifs. Historically, these can be traced to central Asian patterns, Chinese as well as Turkic ones. The dominance of simple, repetitive, angular patterns shows their origin in flat-weaves such as kelims and bands.[10] The centre diamond-shape in many rugs is called '*hous*' like the small water-basin in the middle of a courtyard, and motif segments, no matter their shapes, are referred to as '*gol*', flower, in a corruption of Turkish *gül*, a tribal emblem. This confusion is widely known but dismissed with, 'So what? It doesn't matter.' Neither local weavers nor users of woven things were – or are – interested in history and the meanings of patterns.

Weaving techniques and patterns were not a matter of choice but were in a weaver's memory, since she had learned them while helping her mother and her mother-in-law on the horizontal loom. This loom, used in many parts of the Middle East, is uniquely adapted to a nomadic lifestyle because it can be made by any man, installed and packed up quickly and transported on donkeys to the next camp site. While working, the weaver literally sits on the already woven part. Working from memory made the patterns ethnic (tribal) markers: a woman from the A-people weaves type A rugs. When in a tent of an Oulad Mirza Ali group in southern Boir Ahmad I commented on a new rug that, to me, with its preponderance of dark blue did not look like other rugs from that group, it turned out that the new daughter-in-law who had just finished it was from the neighbouring Teïbi people. The simple Teïbi pattern on an expanse of dark blue was the only one she knew, 'blindfolded', she said.

Variations in patterns crept in by chance, by mistake and by the availability of dyed yarns but not by creative inspiration. As long as a rug was useable and the lines and patterns were straight and regular it was a 'good rug', never mind a little warping or 'abrash', that is, unintended colour differences where the weaver had switched to a new yarn bundle from another dye-batch for the knots, or to fading from sunlight. In the past, rugs and felt mats were used also as covers at night. In addition, rugs delineate space for certain activities such as sitting and sleeping, and signal status when an esteemed guest is ushered to the best rug, while cooking and work happen elsewhere on old, worn rugs, kelims and felt mats. (Felt is the oldest, cheapest fabric, made by itinerant felt-makers.) Maintenance also meant that chickens forever have to be shooed away from rugs and mats, that the heavy rugs have to be shaken out regularly, spread outside in hot sunlight 'to drive away fleas and moths', and when not in use have to be folded and stacked inside along the back wall. In people's comments floor coverings are valued as a basic necessity for comfort, as signs of status and proper, reassuring order, and for the joy of seeing colours. 'One is soon tired of looking at earth-things,' said a woman, shifting her place on the porch to change the vision of a mud-brick wall to that of two rugs draped over a neighbour's veranda rail to dry.

Other than in dyeing of yarns, pigments were used rarely. Playing with colours is not much of an option to this day. Men did not handle or seemed to care about colours. Women and girls handled colours when they made ornaments of tiny coloured glass beads for women's caps, when they strung dried pink rose buds to form small wall-hangings, stitched brown vases with red flowers and green leaves on covers for cushions and clothes hung on racks, and sewed women's clothes with colourful fabrics men brought home from vendors. Women had little opportunity to select fabrics for clothes themselves. Questions about what patterns and colours they liked brought giggles. 'Whatever the men bring home!' they said. Women's few colour activities and their bright clothes affirmed their gender and thus marked their identity, though: '*gol*' (rose, flower), *narges* (narcissus), *lāle* (tulip), *nastaran* (sweet-brier) remain popular women's names, and girls and women are poetically called 'flowers' in song lyrics.

Modernity brought many more colours in wall paints and new items such as school books, coloured pencils, television and movies. The colourfully made-up stars on television may be labelled neat and clean, in sharp contrast to local people's self-defined appearances. They also may be called 'wall-painted' by people judging make-up negatively in the aesthetics of 'good, natural', and in the aesthetics of pious modesty may be declared 'fast, loud, ugly'. Gleefully, and accompanied by loud noises of disgust by the audience, a young woman described the 'looong' – she wiggled her fingers – red-lacquered toenails extending from the silver-coloured sandals of a 'very chic' woman she had met in Shiraz. Such urban acts of defiance of modesty rules put colour into the aesthetics of political protest. Correct, post-revolutionary street attire is uniformly drab and dark because local women's costumes as well as modern-urban garb are covered with black veils if not substituted altogether with rural Persian women's bland, shapeless attire.[11] 'Indoors' and 'outdoors' became colour-coded, and people comment critically on the difference. Overall, in Boir Ahmad the dun-green-brown landscape with mud-brick or cement-brick houses and walls – all called 'earth-coloured' (*khāki*) – continues to dominate the chromatic palette and defines the town.

Hearing (*shenidan*) and Ear (*gush*)

Voices

Animal noises such as from donkeys, dogs and chickens, the swish-swish of milk hitting a pot when a woman is milking, the tok-tok of the motor mill, sparrows loudly chirping in a tree, a crying child, boys yelling, a passing car – all the sounds of life in the village signal that 'a day is rolling along' as it should, as people say. It is good. The sounds are markers of place, of belonging and order, of life moving; stillness is called eerie. Men called the rhythmic 'thump-swish' of the women's buttering sacks[12] in the cool, wee hours of the morning 'the most beautiful noise'. They also smiled and remarked on the warm feelings they had when coming home tired and hearing tea glasses clink. People paused and smiled when they heard a woman singing a lullaby to her baby. On the 'bad' side of noises were those of fights in a house, of people cursing or yelling at each other, of metal clanging (other than from the smith's workshop). As signs of enmity and danger they were disturbing but are expected in the local soundscape, in contrast to strange sounds and occasional political messages and revolutionary or 'sad' music blaring from loudspeakers. These, quietly, were called a nuisance by just about everybody. In 2015, after the government had started to ease the ban on non-religious music, Iranian/Lur pop music occasionally flooding the town from a loudspeaker on a hill entertained as well as irritated townspeople, if for no other reason than being 'out of time and place', as a neighbour said, being 'nonsense' (*bima'ni*).

Laughter is a difficult sound with several choices for interpretation. It can be 'good', coming from a happy child or in a chuckle of polite appreciation, but loud abandonment in mirth may be taken as impolite, an unbecoming loss of control with sexual implications: 'They laughed with each other' means that 'they' were improperly intimate. An elderly man's assertion that laughter is the voice of the devil echoes the opinion of orthodox Shia moralists. A woman's loud laughter furthermore may be taken to reflect poorly on the obvious lack of control of the men responsible for her behaviour. Children, especially girls, who are known to laugh and giggle easily, are often told to keep their mouths shut because an open mouth and uncontrolled noises in good company are 'ugly'. However, the neo-traditional gender ideology and aesthetics in the Islamic Republic[13] do not cancel the traditional appreciation of jokes and funny anecdotes wherever they are voiced: witty asides and stories are great entertainment at any get-togethers except funerals (Friedl 2018b).[14] Funny entertainers are more likely praised than disparaged even if their jokes and stories violate modesty and ethics, as often is the case in countless two-liner songs (*beit*): 'The widow sold the last cow for cloves to put on her navel under the skirts' (implying that cloves smell good and will attract a suitor: widows long for sex). Hundreds of Mulla Nasreddin anecdotes circulating in several languages (Marzolph 2006) and on the Internet are cherished throughout the Middle East but they are not especially popular in Sisakht. A young man in town famous for his 'quick mind and tongue' commented: 'We Lurs don't need the Mulla. We are wittier and dumber and smarter than he is.' People may criticise Islamic authorities' demands to stifle laughter that comes easily by itself, naturally so, and makes one happy. 'The best use of the veil is to keep it in front of the face so that nobody notices when I laugh or yawn or eat or talk,' said a young woman, speaking 'for all girls'.

Music[15]

Although music is appreciated for 'opening the heart' and for 'making feet move', music and dancing were culturally restrained long before the Islamic Revolution made them a wholly religious issue. The only musical instrument readily available in the past was the human voice. The reed-flute, *ney*, ubiquitous in the Middle East, was known locally but used rarely, mostly by shepherds and for many years by a blind local man who played and sang on main street for alms and could be hired to provide musical entertainment at feasts. Music performed by shepherds, by blind singers and by professional musicians hired at weddings tied it and the music-makers to poverty and low status. Except for young children's playful chanting, singing or humming in private is part of a fading way of life, called old-fashioned and embarrassing now. An old woman may be heard bemoaning her aches in a song, her loneliness and the loss of a glorious past, and asking God and her own dead mother to come and get her, but this is not fashionable at all.

Already in the 1960s, adults sang only for 'good' reasons: women sang work songs while hulling rice in a mortar, for example, and lullabies, the most durable of all human singing. Otherwise, houses were 'silent'.[16] Men and women separately sang mourning songs at mourning sessions and 'happy' songs at weddings, including songs about men's infatuation with women, which women sang with as much fervour as the men. Many lyrics praising a brave dead young man or a beautiful bride, for example, fit both mourning and weddings (Friedl 2018a). In the aesthetics of emotions, acceptable ways of expressing love were narrow. Reciting – or just reading – Persian love-poetry (Vali-Zade 2021) was no choice locally. This has changed somewhat with the dissemination of pop songs and love stories in movies, but it is one thing to listen to love songs on television and another to sing them oneself, which some of the elderly call embarrassing and the adherents to 'Mullah modesty' call shameful.

Singing was *a cappella*: one either sang or else musicians played instruments. In the absence of musicians, women accompanied songs with clapping the dance-beat with their hands. While everybody could sing, the men and women who were regarded good singers performed at festivities. Most often, a leading voice sang a verse and the others sang the refrain. At public religious mourning rituals men – only men – sang this way, with a cantor as lead singer. Several traditional lyrics indicate dialogic singing in the past, that is, segments sung alternating by a man and a woman singer (Friedl 2018a: 6), but this no longer fits the aesthetics of modesty in post-revolutionary modernity. Now the choice is between hiring the traditional standard '*sāz o dohol*' (oboe and drum) musicians for weddings, or else a DJ in a wedding hall or a hotel.

Musicians and Dancing

In the days of the khans, musicians were men from an endogamous low-status group connected to khans' courts. This created an aesthetic/moral conundrum: khans reportedly tried hard to retain legitimate power by staying in the good graces of the religious establishment even before the revolution, but they also presented themselves as the bearer of great tribal traditions, which included music and dancing forbidden by Islam. In town, neither the mullah, an outsider married to a local, high-ranking woman, nor his family ever attended wedding parties; the boycott was his compromise in the dilemma between Islamic modesty and local people's customs.

Since the khans' political and economic demise, musicians are in business on their own. Until the Revolution they provided rhythm at weddings for women's circle dances and men's dance-like performances in public for good money; since then they perform in more or less private spaces such as courtyards. There were no women musicians 'ever', people say, scandalised by the idea of a woman handling a musical instrument.[17] The drums' tom-tom at weddings, audible a mile away, was an invitation to good cheer and was called 'very good' even by notorious curmudgeons because it made people happy (*khoshhāl*). A local notable declared that it was 'very good' because it surrounded an important social order (a marriage) with happiness and joy shown by dancers and bystanders. Yet people also remember that religious authorities had 'always' looked at it disapprovingly as a custom that violated Islamic modesty. They readily talk about the conflict between how they and Shia authorities evaluate these customs: 'good' and 'bad' in this situation cannot be reconciled; two aesthetic scales exist side by side, one local and happy-making and the other easily regarded as dull, rigid and powerful.[18]

Sound and dance-movements went together but were gender specific: women did not play any instruments, and men and women had 'always' danced separately, to different music, with women's traditional circle dance-steps more complex than the men's footwork in their dances. Women dancers hold the body rigid, shoulders and hips parallel, while moving their arms in small movements and their feet in small steps, in contrast to men who move their bodies and arms and legs energetically.[19] When musicians were not available, wedding guests provided rhythm with singing and hand-clapping in the past and now with recorded music – DJs are busy people. Except for those who vehemently defend government aesthetics for whatever reason – ranging from punctilious piety to fear of punishment – people like to watch the dances, and the dancers themselves had always said and shown that they cherish the movement, the performance and 'the beauty of it all'.

Rhythm-providing chanting-singing was also used in girls' games (not in boys' games) and, until the 1950s, for circle-dances of sisters at a dead brother's grave. This dancing was called a sisterly duty and an expression of grief that would somehow assist the dead brother in his afterlife.[20] By 1966, adult women in Sisakht no longer danced at graves, but pre-adolescent girls danced at mourning sessions for Imam Husein, moving in small circles to their own chanting, linking arms while bowing and stepping back and forth. Adults ignored them but the girls liked this dancing/singing. Elsewhere in Boir Ahmad such mourning dances by adult women reportedly went on until the Islamic authorities declared any dancing in public unlawful and scandalous. By that time this mourning custom no longer fit most local people's ideas about progress and modernity anyway: people in cities did not dance at funerals. Since then only wailing and singing of mourning songs accompany mourning rituals, and chants (with a lead singer) accompany men's new, choreographed rituals at public commemorations of important founders of Islam. All are sanctioned by orthodox authorities. Their aesthetic value is appreciated generally in town (as is the local, famous lead singer), but there is the popular choice available to argue that the mournful emotional and political messages are not good for the spirit, and that 'crying all the time' at behest of the government is neither healthy nor beautiful.

Into the restrained traditional sound-sphere came canned music in the 1960s, ranging from performances on classical Persian instruments to modern

Iranian pop songs and 'Lur-music'. After a two-decade long music hiatus following the Islamic government's prohibition of non-religious music in public, the laws were relaxed somewhat because they were not enforceable and encouraged corruption such as paying morality-guards for turning a deaf ear to people's wedding music in courtyards. Girls who choose to dance learned the steps from their grannies inside their homes instead of imitating young women while dancing with them in the traditional big dance circles.

Over the past decades, music-making has become professionalised and is left largely to cantors at religious events and to pop singers on compact disks and the Internet. Locally the most popular music now are Luri songs and Luri dance-music. Musicians see in this music an assertion of tribal identity ('This is us!' as a drummer said), but a minority of *hizbollah*-leaning people make a point of shunning 'such noise'. Among young people the trend at weddings is towards big parties in hotels and wedding halls, with modern Western and Persian music that invites women to dance among themselves, 'Persian-style', that is, in variants of fully-clothed belly dancing. Only women dance this way, 'for themselves', as a five-year-old girl assured me. A visiting *hizbollah*-man's suggestion that women ought to dance (only) for their husbands, in their homes, drew chuckles and jokes – 'My old man would get a heart attack if I would do this!' said one of the matrons.

The modern aesthetic of perfectionism works against music-making by amateurs, and city-habits, the mullahs and religious sensibilities discourage non-religious singing and music performances. Only families beholden to the austere orthodox religiosity of the Islamic Republic have totally 'quiet' houses, though, declaring dancing and non-religious chanting and music to be 'bad' because they lead to sinful thoughts and activities. By far most people disagree and call music and dancing 'beautiful' because they lift one's spirits and make performers as well as audience and spectators feel good. Still, the paucity of melodic sounds, of singing even in private, and of any other amateur live music in town is remarkable, 'unnatural' according to a teacher, given how popular singing and music-making are in other small-scale societies they see on television. 'People are embarrassed to make music-noises,' said a discouraged young man who had wanted to learn to play the guitar rather than to code computers.[21]

Smell (*bu*) and Taste (*maze*)

People comment on smells readily, with little disagreement. Perfume is 'good'. The fragrance of flowers, especially of roses, and, as a choice, of opium, is called paradisiacal. Passing gas (*gus*) is embarrassing and hilarious, and local storytellers and merry-makers use the sounds and smells to comic effect. As part of grave aesthetics, mourners may choose to put fragrant grasses on graves so that the dead will not be troubled by their own bad smell of decay. It took about twenty years for householders to accept indoor toilet/bathrooms for fear they might cause 'bad air' in the house. The scents of rosewater on bedding, and of cloves and cherry pits on a bride's traditional necklace are considered aphrodisiacs, while the 'bad smell' of dirt and smoke of – a bit metaphorically – old and poor people, and – fully metaphorically – of rogues and anybody one does not approve of, is off-putting (*'beyom iyā* – literally, 'a badness is coming over me').

Pleasant odours are universally taken as signs of considerate, clean, well-cultured persons and of well-ordered human existence. A perfect host traditionally offered guests rosewater for their hands after a meal to eliminate food smells on the skin. A strong smell in some foods may be taken as a kind of disturbing agent in itself that makes some people sick, and if produced on purpose – by burning food, for example – it ranks as an insult to a housemate. Bad 'natural' smells, though, such as of manure, dirty animals and outhouses reach into ethics, too, as a violation of God's demands for cleanliness and as an annoyance for other people. They also reach into the social order: farmers and pastoral people living with animals regard these smells as a natural, unavoidable byproduct of their God-willed mode of life, but also are well aware that they betray low social standing in the eyes of urbanites and of people working in 'comfortable jobs with clean hands'.

Food, Health and Status

Choice and aesthetics come into the survival necessity of food while it is produced, in cuisines and in how it is consumed. For example, blackberries on a bush around a garden are part of nature, pleasant to see. Picking them is women's cumbersome work. Served in a bowl they become an aesthetic statement about nature, labour, a good kitchen and taste. Experience and customs declare it an undeniable fact that 'good', skilfully handled food is '*khoshbu*', of pleasant smell, and '*khoshmaze*', of pleasant taste, and also supports the body's balances (in the Galenic system). Thereby food is tied to reason, health, wealth and social status, and thus to choices and aesthetics which change over time. Each step in the development of food habits is said to have advanced human culture (*farhang*), starting in the well-remembered past with one's right hand taking food from a communal tray.[22] Within about twenty years, metal forks, spoons and plates had been added for a 'good' *sofreh* (a tablecloth spread on the floor). Food presentation and table manners were elaborated and were soon evaluated and appreciated in terms of how refined, 'good' and beautiful they were: '*malus bekhor!*' (eat prettily/properly) little children heard at meal time.

Around 1970, the amount and quality of available food started to increase. This was especially important for women and children who, by and large, got to eat what men left over. Food generosity also increased. An exceptionally gifted cook in town became a magnet for her little nephews and nieces when she made her famous soups to be distributed to neighbours as a votive meal for a saint: 'I am feeding one big saint and five little mouths,' she joked. In her larder hung a dozen bags filled with dried herbs – different mixes for different kinds of dishes – all together an aesthetic pleasure in terms of smell, cooking competence and the promise of tasty food. The beauty of the kitchen 'links the eyes, the nose and the skills of the cook', said her daughter. Generous cooks are proud of their reputation despite belittling their dishes in a manner of politeness, and are clearly happy about giving their guests pleasure – both, reputation and pleasure, bestowed benefits. While I was laid up in the provincial hospital, one of these gifted cooks, with a pot of chicken-and-barley soup in her lap, travelled there on the bus to feed me. Together with my profound thanks it brought her 'merits for the next world', her sister said, moving taste, food generosity and kindness to religious aesthetics.

The rapidly expanding cuisine options in the wake of modernisation and globalisation broadens the local horizon of experiences by adding choices for 'what goes into the pot'. They create culinary fashions within local Islamic moral and aesthetic parameters.[23] Around 2004, the most popular status-food in town, rice with a stew of chicken, eggplants, tomatoes, onions and herbs (*juje bādenjun*) had supplanted the traditional rice-and-lentil dish with an occasional piece of beef or chicken on top. Later, a *'sāndevič'* place on Main Street appealed to young people, although their elders warned that the sandwiches contained disgusting ingredients and made one sick. The first coffee shop in town, run by a man who had found such shops 'cool' (his word) in Isfahan, became a choice for socialising for some local young men. By 2015, their elders saw this mostly as a waste of money but good nevertheless because it kept the idle young men from brooding at home and misbehaving elsewhere, as a grandmother said, 'speaking for everybody'.

Traditional local foods continue to be appreciated in town despite strong urban influences, such as from a popular television series featuring hosts cooking, serving and discussing the aesthetics of their food performance.[24] Several dishes based on lentils and chickpeas cooked in water with millet or freshly crushed wheat berries and herbs, and topped with butterfat, remain popular although such dishes have been devalued as 'cheap family food' now that many different foods are available. My assurance that I, a foreign visitor, liked these 'old dishes' drew giggles from my various hosts. Such eccentricity also has an aesthetic social side: my hosts took my preferences as well as the simple yoghurt-and-bread meals which the revered director of the former tribal school administration, a high-ranking Qashqa'i man, asked for when visiting local schools, as signs of the much appreciated ability to combine authority and status with respect for local tribal lifeways.

In the past, meals were poor in quantity, calories and nutrition but needed only few ingredients. Even with today's expanding food choices, the absence of hot and pungent spices makes the taste of local foods subtle. Food preparation relied on drying (herbs, berries, fruits, greens); on fire (boiling, steaming, toasting, frying, roasting); on butterfat, cooking oil, salt, onions and herbs such as mint and parsley, wild spinach, artichokes, rhubarb and several greens in the onion family. Dried berries, fruits, herbs, yoghurt and a tangy syrup boiled down from unripe grapes continue to provide delicate sweet and sour notes in dishes. Most skills and knowledge about food were in the domestic domain of women and although the recipes were standard, individual women's dishes and reputations ranked higher or lower on the 'taste' scale. Men roasted meat on spits outdoors, 'using our old hunter's skills', said an elderly farmer. Much-appreciated wild and cultivated variants of native fruits (plums, apricots, apples, grapes and walnuts) have grown well in the sunny, high-altitude environment since beyond memory, but other fruits and vegetables such as tomatoes, green peppers and potatoes have been used in the area only since the 1970s. Labelled 'cold, unhealthy' food they met with caution and suspicion at first but, especially tomatoes, have become quite indispensable.

Sisakhtis were known derogatorily as 'onion-growers' in Boir Ahmad. Along with legumes and barley, onions were the first plantings of settled people.[25] Together with walnut trees, willows and poplar trees along irrigation channels, they established sedentary status, boundaries, a political programme and usufruct rights. Most khans in Boir Ahmad took 'fancy' cultivated plants such as fruit trees and grapes as signs of political aspirations by local chiefs and thus as a threat to the khans' power and order. In Sisakht, the khan's riflemen destroyed trees and vineyards several times. These 'bad' times are vivid in people's memories. 'Remember then . . . ?!' a man gleefully shouted to me from his truck in 2006, ready to transport a load of Sisakht's famously tasty apples and grapes overnight in a convoy to wholesale markets in Isfahan, some 140 miles of mountain roads away. Around 2010, in a dispute with a neighbouring village over the use of a former pasture, one night the malcontent neighbours cut down all the trees Sisakhti men had planted there, vacating Sisakht's claim to the area.

Locally, though, the staple food was unleavened flat bread in several forms, made of acorn meal in the past and during hunger times, and later of barley, millet and wheat. When children said they were hungry, the only handy food choice was half a roll of bread and a drink of water or watered buttermilk, a mother remembered, 'while now I open my larder and the hungry little devils find cookies and fruit and cheese and plenty of left-overs'.

Breads
Acorns (*belli*).[26] *Kalg*, the ubiquitous acorn-meal staple in the oak-rich Zagros areas, is known from pre-pottery Neolithic sites in Iraq. It looked the same there as *kalg* does in Boir Ahmad now and likely was baked/roasted the same way: patties of stone-ground acorn meal mixed with salt and water into a soft, dark, coarse dough are plopped and smeared onto a heated stone or into a concave round iron griddle resting on stones over an open fire (today they are cooked in a pan on the gas stove). I call this bread and the traditional cuisine 'neolithic': acorn meal was used even before grains, legumes and animals such

as goats were domesticated in the Neolithic period in the eastern Zagros. These foods dominated local economies there until four generations ago. (Mashkour 2009). Uncooked acorn-dough may also be added to soups to thicken them.

Despite the elaborate, time-consuming preparation – gathering acorns, shelling them with a special blade, grinding the kernels and leeching the meal in water, all done by women – this 'bread' is bitter and crumbles easily for lack of gluten. It was ubiquitous. Acorns were sung about, and *kalg*'s effect of causing constipation was used against diarrhoea. Five different terms cover different bread shapes depending on how the dough is smeared, plopped or pressed onto the hot surface – it is quite an art to make good *kalg*. In 2015, an old farmer remembered his childhood: 'Without bitter acorns, goats and lentils we children would have died of hunger.' Lacking these memories children now declare *kalg* to be 'bitter and bad'. It seems that over millennia neither taste nor food technology changed much locally until wheat conquered the area.

Wheat (*gandom*). Wheat is a survival necessity, a cash crop, a measure of wealth, produced by men's skills and efforts that are judged by others, and was taxed by the tribal chiefs. (Acorn-products and gathered foods were not taxed by the khans, who, however, expected 'gifts' of gathered herbs, honey and game.) Roasted, salted grains have been a food choice since antiquity, and are still taken along as snacks to the fields and on travels. Location and skills in the production and quality of wheat had the aesthetic component of resulting in different tastes: the miller and several other people can identify the area where the wheat has been grown by the taste of the bread. While men grow the wheat (with women's help in weeding and at the harvest) and the miller then mills it in a water-driven and, later, a motor-driven mill, turning wheat into bread with water and salt is women's work. Many households still have a grinding stone. In the 'old days', and nowadays when needed for certain dishes, with measured, rhythmic movements women grind and crush washed, dried wheat kernels into grits and coarse flour. In 2004, a strong neighbour lugged a suitably flat, very heavy rock on his shoulders from a high pasture the long way down to his house to replace his wife's broken grinding stone.

Wheat bread (*nun*) was the most important food staple in Boir Ahmad until about a generation ago, and frequently the only choice for stilling hunger. The earliest form, we were told, was that of a thick pancake, made of a soft dough roasted inside a concave griddle, similar to but much better tasting than acorn bread. It remained an occasional food choice: eaten while warm, children and old people like it. By the 1950s, the choice of thin, crisp, large round breads, *nun tiri*, 'rolling-pin bread', was most popular. Strength and patience are needed for getting the wheat–flour–water mix right, kneading it until smooth, rolling identical dough-balls between the palms of the hands, flattening them on a round bread board into paper-thin, large disks with rolling-pins, and roasting them on a hot iron griddle without burning or tearing them. The shape of bread is a gauge of a woman's skills and has the intended aesthetics of perfection: a torn, shapeless bread with thick rims was the work of a girl-beginner, a sloppy housekeeper or a sign that the dough was cheapened with millet flour. The rhythmic knocking of the rolling pin on the bread board makes an enjoyable noise, indicating a woman's industry and the promise of the welcome sight, smell and taste of fresh bread. Deep sighs by the bakers after getting up from squatting for hours and stretching their backs and limbs are the signs of the physical discomfort and exertion of baking. Elderly women can no longer do this work. If participating at all, they take over the turning of the toasted sheets on the griddle with a long, flat iron spit to prevent burning.

After this thin, crisp bread is softened with sprinkles of water and then rolled up, it is a bit tough to chew but tasty and 'good' for people who have teeth – which left out the old and the very young. It indicated status because wheat was expensive in the market. By 2000, commercial bakers in town were baking urban-style wheat bread with slightly fermented dough, round and flat but soft and much thicker than the local bread, and subsidised by the government. Not only cheaper than home-made bread, it also was declared healthier because of the sourdough which controls stomach problems people had complained about in the past. In 2015, bakers' bread was so common and so low on the rungs of the status ladder of food that it no longer appeared at festive meals at all – rice was a much more appealing choice.

At the same time, a new-found emphasis on 'natural' food and tried and true customs made the old acorn-meal patty, bitter, dark-ugly and crumbly as it is, re-appear as a fashionable, nostalgic status food. A young teacher who had bought some dough from a woman in a southern village assured me that '*Kalg*-dough is expensive but it keeps well in the freezer'. The even more expensive rice was edging out all bread, though, and for the same aesthetic reasons: it tastes better, people said, and it shows higher status. In 1971, the women we met in a tent-camp in southern Boir Ahmad declared our gift of a bag of rice a rare windfall goodie and instantly turned a kilogramme of it into a big, communal milk-rice meal for themselves and the children in the middle of the afternoon while the men were away.

Rice (*berenj*)
Rice is the preferred staple now, 'normal' but expensive,[27] especially the kind grown in a few valleys in Boir Ahmad that are warm and wet enough to sustain small rice fields. This rare, medium-long rice (*ćampa*) is taken to be especially tasty and healthy, much better than the hulled white rice imported from the Far East. Thus, the kind of rice one eats conveys one's social standing now, but recent reports from Sisakht indicate that the local diet is changing in quantity and quality again due to rising poverty, with a marked increase in bread consumption and money-based differences in the kinds of food eaten. 'Hospitality has become difficult,' reported a friend when listing the hardships of the day.

Salt and herbs
Salt, dried mint, dried wild onions and other herbs continue to be the main flavouring for nearly all dishes, and therefore the salt-bag and herb-bags are 'the most important things in the kitchen', a grandmother said, obviously proud of her larder, and blessing her granddaughter who had brought them. Women collected and dried herbs in the spring, and men used to bring bags with salt on donkeys from salt-outcroppings high above the village. This salt does not contain iodine, though, and on doctors' recommendation people buy iodised salt in the bazaar now to prevent the endemic thyroid problems of the past.

Meat, fish and eggs
Meat has its own aesthetic hierarchy based on taste, on purported health benefits and price. The 'best' is declared to be game (partridge, wild sheep and goats) which, however, no longer is available legally but retains its symbolic value of the hunt as a quintessential manly occupation. Next in goodness and price are lamb and mutton, considered 'warm' and thus beneficial in the Galenic medical system. Next down on the cuisine ladder is chicken: if it is

local, it is *tabiï*, 'natural' and thus good, but rare; a 'factory' chicken (from an industrial poultry farm) bought in the bazaar is relatively cheap and acceptable for a respectable meal, but it is *masnuï*, 'artificial', or even *shimiï*, 'chemical', and this is not good. Fish comes from one of several fish-farms in Boir Ahmad. It is billed as healthy but is expensive and not a popular food choice. The least valued meat are beef and goat meat, both considered 'cold' in the Galenic medical system and said to give strength but to cause arthritis and to make 'cold'-related ailments such as '*rumatis*' worse.

Chicken and eggs continue to be under women's care and control. Women build chicken coops with mud, augment the hen's scratch-and-find diet with little bread-dough balls, have an egg at hand for a quick (*hāzerī*) meal, for breakfast, for an unexpected guest or for the husband when absolutely nothing else is available for his dinner. A woman with eggs to sell will pocket the egg money. However, eggs and all meats are expensive and have become 'unaffordable' in the 2020s. Their consumption separates the rich from the middling and poor, and most main meals continue to be based on rice, vegetables, legumes and bread.

Drink
Besides water (*ou*), buttermilk (*dugh*, a byproduct of buttering yoghurt) and dried cheese balls (*kashk*, made of buttermilk) that were crushed when needed and dissolved in water, were the common drinks. Before modern plumbing, women lugged water from irrigation channels and wells in heavy goat-skin bags. This was very hard work and sometimes the 'natural' water caused diarrhoea, but it was free, while now people complain that they have to pay for the tap-water in a courtyard or a modern house – 'pay for our own water!' Milk, mostly from cows and goats, was rarely consumed at all and never raw. Rather, women boiled it and turned it into yoghurt, poured what was not sold into a goat hide buttering sack and sloshed it on a tripod, separating butter from buttermilk. Water and buttermilk were cheap and declared good as long as they were cold. Before refrigeration this was difficult to achieve in the summer and was a health-and-status matter: tepid, still water and drinks counted as unhealthy. Occasionally, the chief's house got ice from men lugging bricks of ice down from ice-pits way up Dena Mountain. Alcohol, forbidden in Islam, was no issue in town but is known as a choice medicine for an upset stomach

(our reputation as anti-alcohol advocates helped us with Islamic authorities). Soda-pop is for sale in the bazaar and is served in some houses to guests but is declared to be bad because 'it takes money out of everybody's pockets for nothing', as a hostess complained.

The most cherished drink, though, is tea, introduced locally less than 100 years ago. Golden-black and slightly spiced with cardamom, the look, smell and taste of tea and the tinkling of tea glasses rank high in the pleasurable experiences of daily routines and hospitality. Tea and pieces of hard sugar hacked from sugar cones were served at meals and throughout the day when asked for. Tiny toddlers soon were hooked on sugar for life. Tea remains the sine qua non offering for guests, and for many people remains the main source of comfort, energy, stomach problems and debts: tea and sugar cones have to be bought in the bazaar.

Food economy and health
Bazaar merchants 'helped' (their expression) local people by exchanging people's meat, yoghurt and wool products for cash items such as tea, sugar, rice and cooking fat. They undervalued local agricultural products they bought and overvalued cash items they sold. Once caught in this economic circle, the agro-pastoral people had no way to escape it. Much of this exploitation ended with 'progress', when cash-based jobs became available in the 1970s and government-affiliated banks started to lend money to local people at manageable interest. The debt loads of people, however, has remained very high according to local bankers and householders themselves. However, until the recent economic downturn, borrowed cash was needed less for essentials such as tea but for 'better living' such as travel, clothes, children's education and modernising houses. In contrast, in 2022, people said that 'now every penny goes to mere living'. Yet they also build new houses with loans that make 'everybody indebted to the bank for life' and to the government for the earthquake loans it provides. 'Debts are a constant headache and won't let us sleep,' has become a proverb.

Not only calories but also protein and vitamins were scarce in the traditionally available foods, especially so in winter, and people unanimously comment on their ill-health in 'the old days'. They had no illusion about sub-nutrition. Young children and old people had an especially hard time getting enough nourishment because the food culture was not adapted to their needs. Emaciation and weakness in old, toothless people and the high mortality among weaned, underfed, sickly, whiny toddlers were taken as normal for these stages in life – not good at all but to be expected. 'I have seen my first normal-weight new-born in this village today,' the local physician told me in 1975. People knew they were poor and ailing, and that 'everything' got worse as the pastures became over-grazed, the khans more oppressive and the families larger, but other than leaving Sisakht there was 'nothing we could do', they remember, there were no choices.[28] The elderly comment with approval on the increase in food now, especially rice, which is 'much easier to chew than bread' and therefore 'much better'.

In the last two or three generations sweets and fat–salt–sugar based snacks have become favourites among children. Parents blame these for rising obesity, ill-health, bad teeth and a drain on available cash resources. Over-eating as a facet of the aesthetics of modernity is in direct opposition to the value placed on 'health' and the ethics of frugality in Sisakht. It speaks to the high value placed on 'reasonable' living there that by 2006 hostesses had curbed their habit of urging guests to 'eat more!' and that several hosts asked us not to bring sweets or soda pop as a gift because it was bad for the children. By 2015, some had even stopped offering soda pop. On their own initiative, women also choose to boycott chewing gum, and most hosts stopped offering cigarettes to visitors. However, the display of sugary delicacies by two confectioners in town continue to be mouth-watering as well as nice to look at and are 'stealing money right out of our pockets', as a father said.

Touch-Feeling (*hes*)

Pleasure

'Soft, warm, smooth' are good, likeable, pleasure-creating (*khosh*) feelings, such as one gets by sitting on a new rug. For an elderly neighbour, a soft cushion at a fireplace was 'like a place in paradise' after a long, cold work-day in the orchard. Friendly, helpful, contented housemates make for a 'warm' house, while unhappy housemates at odds with each other create a 'cold', uncomfortable house. Friendship is gauged by how 'warm' it is. An old woman I visited complained about suffering from 'cold all the time' despite blankets and a good heater. Her daughter-in-law aptly translated the 'cold' complaints as loneliness: 'Nana wants us to sit with her all the time and listen to her.' When a toddler balked at the suggestion of kissing her great-grandmother, everybody understood her: a wrinkled cheek is 'ugly' to look at and unpleasant to touch. In contrast, caressing young children gives one a fine, smooth touch experience, and wedding songs sing about the groom's pleasure of putting his hands on the 'belly' of his (very young) bride.

Touching, though, means intimacy, and this is placed into a narrow frame of sexual morality and difficult aesthetics for adult men and women. While touch-based signs of endearment, such as embraces, are perfunctory gestures between women, rarely will a woman as much as shake hands with a man, including male relatives. In the post-revolutionary practice of modest gender interaction, such a hand shake would mean a lot more than a hearty or polite greeting. In 2015, when a young man I have known since his birth and who had become a prominent public figure, *coram publico* grabbed and shook my hand warmly at a big funeral, he not only told me that he was glad to see me but also told everybody else that he stood above petty rules of so-called modesty, and that he challenged any criticism. He made a public political statement – made relatively easy, I have to add, because I was an elderly, foreign woman.

Even married couples are unlikely to touch each other in public, and despite a general easing of sexual mores in Iran,[29] locally, a young couple holding hands in public still may provoke comment and signs of unease in others. Such a display of intimacy is not a good choice; it is called 'a bit ugly', making people look away in embarrassment because it offends traditional local habits and sensibilities and suggests moral shortcomings. In crowds, close contact cannot be avoided. Crowds provoke anxiety, and women tend to bunch together when standing in line at the baker's, for example, often yielding space to a man even before he pushes them aside. Locally, sexual harassment of women is checked by men's need to guard their reputation in a small place where everybody knows everybody else, but it is ubiquitous in Iran generally. Women, especially young women, make a point of appearing outside 'in flocks, like sheep', as a young man said whose attempts to talk to a certain young woman were frustrated by the constant crowd around her.

Most touch–feel moments happen in the process of work: one is glad when dish-water is not too cold or too hot, a dough is smooth, a load is well balanced on a donkey, the rough skin on one's hands is not broken, a wound is healing. Letting rice or lentils run through one's fingers while sorting them on a tray feels good, as do warm sun rays on one's back while repairing a tool in winter or feeling a cool breeze in a shady place in summer. Elderly men sitting along a wall in the wintry sun or in the shade of a tree in summer's heat bring a smile and friendly banter from male passers-by.[30] Women, in contrast, especially young women, hestitate to exhibit themselves in public spaces; to 'strut around' could be taken as a sign of unwarranted leisure and lack of decorum, and therefore called 'ugly'.

Pain

Anything hurtful is bad. This makes pain a useful tool of control and punishment: pinching and pricking one's disobedient child with needles used to be mothers' common child-rearing devices, as were beatings by fathers and elder brothers, and slapping, pinching and hitting among children. We were asked often how we managed our two daughters (and each other for that matter) without hitting or yelling.[31] Violence had positive aesthetic value in boys' games that gave winners the right to 'punish' losers, which caused great hilarity and often considerable pain, and also in the men's stick-dance performed at weddings. This is a fight between a man with a stick trying to hit the legs of his opponent, who, with the help of a long staff, jumps and dodges blows, all to the beat of music. Over the past two generations, violence has diminished as an educational device, and parents and teachers say that the choice to call it old-fashioned is gaining popularity.

New, lenient educational philosophies encourage parents to grant children great 'freedom' (*āzādi*) in behaviour and to adopt markedly permissive attitudes towards them. This works well for many, if not most, children, but enough youngsters abuse this freedom, people complain, by being loud, selfish, demanding and disobedient, to give children generally 'a bad name'. In the past, children were called *fuzul*, mischievous, and this behaviour was expected, but now the many headstrong and disrespectful ones are said to rob their houses of cherished quiet comfort (*rāhati*) and make life difficult for everybody. This new ubiquitous trend towards upending the domestic status hierarchy is widely deplored, and pious older people proclaim parents' abandonment of parental authority to be an obvious violation of God's order.

This not only has practical domestic consequences and ethical and theological ones, but also challenges economic aesthetics because many young people now are called 'lazy'. A grandfather complained: 'The many children in the past – oh, the noise and punishments and destruction and dirt! It was difficult then. And now we have only few children, and they go to school and are clean and healthy but they are expensive, they care only about themselves, they are disrespectful and offensive, and this is hurtful, a headache, no good, no good!'

Of all pains, the touch of fire is so terrible that burning is taken to be a torment in hell rather than a purifying device as it was in ancient Persian tradition. Burning accidents around open fireplaces, while handling scalding water and heavy, hot pots, happened frequently, mostly to women and children. Some women at the end of resources and patience with domestic violence in their in-laws' houses chose to burn their arms in a gesture of self-immolation.[32] Suicides and suicide attempts of women were frequent, mostly hanging by a rope and drinking agricultural poisons. The considerable improvements of life conditions make self-harm of women 'no longer necessary', said a nurse (for local men self-harm was not an issue in the past). Although everybody understands the motivation for such painful acts of protest by women, the protest is called ugly and has the bad consequence of ill-repute, then and now. A burned arm, cuts and bruises indicated loud dissent, and likely caused more pain when the hurt woman's father or brothers tried to protect her or else, just as likely, berated her and beat her up to silence her: a noisy, talked-about house, be it a discontented woman's father's house or her in-laws' place, brings many kinds of pain.

Until modern medical interventions provided fairly successful choices to deal with pain, ailments were 'always nearby' in the past, as a grandfather remembered. The main causes people – and local physicians – gave for ill-health and 'weakness of the body' were hunger, malnutrition, over-work, accidents, violence and old age, none of which could be avoided. '*Piri-dardi*' (old age is painful) is a popular saying. So many of the malnourished, sickly toddlers in the past were cranky, listless and whiney that their behaviour was taken to be normal for this stage in life. People commented that happiness obviously was no hallmark of the very young, and that hard work brought aches and pains for adults as a matter of course: pain was unavoidable. Local bone-setters and wise women who knew about the benefits of medicinal herbs helped somewhat, as did the belief in amulets, beads and some saints, but so did the fact that people died younger in the past. Thereby they missed at least the usual infirmities and ailments of old age, 'from bad eyesight and tooth aches to bent backs and arthritis', as a local physician summed them up.[33]

Given people's life circumstances, the choice opinion about differences in wellbeing was that enjoyment of good health and feeling well were a prerogative of the young, the rich, the smart, the educated. For most of the others a pain-free, carefree and beautiful life was out of reach because God's plan allotted them a difficult life with little aesthetic merit. Progress added choices for achieving and maintaining good health with better food, less back-breaking work and modern medicine, but ailments did not disappear. For the pious this is proof of God's design, which, however, also includes the choice to expect that God opens doors to deal with adversity, and one therefore better take a pain in the body as a call to find a good doctor.

Pain caused by an accident, disease or unsuccessful medical intervention begs the question of theodicy more urgently. Evoking God's punishment for a hurt person's (or an ancestor's) sins, even for unavoidable sins such as killing an animal for food, is a popular choice but brings no pain relief; doubts in God's purported kindness is another choice, and invoking God's inscrutable Will is the choice left 'after all thoughts are thought and all words have been said', as a man bent by a back injury summed it up. God obviously built pain into the fabric of life but then let doctors and scientists make medicines and health clinics, and one thanks God for them and keeps up one's hope even if the modern, costly health interventions do not always help much either.

3

Aesthetics of God's Order

Introduction: Necessity, Benefits, Contradictions

A common local assumption asserts that without order the world would be chaotic, and this would be bad in every respect. This order (*qānun*) is said to come from God as a law (*hoqm*) and is expressed in traditions (*rasm*, *ādat*). Common-sense logic and Islam agree that God created an ordered world and made ordered life possible by limiting what people can perceive and do but also by what they are permitted to see and do. This is the basis for local traditions that may vary from place to place and is declared a fact by believers as well as by people who are critical of the 'mullah-religion'. Denying this fact makes no sense because nothing can come from nothing. Believing that things can exist without having been created is said to be unsettling, wrong and bad.

Although at times interrupted by God's wilful episodes, God's order is called reliable and reassuring. It is abundantly manifested in nature and in everything natural (*tabii*) as well as in God's directives for human behaviour. Except for a few local agnostics, the common understanding is that God's demand of 'dos' and 'don'ts' are quintessentially necessary and good. This is a basic assumption, a dogma, a given, not a choice, and can be demonstrated by looking around, as a neighbour assured me: every single thing one sees has its place, every tree knows when and how to grow, every animal is able to survive and bring up its young. Men and women are created to be different and therefore will behave differently, naturally so, and this is good, too. Whatever is not good in nature, such as a wheat pest, a mudslide, an earthquake, lambs and kids dying of diarrhoea, wolves eating sheep, the aches of old age, is ascribed to God's inscrutable Will, which is unassailable, beyond argument and human understanding.

For people who like to ponder such ideas, a problem arises: why does God make pests that wilt wheat and wolves that eat lambs and '*mikrub*' that sicken people, but then also lets people invent medicines for the sick and insecticides against blights, and bestows on some people the power to write amulets that will bind a wolf's jaw? There are two main choices for answering such questions: the empirical-minded realists say that God gave people brains and arms and legs with which to find their way through life, and never mind why His order is the way it is. Pious scripturalists say that trust in God and gratefully doing His bidding will make for a good life, and that poverty and ailments may show that God is angry or else that the afflicted are not applying themselves: a comfortable life is possible by following God's rules. These options are equally popular and are invoked, often by the same person, to fit circumstances and the needs of the moment (R. Loeffler 1987). Only a few serious doubters are troubled by the contradictions. The general consensus is that the choices are there to be used to one's advantage – this makes them good and reassuring.

In the vast domain of God's order I will single out three basic concepts that are taken to firmly structure life on earth: beauty, work and time.

Beauty

Ethics and Morals

The terms used for beauty, such as Luri *malus*; Farsi *qashang*, *zibā*, but also *pāk*, *tamiz*, meaning 'clean', suggest a firm link to goodness and ethics especially when applied to humans. In contrast to other natural things and beings that cannot choose how to behave and thus are likely without sin, human beings are taken to be endowed with reason that lets them discern and judge. This enables them to make right, God-pleasing, good-beautiful choices. Failure to make them points to sloppy thinking and to giving in to ugly, sinful tendencies. There is no beauty in this: lack of ethics is also lack of aesthetic value.

The common assumption that human activities are circumscribed by explicit ethical and moral considerations leaves no choice: people's actions are 'good' or 'bad' not only in terms of taste and preference but also in terms of their observable morality. The shape of this morality is formed by tradition, that is, by habituated assumptions and actions (*adab o rosum*); by one's dealings with others, whereby service to people (*khedmat be mardom*) ranks very high; and by personal conduct and interests. The most basic and popular rule for moral content of aesthetic qualities is that more goodness means more beauty and therefore that 'bad' is 'ugly'. Believers insist that God and the Quran are the apex of beauty, wisdom and goodness. Whatever else is truly beautiful is very likely also good: a green pasture, a herd of sheep 'with full bellies' (meaning well fed and pregnant), a smiling baby, a kind word, straight furrows in a field, a well-performed song, a neat woman, a pile of spic-and-span dishes, a roof covered with drying apricots, a bag of wheat, a kebab on a skewer over a fire, a sleek horse, a new car, a big, orderly crowd at a funeral – all are pleasing and called 'good', and so are the creators and owners of the useful order, of the beautiful things.

Beauty of People

From here it is only a small move to put human senses into a moral frame: looking good, smelling good, talking well, being amiable, and the effort to bring these features about can be taken to be a duty: a wife ought to make herself and the home attractive for her husband. This is according to the resident mullah (R. Loeffler 1988: 23) and to urban tastes, and as praise of ideal wifely behaviour it is also sung about.[1]

Beautiful children are their parents' darlings, and to treat children according to their attractiveness is taken as a normal fact of life. 'He is ugly and the teacher doesn't like him,' was the matter-of-fact explanation for the low grades a little boy got in school. And when an aunt fretted about the impending marriage of her very young niece, a neighbour offered consolation: surely the in-laws would like their new bride and treat her well because she was so pretty. Beauty may have religious merits, too. Every time my hosts saw one of their neighbours, a poor woman with a much-envied knack for always looking neat, clean and attractive, they blessed her for uplifting the mood of everybody who saw her. 'Sunshine' (*aftāb*) is a personal name for women. For an elderly neighbour, visits by her pretty, sunny granddaughter 'turned on the light' in her life. In this expression, several aesthetic lines merge: the granddaughter was pretty; she provided entertaining stories from news on the radio and from relatives and neighbours; she was empathetic, helped with chores and was a reliable messenger. This made the lonesome old woman feel more like 'belonging', she said. The girl was good and beautiful on many counts.

For all its merits, though, the pursuit of attractiveness in Iran often turns into an expensive, 'narcissistic obsession with beauty', a 'disease', as a local psychologist called it, and an 'ugly sin' in the opinion of supporters of the Islamic government's religious standards.[2] Urban choices to create and enhance beauty locally became available within the last two generations together with their economic implications. A jealous local physician regretted having limited his training to family practice because 'The really wealthy doctors are cosmetic surgeons.' The modern make-up of a bride may be declared to be a kind of lie because it turns the homeliest girl into a movie star, as a bride's astonished sister said. This transformation requires the better part of a day at the beauty parlour, and in 2015 cost the groom a month worth of a teacher's salary. A local banker summed up the choices while talking about people's debts: 'The expensive beauty is sinful for the very pious, ugly (*zesht*) and dumb (*bi-aql*) for those who don't have the money to buy good looks and for the enlightened (*roshan fekr*) who have better things to do than grooming; and the government calls it illegal. Most people in town do what they can to look well without great expense – they simply can't afford to look like movie stars.' Unless handled with circumspection, beauty can easily lose aesthetic merits.

The proverbially best look for women is that of a fourteen-year-old of 'good colour', meaning healthy and well-built – a slim, pale, slouching woman may be weak and unable to work hard, as a mother of three daughters explained. Beyond this traditional ideal there are other choices now. 'I want to look like the women in California,' said a girl in her teens, speaking, as she said, 'for everybody in my school'. The cherished marks of beauty are, indeed, a mix of traditional features and the global aesthetics of modern beauty queens. The dissenters, mostly *hizbollah* women quoting religion, but also some young people who call themselves 'reasonable', dismiss this ideal as 'Hollywood make-up'. Locally, traditional sensibilities, an often stated preference for 'natural' over 'artificial' (such as in 'natural beauty is best'), and lack of money keep women from using expensive beauty enhancement, except when made up and dressed as a bride to the point of being totally unrecognisable. 'I thought his bride is Maryam! Where is she?' joked a cousin at Maryam's wedding.

On a woman, the only hair ought to be on her head, especially beautiful if it is brownish rather than black, and on her eyebrows. Elsewhere on the body it is said to be 'dirty' and therefore has to go, as per God's order for cleanliness.

A bride's 'white belly' (meaning no pubic hair) was sung about in wedding songs, and scraping and plucking out-of-place facial hair and all body hair is a woman's chore in the bath house. Sisakht had a communal bath house since its beginning, said the barber who is in charge of it now. Indeed, the bath was one of two regularly used public communal buildings.[3] Women especially cherished it as a place where they could socialise in comfort while doing the aesthetically important chore of self-cleansing with the help of the bath attendant (the bath-keeper's daughter): the bath is 'good' for religious as well as social reasons. 'I always was the first to notice when a woman was pregnant,' said a grandmother about one of the benefits. Showers in homes have become prevalent and are taken as hallmarks of modernity and progress, but they lack the communal aspect. In a far-off summer pasture the women even built a make-shift bath place themselves. If not in use, the empty bath house was 'a bit strange' and had the reputation of being a likely jinn-place. Indeed, even modern, indoor bathrooms and toilets have this vague aura of danger: young children who need to use them become whiney and demand company. 'They learn this nonsense from each other,' said an eldest brother about his siblings; 'All the dumb kids are afraid of the bathroom.'

The beautiful woman's skin is clean and white, without blemishes such as freckles. Dark skin is taken as a sign of much menial work in the sun (*sesokhte*, burned black) or else of inheritance from low-status parents: 'Ahmed's daughters are strong but a bit black,' goes a ditty. The nose can be made small by surgery, but this effort is sometimes unsuccessful: 'Last year my nose was too long and now it is crooked!' said a bemused young woman who had sold her earrings and bangles to pay for a beautiful nose. Cheeks ought to be rosy, the lips full (tattoos are available to improve them), the back straight and the gait should be strong and easy. None of these details are pressing concerns locally but they are discussed as signs of health and strength, and furnish realistic choices for enhancing one's attractiveness. Virginity is not visible but expected as a matter of course until marriage and if need be, surgery is available in the city.[4] The eyes are most beautiful if they are dark and round, with eyebrows 'ram's horn'-style (meeting over the bridge of the nose) in the past and now curving elegantly. This can be achieved by plucking and tattooing, but sometimes the brow ends up a bit lopsided, which is 'very bad' and prompts curses on doctors and tattoo-artists. In contrast to these new tattoos, traditional ones (*khal*) consisted mostly of dots and short lines on the face, hands, wrists and feet, and were meant for health, beauty, control of pain and to make one likeable and successful (Deter-Wolf et al. 2014, discuss the history of this old body-art).

Beauty in men is less of a public issue, but it is noted. 'His grandmother always burns wild rue for Ali because he is so beautiful,' said a young man about his cousin, mixing jealousy with poking fun, and several people commented on the misfit between an 'ugly' wife and her 'very *shik*' husband, a new doctor in town. Cosmetic surgery for men is known to be available, too, mostly used to remove skin blemishes and wrinkles. Young women may opt to make vows to saints for help in getting a suitor who is 'rich, good-looking and salty' (*bānamak*, sexy-attractive). 'Look at his tiny white hands!' a young woman murmured with disgust about a visitor's hands, and another one named a suitor's sagging shoulders and odd walk as reasons for rejecting him. The attractive man ought to be young, tall, straight, without faults such as a bald head, a limp or bad skin, although high status and a good income will cover many blemishes, as a mother of two daughters in town said with a straight face in 2015.

God's Will in such beauty issues can be problematic for people who are bothered by their own thoughts. A grandmother made fun of them: 'God makes a woman in a certain way but if she is too beautiful it is a bother for everybody, and if she is ugly, thin and with freckles on her nose it is another kind of bother for her and for the husband who has to look at her every day.' In 2015, a high school student found it absurd that: 'God makes a girl ugly and then makes surgeons to make her beautiful, and then orders her to cover herself from head to toe to prevent sinful passion in men.' Like everything else, beauty is for sale now and depends on money, which means that 'ugly people who are poor have to stay ugly, and that's that', in the conclusion of a young man. Justice has an aesthetic component, too.

This is the flip-side of any beauty: although high on the aesthetic vision scale, good on principle and meritorious when contained in one or another of several morally acceptable frames, beauty is potentially dangerous. It may lead to disquiet, jealousy, distress, such as when a man becomes infatuated with his shiny car or a beautiful woman beyond his reach. It may make a person 'get lost' in contemplating an alluring object or experience, as happened to a local man who was said to be so taken by the meditative work in his beautiful orchard that he neglected his other duties and his family. Given human nature, beautiful things are said to attract envy and theft, inevitably so: 'Whatever your eyes see, your *del* (seat of emotions) wants,' goes a proverb. A joker in town said that our family was different because when Lurs entered a room, their first idea was to see what they would like to steal, while we obviously had no such urges. Until recently, to ward off any potential bad side-effects of praise, such as a mishap, admiration was accompanied by an exclamation of '*mashallah*' ('God has willed it').

Attractive presentation of oneself and one's belongings, meritorious as it is on principle, can turn easily into undue self-promotion (*veshd*) and may attract the evil eye,[5] envy or, in women, unwelcome attention from men, as well as gossip and a charge of frivolity and sinful flirtation. In 2015, a well-to-do man in town drove an old, rickety car so as to prevent 'unhealthy attention from the authorities' which a new car would elicit, he said; a young man obsessed with his immaculate appearance, especially his hair, was told by his uncle to tone down his grooming lest the evil eye would strike him for sure; and an exceedingly attractive high school student complained that no matter how much she covered herself and avoided looking at anybody on her way to and from school, men were ogling her and this ruined not only her reputation but theirs as well – the behaviour was ugly, and the cause, her beauty, was a bother and a danger for her. This flip-side principle pertains to everything that is pleasing: people, animals, a field of wheat, a tool. People tell the story that when the first tractor came to town they admired it so much that either the evil eye or the combined power of their admiring gaze made it turn over and nearly kill the driver.

Beauty of Nature

The best example for the God-given, useful beauty of nature (*tabiat*) is in the variety of trees, including many fruit trees, people found when they moved up into the highlands. The Zagros area is 'God's orchard', they say. An official in the local agricultural office named these native trees: willows, plantains, oaks and several conifers, and also wild apples, several plum varieties, apricots, walnuts and almonds. Now cultivated in orchards, these count as God's shared wealth (*neimat-e khodā*) together with the many edible wild plants that provide taste and *vitāmin* to bland basic dishes. The very first thing settlers did – and still do – in a new place was to plant willows, walnuts, plums and apricots as signs of culture and in order to stake a property claim. Trees in the woods provided firewood but are increasingly crowded out by agriculture. 'Now that we have gas to burn, the oaks are useless,' said a man who, with government support, replaced the 'old trees' with apple trees, turning a communal dry-oak forest into his own, irrigated orchard.

For all its God-given goodness and beauty, nature, too, produces practical and cognitive problems. A strong anthropocentric bias lies in the God–nature–human relationship: God made nature for itself – from mountains and rivers to grass and animals – but also obviously for people's use, which means that whatever nature provides for people proves God's benevolence and foresight. This is a basic assumption. Furthermore, while everybody appreciates a spring-pasture red with wild tulips, a green field, pink blossoms on apple trees and orange apricots drying on a flat roof, everybody also knows that like most pleasant natural phenomena, beauty in nature is of short duration, comes alive and dies quickly. In addition, many natural features and occurrences harm people and make life difficult, from earthquakes and mudslides to accidents and diseases.

Indeed, nature in the raw, as wilderness, is dangerous for people and on this account provides little aesthetic comfort. *Biābuni* ('place without water'), an uncultivated wilderness, refers to uninhabited or uninhabitable places, and conjured jinn, wolves, snakes, bears, boars as well as robbers and bad people in the past and a little bit to this day. 'Disappearing over the mountain pass' is a metaphor for death but also for men who flee domestic problems; to 'take to the mountains' means banditry or hiding from enemies; to be '*ve sahrā*' (outside the house or settlement) meant play-space for children near the house but also the potential danger of a liminal space. The toil and trouble of making a wilderness arable and of planting crops are taken to be pleasing God. *Ābād kardan*, to make habitable, is a well-used verb, a duty, orderly beauty and religiously meritorious, and has deep roots in Persian cultural history, as many local people like to point out. They credit Zoroastrians for an ancient irrigation channel on the Sisakht plain that they restored and use to this day.

As the sphere of tamed nature around the village grew, the danger zone receded, and when studying became an option for some young people, male students in need of study-space often took to the near outdoors and the orchards to escape the crowded, noisy courtyards. For them, *ve sahrā* meant a quiet place to study. And for young men who wanted to 'cook and smoke a little' (controlled substances) quietly, 'a tiny fire in the woods' was an attractive, safe place. Women's outdoor choices were much more limited. Women were outside the house for obvious, valid reasons such as fetching water or visiting a relative, and left the settlement only with other women, such as for gathering wild vegetables, weeding a field or hiking, in a combination of work, exercise and the pleasures of good company and fresh air, as they say. Safety still is in numbers for them. To be outdoors in a women's group one feels safe from predators (including men), women say, 'it is a good habit'. For men watching groups of colourfully dressed women from afar used to be a safe pleasure sung about in songs and living on in joyful memories of the old days.

By 2000, the 'biological interface with the environment' (Tyson 2007: 26), and attitudes towards nature had expanded beyond utility, fear, toil and secretive projects: outside the borders of fields and orchards, nature now provides pleasurable, attractive choices for exercise, for picnics and for leisurely harvesting of edible plants for fun more than for necessity. By the turn of the century urban middle-class people's habits of hiking and mountaineering locally were accepted as 'good, healthy' entertainments by some local young men, but hiking also took on political ballast. Outdoor-oriented environmental activists together with the 'Greens'[6] were officially declared to be a threat to the government. Several young local people who occasionally hiked together for fun, health and to enjoy 'the beauty of the peaks', as one said, got into trouble with the authorities, and this turned nature into politics, a good activity into a bad experience, and health and beauty into a headache.

Aesthetics of Domestic Order

Gardens[7]

The benefits of enhancing nature's beauty are most appreciated in gardens and orchards (both called *bāgh*). Pious people say that creating and tending a beautiful garden earns the gardener religious merits (*savāb*) by combining fragrances, colours, cooling water, shade and pleasing order that otherwise can be expected only in paradise. People who are inclined to 'think a lot', and who are aware of their Persian cultural roots, say that 'garden' has two meanings:

the old Persian one, which gives people the mandate and ability to make nature into an image of paradise or treat it as a step to the perfect paradisiacal garden; and the Abrahamic one, which conceives the world to be rather dark and dangerous, a place far away from the heavenly gardens attainable – by some – only after death. The ensuing, often contradictory choices for imagining one's natural, God-given existence 'fill a big cauldron, all mixed up', in the words of an elderly man who had 'seen it all'.

The ancient Persian attitude towards nature and gardens is alive in Boir Ahmad as a common-sensical way to make nature useful in a practical and aesthetic sense: food is 'good' and so are trees and flowers, and gardens are the best, said a visitor, cherishing the memory of the gardens he had seen in Shiraz. The work, time, money and patience needed to design and maintain a garden such as the spectacular Bagh-e Eram in Shiraz[8] or the famous Ćeshme Belqeis in central Boir Ahmad (built around a spring named after Belqeis, the wife of the local khan), link religious merits to wealth and status: rich people have the financial and social means to create and maintain representative gardens and will reap the benefits of fame and religious merits for this work, while poor people can not earn such merits. A few local people place the issue into a justice versus injustice dialogue, but it can be easily pushed aside with a reference to God's Will or else by making fun of it. 'For every seed he plants, my uncle expects a kiss from a houri in paradise', joked a young man about his ambitious uncle's tiny front yard. Mostly, though, the discussion gets a positive spin: if gardens make visitors happy, the owners ought to get a just reward 'here and later there' for tending it, said a fruit grower, pruning his apple trees. There is no famous garden in Sisakht, but local chiefs made a point of living in a big house surrounded by trees and flower beds, as do well-off owners of Gulf-style villas now, although the rocky soil, the high altitude and lack of skilled and willing garden workers make maintenance difficult.

Dwellings
Buildings count as opposites of raw nature and as an improvement on it. As places of comfort, order and safety they are good on principle and 'very good' when well maintained. There is hardly any dissent from the opinion that taking care (*safd kardan*) of one's things is a duty, a virtue and good to behold. In the early 1970s, the villagers, poor as they were, decided to pay a street sweeper to

keep the alleys clean. This was called 'good': a sign of progress, of obedience to God's demand for cleanliness, and pleasant to look at, an aesthetic satisfaction all around. For the same reasons people built outhouses in the 1960s when the first government-appointed physician in the local health clinic, a young man from Tabriz lauded for his competence, integrity and authority, persuaded them of the health benefits. A few years later, with government help the villagers also installed water pipes to get clean water to every courtyard, and when electricity came to town in the 1970s so many people blessed Mr Edison for having invented it that the blessings 'surely lift him up to the highest-ranking angels', as a neighbour quipped. Once again, progress was called a great lifestyle improver, and 'good'.

Inside a tent, hut or house, the foremost intended aesthetic is cleanliness and order, even in the smallest, simplest places such as a branch hut in a herding outpost. There, a clean fireplace, scrubbed pots, a swept dirt floor, shooed-away chickens, and a rug and tea ready when needed marked a good housekeeper, be it a man or woman. In better equipped, new homes, progress and status are asserted further by providing separate sleeping spaces for children, indoor plumbing, a modern (*opén* – the English word is used) kitchen with cupboards, and a table and chairs instead of a rug on the floor as an eating space. In the local middle class it has become de rigueur to arrange two sets of sofas and chairs to provide different spaces for men and women visitors in a parlour (*salon*). In formal settings the separation of unrelated men and women was dictated by tradition and common sense. Women likely occupied the domestic work space, such as around a fireplace on a veranda, while men congregated in the 'good' space of the tent or house. The separation was natural, they said, a matter of convenience. It did not make women's interaction with men impossible, but let women visitors talk among themselves 'instead of listening to the men'. Except for close relatives, this gender segregation is upheld also in modern houses – it continues to be a matter of propriety and convenience.

Propriety here is based on the assumption that men's innate sexual inclinations and women's purported innate inability to withstand men's advances make rules necessary that limit interactions between unrelated men and women. Under the missionary influence of the Islamic government, the aesthetic bar of sensibilities shifted towards an even heavier morality. Especially for *hizbollah*-leaning people, socially mixing unrelated males and females of any age, for whatever purpose and especially in public became morally problematic, and this bent the aesthetics of modesty towards the separation of boys and girls in school, women patients from male doctors (if possible), women dancers at weddings and women mourners from male ones, and also of male and female visitors at home. There is little choice. Walls and well-defined indoor spaces contain order one can easily declare to be natural in the sense of intended by God, and thus to be beneficial and beautiful.

Work (*kār*)

Merits, Ethics and Controversy

Experience shows that labour, work, toil and exertion are built into God's order to sustain life on Earth. In Sisakht, these are taken as a given and thus as deeply embedded in aesthetics, but they also are deeply controversial. On the one hand, *zahmat* (toil, hardship, trouble) without a choice is said to be absolutely necessary to make the world go 'round, to fulfil people's duty to make the world liveable (*abād*) and keep everybody fed and orderly', not to speak of living well. On the other hand, the fact that one is forced to work as per God's Will and demand, and has to cope with the painful physical costs of labour makes people worried, tired and uncomfortable. The little beauty people report seeing in physical labour lies in the potential religious merits of some work and in some products of exertion. The fruits of labour (such as grapes and apples, a sack of wheat, a good meal, a car) provide the pleasure of satisfaction, but the work necessary to achieve it is 'just work'. A local man, well-known and appreciated for his skills in making perfect mud-bricks for house walls with rhythmic, steady movements that were a pleasure to watch, saw his job on a hot summer day as an exhausting toil that stressed his back – he was hot, tired and aching, and for him this counted the most. However, the rows of his neat bricks lined up to dry in the sun were a joy to look at, and passers-by praised him: 'May your hand not ache' (*daset dard nakone*); 'May God give you strength' (*khodā qouve*); and 'Don't be tired' (*nakhaste*), they said.

The first of these phrases is also used routinely to express gratitude, regardless of the exertion used for the rendered service. With it, 'thank you' combines gratitude with a wish for absence of pain.⁹ Such phrases of encouragement implicitly acknowledge the cost of hard work and count it as a *narāhat*, a 'non-comfort' that pious believers locate in God's order as a punishment for Adam's misbehaviour in the Garden of Eden. In contrast, *rāhat*, comfort, is a caring host's admonition to a guest ('make yourself comfortable!') as well as a promised feature of paradise. Paradise is the place for wellbeing without toil. Everybody says so, more or less seriously, even agnostics, doubters and critics of religious doctrines.

One can see a kind of beauty in one's work if done in a pleasing, clean environment, in good company, promising good pay or excitement such as in hunting, for example, or if it is inducive to contemplation, such as in harvesting an orchard, ploughing straight furrows, gathering edible plants in spring, weaving in the shade of a tree, tending tomato plants in a greenhouse, doing chores while sitting comfortably. Comfort makes white-collar work better than any other work. Neat and clean teachers and doctors, traders and clerks are said to be good to look at in contrast to dusty farmers and labourers, and this beauty has merit.

Since the 1970s, when education offered a choice to attain a 'better life', ambitious parents increasingly try to steer their children away from physical work. In 1995, a local widow refused to tell her sons, who attended high school, to plough a field because, she said, she did not want the boys to see themselves as farmers – they ought to study (several times she secretly worked the field herself, at night). In 2015, the young son of an ailing farmer was working long hours by himself in the orchard during his summer vacation. His mother was proud of him but made sure that everybody understood that he was not a farmer but an 'A' student in an elite boarding school, destined for university studies, and that his toil was beyond what one ought to ask of him and therefore had religious merits and God's blessing; the orchard indeed did very well. (There is also an entirely practical reason for these women's behaviours: they were afraid that if one of the husband's brothers helped the young nephews, as would be right and proper, he later might try to claim the harvest or even the land on account of having worked it.)

One can rarely choose a specific kind of job in Boir Ahmad or how to do the job available to him or her: a young daughter-in-law has to do her in-laws' bidding; a worker has to obey the foreman; a blacksmith has to learn from his father about metals, heat and bellows; a brick-maker has to work with mud; a miller has to know about flour and how to run the motor-driven mill. Likely they all have their jobs and skills from their fathers. The elders, though, are not of much help for skills needed in modern jobs. Soon after public schools opened in the village, in the early 1960s, the attendance rate climbed to 90 per cent for boys and, a bit later, also for girls. The option was less a choice for them than a necessity. But basic education is no longer enough for a good job, and access to higher education depends on grades on the university-entrance examination (*konkur*), an annual major headache for graduating high-school students; on available slots in university programmes; on what fields of study parents see as advantageous; on what parents can afford financially; and only a little bit on a student's own preference.

These circumstances create opportunities for bright rural and low-class children but also anxiety, mis-matches and misgivings. A student with a *konkur*-grade a notch too low for 'anything good' such as engineering, saw his life 'ruined' (*kharab*) when he only was accepted in a less prestigious, 'boring' agriculture programme in a far-away provincial university. A medical student followed his parents' advice to choose radiology as his specialty solely on the grounds of good income and working hours. A young local engineer refused a job offer and chose to stay at home sulking because his parents had not allowed him to study languages when his good grades had qualified him for the much more prestigious and lucrative engineering field. A student who had qualified for veterinary medicine, years later told me he had a desk-job and luckily never had to treat an animal; and a young nurse described in words and facial contortions how much she disliked touching sick people. Teachers, however, often told me that they liked 'making children literate' despite the low salary, and also that they liked the long vacations. A well-off, well-regarded and successful man in town chose to develop his herd and fields into a thriving business instead of looking for a 'chic' occupation. Although approved of and even admired in town for his success, people may refer to him also as an old-timer, a term that carries no great compliment.

People's reactions to their chores and handling of their jobs suggest that the necessity to work and the structures around work are firmly anchored in ethics and daily routines but that little joy is expected in work per se. One does not have to 'like' it, and it has no religious merits either unless it is heroic or one uses the gains for alms and religious purposes. Work is a necessary duty (*vazife*), an obligation (*majburi*) and 'good' because it keeps people alive and the world turning. 'Work was survival, and opportunity was the future,' K. Loeffler (2022: 126) remembers of her years among young people in Sisakht, and people shake their heads when they remember their parents' and grandparents' hard work. Because laziness clogs up life, it is declared a bother for others, a sin. '*Ma bikāri?*' ('Have you no work to do?') is a frequent, dismissive criticism of a gossip or idler, while an industrious person who always finds something to do is complimented as a *kārkon*, a 'work-doer'. Neglecting one's duties is sinful and for a farmer is tantamount to self-harm, which pious people declare to be especially offensive to God. People readily call neglect of duty by white-collar workers sinful, too, but lackadaisical performance of clerks and bureaucrats is of little material consequence for the slackers and hardly invites comment: a lazy postmaster gets a salary anyway, as does a teacher who leaves the classroom for hours while going about other business, or a clerk in an office who lets unfinished business pile up on the desk. 'They have an easy life,' people say.

In contrast, farmers, herders, craftsmen and workers cannot choose to neglect their work without serious, bad consequences, and neither can women.

Women and Work

Regarding the aesthetics of women's work, again some structural features matter more than individual people's likes and dislikes.

The traditional economy was based on the interdependence of men and women. Women said they turned what men brought home into necessities for living by preparing food, processing milk and keeping a larder for winter, but with the catch that they were responsible for feeding everybody regardless of how much or little the husband provided (the gathering of acorns, greens and berries, mostly done by women, was important in the traditional economy partly for this reason). They furthermore produced the items providing comfort, such as floor coverings, bedding and clothes, and were caretakers of the young, sick and elderly. Even with mutual help from other women in the household and from children and siblings, women were visibly over-worked, under-fed and exhausted, and they complained about it. The daily work load was lightened when done in good company, such as when, in the past, two women choose to team up hulling rice by pounding it with heavy wooden pestles in a wooden mortar in a fast rhythm kept by singing a work-song; or sitting around a big tray cleaning lentils; or baking bread or collecting acorns in the autumn and wild spinach, mint, onions and artichokes in the spring. Even shaking out rugs and lugging water in heavy skin-bags were declared to be less of a drudge when done in the company of other women. Not only was the social frame pleasurable, but the outcome, the news learned and discussed, questions asked and answered, help requested and accepted, the smell of a stack of fresh bread, cool water to drink, a tasty barley–lentil soup, clean rugs on the floor – all were sources of satisfaction.

As this work petered out when chores like milking, hulling rice and fetching water disappeared in the wake of 'progress', women started to complain about isolation and about 'having nothing much to do', meaning that much of what they did now had few aesthetic merits. Eventually, spending 'a lot of time and money' on the telephone with relatives, and on new busywork in home-making became emotional necessities for some, a chore to keep up with the neighbours for others, and boring nonsense, too. Cell phones and the Internet increased choices for filling time even more, as do cars and travelling. All these activities cost money – women need it without adding to the domestic economy, as a social worker concluded (Archer and Ware 2018, discuss this global development). 'I am to believe that God wants it that way?' said a young man who was critical of 'bad, modern developments' and of his adolescent sisters' leisure time.

Tradition meant a man counted anything his wife produced as his own, including children and a wife's wage or salary. For tea, sugar and items needed to fulfil his obligation as provider, a man sold or bartered the rug his wife had woven, the butterfat she had cooked, the wool yarn she had spun. The unpaid work of women in the local economy was a matter of course. Starting in the 1960s, when a few women earned money as teachers, a father or husband likely converted her cash income into domestic necessities and some luxuries such as a washing machine or a television set that benefited the women, as men pointed out, and also for buying land. A woman's salary was in a man's pocket, people said, and a woman had little say in how it was spent unless she made it a more or less contentious issue.

In 2015, the best-reputed, most peaceful local households of couples with two salaries were said to be those where the wife did all the housework – 'of course' – and let her husband manage her salary 'for us all', as one such woman said. It was difficult, she said, but as long as a husband 'listened' to his wife and children, everybody likely felt well-represented and taken care of. The households where a wife insisted on controlling her earnings or demanded cooperation for household chores from the husband were much more likely to be plagued by strife. 'My wife is a teacher with money in her pocket, my dinner is a scrambled egg, and she is not sweet,' goes a popular ditty of complaint. Smart young women make use of Sharia law by insisting on a clause in the marriage contract defining the use of their present and future potential salary. 'It makes the girls feel better,' said a mother of such a bride, but it also angers many young men and their families because they take it to imply lack of respect for the groom, and this is not good.

Legally and by custom, children belong to the father's paternal kin group and the mother is obliged to take care of a son for seven years and eight years for a daughter. In case of a mother's death or a divorce, the full burden of childcare falls on the father. Usually in such cases the father's mother takes care of the children until the father remarries (in some cases even longer: '*Nana* is nicer than father's new wife,' explained one such grandmother, lifting her eyebrows). The law is not an urgent issue in town but women talk about the possibility of 'losing the children' in case of a divorce; they express anxiety when watching sob-stories in soap operas on television, and grandmothers over-burdened by the care of grandchildren voice misgivings. This 'ugly' prospect is the main reason for elderly women to try hard to prevent calamities such as a divorce in the family.

All in all, in the past the lot of women was very difficult, elderly women say in hindsight, and is a 'bit better' or even 'much, much better' now. The combination of hard work, bodily and emotional violence (such as from husband and in-laws), and lack of choices in living arrangements and movement drove up the suicide rate of women. 'What else could she have done?' was women's telling commentary on a suicide, together with scolding the dead woman for abandoning her children. Local people of all walks of life, including doctors and psychologists, credit progress in the economy, social relations and law since the 1970s and the Islamic Republic's Sharia laws for the noticeable increase in wellbeing of women. In 2006, a local woman with an abusive, controlling husband and a five-year-old son told me of her exit-plan, as she called it: the day the boy turned seven she would walk out, leaving the husband to cope. 'Either I leave or I'll kill myself,' she said. Five years later she had done neither. She had learned to handle the situation better, she said, meaning that public opinion, the police, her supportive mother-in-law, an outspoken brother and the opportunity to earn a little money had offered her choices that women in earlier generations in her situation did not have.

A husband's full responsibility for his family's upkeep and his concomitant entitlement to all household income is still in effect but is being questioned now. It was – and still is – used to justify as well as criticise the low job participation of women in Iran generally: young women say that a husband's duty to provide gives them the choice to deny 'working outside' once they are married, and many opt for this choice in order to avoid the misgivings which a double-shift of job and housework, and fights over money may cause. 'Why should I try to get a job when my husband is obliged to take care of me anyway?' asked a young, married, childless woman in 2015. And when recently I asked a local, college-educated young friend about her work status, she said that her husband was doing well and it was not necessary for her to look for a job.

A man whose wife has a paid job has the choice to feel proud of her, to be glad for the extra money, but also to say that his reputation might suffer as it implies that he cannot provide well for his family. 'It doesn't look good,' a struggling householder said. The prejudice is modified by status: a married woman physician, for example, has high social status and a good salary, and never mind the housekeeping, whereas a secretary in an office earns too little to justify an 'empty home' with imperfect housekeeping and exposure to unrelated men in the workplace. A well-off local entrepreneur who did not let his wife teach was explicit: 'A job as a lawyer would be acceptable, but teaching little kids – no, ugly!' he said. One of the first local women teachers said she had no problems working because the male teachers in her school were all related to her. Such arguments have merits in town.

Many anecdotes exist about husbands' objections to a wife's job, but they do not figure in the official, standard reasons given for housebound women, namely, lack of jobs and lack of child care. Both are dubious reasons: the job aversion of married women is a tradition even for women with no or only one child. To stay at home after marriage remains a popular gender principle in Iran. However, women predict that the growth of Internet use and the informal labour sector will eventually offer them more opportunities for paid work that fits gender aesthetics. In 2020, a local former teacher said she was making nearly as much money at home tutoring high school students on line for the university entrance examination as teaching in school, and her husband was very happy about it.[10]

Well-meaning women defend men's short tempers with '*estress*' produced by the many responsibilities men have to bear, such as the obligation to support their families and provide spouses for children without counting on a wife's income. For most men, the aesthetically and ethically right balance between work, income, providing for the necessities of life, fulfilling children's demands, and being kind at home is difficult to achieve, people say. Deeply anchored in a man's identity, pride and social standing, these expectations are a heavy burden for agricultural smallholders as well as for salaried men, and are a well-spring for satisfaction and authority for those who are successful. In 2015, a local town administrator summed up the ubiquitous money problems: 'Now men are depressed, too, not just women. The young ones are angry because they can't afford wives, the others because they cannot keep up with their families' expectations and are overworked.' 'Am I glad I am not my teacher-brother!,' said a young woman about the plight of her brother's pressures from his wife and two children who were expecting a good life on his small salary. The inflationary economy and high lifestyle aspirations make many adults say that they feel poor and 'stuck in one place'. The local suicide rate for men, nearly zero three generations ago, now is rising while the one for women is falling.

Nobody sees beauty or satisfaction in such conditions. For pious people, the correct choice for dealing with these problems is to be content and grateful to God for what they have, little as it may be, but, as a *hizbollah*-leaning man said, 'The problem is that the children want a better life, and this is very difficult.'

Leisure and Discontent

The opposite of work is called 'sitting, being comfortable'. This condition may be taken as a privilege, as a well-earned rest or else as a sign of laziness. It implies that work obligations are taken care of by somebody else. A woman whose daughter-in law does the housework is able to 'sit a lot' (and may like the leisure and bossing the young woman around but also likely will complain about the pains of aging), while a young mother taking care of everybody in the house is 'running all day'. Khans proved their status by 'sitting on pillows' surrounded by servants, retainers and riflemen who were standing. It took several school generations until 'sitting and doing nothing' such as reading or studying became accepted as a kind of work. Furthermore, sedentary work with paper and computer is less of an urgent chore than are milking goats and ploughing fields, and means easy income with clean hands and no pain in one's joints.

The ambivalent implication in 'work' figures in the standard, popular explanation in Iran for unemployment, 'there is no work!' (*kār nist*). There actually is plenty of work available, as older people, parents and government officials point out but it is hard work and badly paid, if at all, and thus uninteresting for the young. In people's complaints about idle youngsters, and despite many exceptions, young men likely chose to ignore relatives' need for help in vineyards as an unpaid chore, a trouble and exertion (*zahmat*), bad luck (*badbakhti*), an embarrassment (*khejālat*, *sharm*), best avoided. Wage-labour jobs such as in construction or factory work are said to be good for poor landless men and Afghani migrants or refugees. Nobody in town wants to be known as a paid servant, and only a couple of the poorest local women chose to help in the fruit harvest for a wage. Shepherds were hard to find after local children went to school, and this contributed to the near abandonment of herding in the 1980s (it now is managed cooperatively, with chores rotating among the owners).

The local social class-component regarding manual work is shared widely and fits into the aesthetic scale of modern progress values in Iran. In 1965, a professor of engineering in Shiraz was puzzled by his mostly urban, upper-middle-class, male students' unwillingness 'to touch a screwdriver', and fifty years later the same class-bias emerged in a discussion about work I had with administrators in the provincial governor's office. The urban officials I talked to furnished examples from their own experiences in their hometowns but said they were astonished to find similar class prejudices and worries among 'modern tribal' people.

The split in the meaning of 'work' into manual labour for one's upkeep that is hard and uncomfortable, and into white-collar jobs that supposedly lead to a 'good' life but are difficult to come by creates stress and troubling thoughts for most people. In 2020, a local physician said about this existential discontent that anxiety and disaffection had settled 'in every house', and he rarely met patients who were not depressed in addition to their physical ailments. This state of affairs is not good at all, people say, it is sad, ugly and has no easy alternatives. For the pious, furthermore, discontent means ungratefulness (*nashokri*) to God, which is considered a grave sin and for some turns the unhappiness into a moral burden.

The ambivalence in the ethics of manual work combined with status ambitions appears also in stories in the Iranian diaspora: a local young woman studying abroad claimed there that her father was a fruit-exporter when, in fact, he was a retired teacher who tended an apple orchard for extra income; a local young man who studied in Tehran joked about hiding his 'dirty farming' background by claiming to be from Shiraz; and a young woman quit her job as a waitress in Europe as soon as she was married because, she said, 'it was unpleasant work and did not pay well'. Yet working hard, being content with one's lot and being grateful for the life one has are universally considered praiseworthy signs of a well-ordered, pious mind. There are people whose cheerful attitude towards their chores lightens many difficulties, but they cannot silence the general grumble. 'I wish I could be like my grandfather who is always in good spirits, no matter how hard he works!' said an unemployed local young man who complained about 'always being tired and worried about money and work and everything'.

However, after the earthquake and the influx of loan money, the 'can do'-spirit of Sisakht is reviving, people report. They talk of building new houses, of buying apartments to rent out, and of becoming contractors (rather than workers) for public projects such as a big bridge over a mountain stream near the town. 'We'll see what will happen tomorrow,' they say. There is a tomorrow now, and the choice to expect better times is available.

For the philosophically inclined, in God's order of things the all-encompassing, basic and inescapable principle of time always changes the human condition.

Time

Like God, Time Just Is

In this third example of God's order, life and death, work and rest, duties, needs and all movement exist in a reliable, given time structure. This is 'plain to see', beyond any argument. People who wonder about time emphasise that it is built into causality and movement. I counted some one hundred Luri and Persian time-related words and phrases in use. A few dozen terms also imply space, such as in verbs including movement: to stay, get up, walk, plough. The ways time-words are used suggests that time is taken as a basic, God-willed ordering device, an aesthetic constant fitting the experience of moving steadily in reliable increments as shown by the sun and the four seasons.[11] Indeed, it is so obvious a fact to be a truism to say that whatever we can perceive with our ears and eyes is subject to the relentless progress of time, from dawn–day–dusk–night–dawn to birth–young–old–death, from growing wheat to walking from here to there to singing a song, and that all movements (except, maybe, in circles) have a beginning and an end.[12] People who assert that only God has no beginning and no end take God's non-stop-time of eternity as a sign of highest divinity.[13] But even less pious believers argue that time must have been part of creation simply because it exists, and, like all creation, will come to an end or else will repeat itself in a circle. 'Time is a tool of God, it is good,' said a local craftsman. There is little choice in dealing with time. People do not talk about saving or spending or wasting time, for example. A young teacher joked that it was the only good thing nobody could boss around and nobody could pocket for himself.

In terms of time-philosophy, the unquestioned bias in local ways of handling time is presentism in the sense that what is empirically 'real' is here and now. The past is no longer, the future is not yet, and everybody is on a path from here to there with the hope of 'arrival', be it at success or a good place. The much-used term *pishraft* for development literally means to walk forward (just like Latin-derived English 'progress' does). The arrival is up to God, though: expressions such as 'God willing' (*inshallah*), 'If it pleases God' (*meile khodā*), and 'Nobody knows' (*hishkes noune*) are used often when discussing time issues. In local time-language, the present extends a little into the future to include what is about or expected to happen. 'I will leave now' is expressed as, 'I have left' (akin to 'I'm gone already' in English); 'then' (*uso*) may refer to a happening in the past or in the future (akin to the English use of 'then'). For what will happen soon one often uses the present tense: 'Tomorrow I go to the health clinic'; 'Next year I start school'. It implies that one is ready to face what will come next, that one is as open to what the day will bring as to remember what has happened earlier. Motion-related verbs furthermore imply time and are used with a destination: I do not just 'walk' but 'I walk to the store' (psychologists link such use of motion-related verbs to goal-orientation).

Calendars and the Year

One of the two calendars used in Iran is based on the cycle of the sun with the year beginning on the spring equinox, with twelve months, four seasons that support agriculture, and with equinoxes as sign posts validated by observation – they make sense empirically. The other is the moon-based Islamic Hijri-calendar based on the phases of the moon with emphasis on important religious events. The moon-based year is shorter and thus such events are moved backward in respect to the solar calendar. For agricultural people attuned to sun, rain and snow, the sun-rhythm is naturally compelling, while the moon-rhythm, clearly also fixed in God's plan, is made compelling by religious authorities. People make the point that the Islamic calendar's shift of rituals and festivities is also at odds with the standard (Gregorian) calendar used in the modern, globalised world. 'Although it is always the same time, people mess it up,' said an elderly merchant about calendars.

In both calendars, months are divided into seven-day weeks. The first day of the week, *shanbe* (Saturday), is considered to be an inauspicious day for starting new projects such as travel.[14] Wednesday, too, may be declared problematic, while the other days are neutral in terms of luck but may be good or bad in the personal aesthetic parameters established by individuals' experiences. 'When the first person I see on a Tuesday morning is a good guy, I know it will be a good day,' said a neighbour. One pays attention to the calendar. Thursday afternoon (*shou jom'e*, 'evening before Friday'), is the time to visit dead relatives in graveyards, a fixed weekly routine especially for women (most men delegate these duties to the women in their families). In these modern times of schools and offices, Friday is a holiday except for farmer-herders and women who point out that they have to do their chores every day. It is the day when a preacher leads the Friday prayer and gives a sermon in the new mosque. The mullah who had been in Sisakht for two decades before the revolution rarely came to the old mosque, an unadorned, large, one-room mud-brick building, and rarely gave Friday sermons because the men were too busy to attend, he said (women, implicitly and in practice, were not expected there).

In the cognitive calendar-map of the cycling year the equinoxes are fixed points: 'We moved back from the pastures forty days after the first day of autumn,' for example, or 'My son was born in the middle of summer.' While herding was important still, one of the goat herders in a snowy winter pasture where the hungry animals browsed on trees and bushes, each morning with his knife marked the first rays of the sun where it hit the wall of his hut a bit earlier each day, as a reminder that spring would come, reliably so. He said he was counting down his own life, day by day. The annual festive, day-long move outdoors thirteen days after the spring equinox to avoid potential hostile powers roaming the village on that day, called 'thirteenth outside the door' (*sizda ve dar*), was one of the most joyous, happy-making holidays of the year until hardliners in the Islamic Republic repressed it, to the dismay of nearly everybody in town. The Persian outdoor fire ritual 'Red Wednesday' (*čarshanbe suri*) is staged on the night of the last Tuesday before the spring equinox/New Year. Although not (yet) popular in Sisakht, it is meant to secure good health with the phrase, 'Your rosy-ness for me, my yellow-ness for you' (fire is red, the colour of health; yellow means weakness and ailing). It combines old rituals such as for good health, remembrance and avoidance of souls of the dead, and purification by fire, all happening on Wednesday, which for some people is a faintly unlucky day.[15]

The Abrahamic use of 'forty' connotes a lengthy, important period such as the purported time of chaos in the world just before the Twelfth Imam will start the Day of Judgement. In local usage it is often the actual number: *čellom* ('the forty') is a commemorative ritual forty days after a person's death, and also marks the post-partum period of seclusion, rest and no sex for a new mother. The ritual bath at the end of this period is obligatory but the rest-seclusion was somewhat illusory for most local women who had to manage a complex household with little help. Remembering her mother, a neighbour made this 'forty' a matter of lifestyle when she told the story of her own birth on the migration from a winter pasture back to the village: 'My mother was riding on a donkey with me in her arms an hour or so after giving birth – where was a forty-day rest period?'

The two ways of locating time in the calendars often overlap and collide in their respective activities and meanings, causing rivalries (R. Loeffler and Friedl 2022). In such cases Islamic authorities disparage cherished pre-Islamic solar-calendar events such as the New Year celebrations as heathen and frivolous. Nevertheless, given how deeply rooted in Persian aesthetics they are, authorities more or less quietly tolerate them 'for the time being', as a theology student said. When the death commemoration of a prominent local man in Sisakht coincided with New Year festivities, his sons took the party to the cemetery by spreading the customary special seven items (*haft sin*) on the grave and hosting visitors there (R. Loeffler and K. Loeffler 2022).

Blocks of Time

Counting time in days and seasons is dictated by observation, experience and common sense. There are no other choices. Counting it using hours became a choice when the wrist watch became a status symbol for men (Persian *sā'at* means both hour and time-piece) and a sign of modernity and progress. It was handy for occasions when precise time had to fit a precise location: school starts at eight o'clock in the school house; the bus to the provincial capital arrives at (around) four o'clock in front of the butcher's store; the news on radio and television come up only at certain times. When a first-grader insisted on leaving for school at the crack of dawn, he argued that school started in the morning and he must not be late. 'I'll teach him what eight o'clock means,' said his elder sister, rolling her eyes.

Meanwhile, hour-periods have become familiar and unavoidable, and can be pinpointed anytime, anywhere. But one can always see time move also when watching the sun and one can feel the move when dealing with chores and social life that require set blocks of it. Any cook knows without a watch how long it takes to steam a pot of rice or to roast kebab to perfection over an open fire. One knows how much time is 'good' for a polite visit or a nap or a dance. Prayers, sleep, pregnancies, apples on a tree, a song are linked to time with few variations or choices. Any farmer can tell how much (*mahli*) or little (*kam*) time (that is, measured in volume) it will take to harvest his wheat with a sickle or burn a tree enough be able to smash limbs and trunk, which in the past was the only way to fell a tree. But although time is known to be an autonomous, unvarying movement, one may experience it at different speeds, too: 'It took me a long time to read this'; 'Where did time go?' If one is impatient or bored, time seems to slow down, and if one is hurried or clumsy it seems to accelerate and is hard to keep up with, but these experiences are said to be a person's doing, not a quality of time. Patience (*sabr, tāqat*), the ability to ignore the passing of time occasionally, is declared to be a beautiful virtue, proven to be eminently useful for 'staying upright' when life becomes challenging.

Blocks of time cannot be slowed or hurried much, be they 'dawn' or 'noon', 'early evening' or 'night' (all with their own names), or hours tracked by watches or needed for set chores. Before radio, wrist watches and cell phones, the only public time piece in the area was a big clock on a beautifully tiled tower in Yasuj, the provincial capital. It was pretty but superfluous and soon vandalised. Urgent chores often break the obligatory prayer routine, leaving people with the choice between sin or God's justice: after all, God himself had ordered their hard, time-consuming work that sometimes is at variance with prayer-time. The newest challenge to time's own pace, people joke, is cell phone-time: '*wotsupp*' time for keeping up with relatives a courtyard or a continent away range from brief messages to long sessions in slow afternoons. The cell phone more than any other gadget is the tool for organising events and tracking social and political developments in town. Its use is not a choice but a necessity, people say.

Beyond time's basic rhythm, people often talk of lengthy periods, of 'ages' (*doure*) defined by general themes and socio-political conditions. Recollections of these eras colour people's memories of the past as well as their lives at present. Three such eras stand out:

- The '*doure khānal*' was the time of the khans, the old times when khans wielded power for better or worse; the time of bloody skirmishes and the glory of festivities in the khans' forts; the time of poverty, hard work in sun and snow and its rewards and disappointments with fields and animals. It lasted into the 1960s. Most people in town remember this time with nostalgia as well as misgivings and with hostility and curses especially towards one of the last local chiefs.

- In the early twentieth century the '*doure Shah*' started, overlapping with the first period. It was the time when the Pahlavi governments firmed up control over the tribes, eventually bringing schools, electricity, roads, water, physicians and 'progress' to the area. Looking back, only few people disparage that time. Some still mourn the loss of young men persecuted as communists by Muhammad Reza Shah's secret police. The chiefs' relatives who lost out in the land reform remain angry, and some old people like to remember the 'shameless dress and conduct' especially of young urban women at that time. Progress time in this era sped up after 1963, when the last paramount khan was dead and the nation's administration integrated the area fast and firmly. The political turbulences of the last years of Pahlavi rule had little impact locally.
- The '*doure akhondal*', mullah time, started after the Revolution (1978/79) and is marked by the Islamic government and its much criticised, heavy-handed rules. It started with a terrible war with Iraq and brought many economic difficulties but did not stop socio-cultural progress. Rather, entitlement thinking and lifestyle aspirations that had started under Muhammad Reza Shah continued, as did opportunities for education, including higher education for women, and the decline in the birth rate that firmed up social adjustments such as nuclear families, the widening divide between rich and poor, and emigration of educated young people. Until 2023, local criticism of government policies and challenges to the authoritarian rule of the mullahs did not reach the level of violent protests, mostly because people feared – and still fear, they say – that social chaos might follow the demise of the regime.

In the last two generations a new choice appeared, the '*doure baćyal*', the era of the children. People use the term half-jokingly but with deep sighs, and list a string of features and problems: rising lifestyle aspirations, the rapid decline in the birth rate that makes the few children in small families very precious, and the rising wants and purported needs of these children which tax their elders' patience and wherewithal. Adults used to count children as servant-helpers and as assets, while now they may regard them as valued luxuries. Especially sons are said often to behave like 'shahs' at home, avoiding manual work and demanding services, comforts and a good future from their parents yet being unable to take care of them in old age. Tensions and bad feelings in the aesthetics of family life are expressed in sayings such as, 'My father had ten children and ten thousand worries; I have one son and ten thousand worries.' In the steady decline of the economy in Iran such tensions are increasing.

In people's memories and stories these culture-cluster periods stretch from now (*iso*) backwards in a straight, fading line of history (*sargozasht*) of past time (*u zaman*), of then (*uso*). 'Do you remember?' reaches back less than a lifespan, and time may have hit another before and after point locally with the earthquake in 2021, with rising emigration and the ongoing opposition to what many people call the repressive and economically inept leadership in Iran.

The lifecycle

Life's important time clusters are treated as given without choice: infant (*kućilu*); young child (*baće*, a term often meaning boy and unmarried young man); boy/girl (*kurr/duar*); young adult (*javuni*) and young chap/girl (*ćaqlei/duar*); married man/woman (*merd/zan*); old man/woman (*piremerd/pirezan*). All stages have gender-specific aesthetic domains of behaviour, skills and also emotional reactions to them. People of all ages observe and readily judge gender- and age-specific conduct of others – 'Auntie Maryam is the best!' – and one's approval or criticism by others influences self-image and well-being: 'Just because I am wearing a Lur cap my nephew has to call me "old man"?' complained a neighbour. 'Goli always hits me, she is ugly and I don't want to play with her,' said a little girl about an older playmate who was not as kind and helpful as expected; and a young man who had 'no servant to do it for me' was shining his shoes before heading out so as to prevent shaming his family. Until recently, 'child' directly turned into 'young person', an elastic term based on youngsters' competence and reasoning power that made them useful for doing chores – girls earlier than boys. There was no term for teenager in use: a girl in her early teens turned into 'married woman' (*zan*) as soon as possible, and unmarried young men remained 'boys' or 'lads' (*ćaqlei*). Not age in years but married status, strength and skills 'make the days roll along' and define 'young' and 'ripe' and 'reasonable'. Numbering age by years became important when the authorities insisted on a paper showing a date of birth such as for a girl's marriage permit or for an application to college. One could fudge them easily, if necessary.

Women were 'old' when they could no longer bear children, balked at providing sex, and their hair turned white and needed to be dyed, sooner for some, later for others. Men were old when they could no longer work reasonably well. This development is seen as not good but unavoidable. Hardly anybody talks about beauty or advantages of old age. Aging is connected with wrinkles, bent backs, aches and pains, isolation and few rewards. Old people are praised and honoured loudly for being old and wise, but behind their backs relatives often choose to call them demanding or ugly, especially so old women, who also proverbially were ill-tempered and grumbling. The traditional Lur term for old woman, *dālu*, has become an offensive swear word. Gender-based difference in how old people spend time encourages these stereotypes: while an old man can 'sit and talk', that is, can rest comfortably anywhere and anytime, his elderly wife likely has to perform many of her usual duties of caring for house and husband despite her own aches and pains. 'Nana likes to rest on her rug in the afternoon – it's all she has!' defined a grandmother's approved space for idle time in the house. Tired, elderly women may become resentful and short-tempered, and this is taken as an unavoidable effect of time but also as a gender-attribute.

Except for life's milestones of birth, wedding and death, people did not mark age-related events. In daily life a year, let alone a day, does not make much difference; 'young' and 'old' were indicated by appearance and work abilities, and these change slowly. Two wrinkled, bent and bald old men in town, friends since childhood, said they were both seventy-five years old. According to their children neither was over seventy, and one was three years older than the other, but this did not matter at all in how they felt or behaved, smiling easily, walking together in the orchards, sitting in the sun, slowly visiting all the places that anchored their lives in their memories. Birthday parties for children appeared around 2006. Although said to be 'very good' on the progress scale, they are rather stilted social affairs in a feted child's house, with children sitting around a table or against walls on the floor and eating a store-bought cake, as seen on television. Mothers feel compelled to compete with each other's birthday performances and to record them on video. Such lifecycle events gain time-defying permanence by being captured on camera or cell phone, and showing such videos at parties has become part of domestic hospitality aesthetics.

Arrow, Cycle and Decay

The time-arrow moving straight ahead in one direction with signposts in growing, ripening, aging and in days and periods following one another is one local time-movement people feel compelled to adjust to.[16] The other is cyclical, such as in day–night–day and in the annual cycle. It is based on experience, but as a choice appealing to many people also extends beyond the observable to include God's likely re-creation of the world itself and of new people after the end of 'our' time.[17] This choice allows for the hope that God will make all new living beings' life-time easier in the next world. Optimists joke that surely God will make the new people better than the present sorry lot. 'With time and practice, even God's work makes progress,' said a grandmother.

Time beyond death

The most popular option for looking at the flow of time is the expectation that probably already after death but surely after the Day of Judgement all people who have ever lived, and maybe even those in hell, will move to eternal bliss-time in paradise. About this a local young, professional man summoned psychology and aesthetics when he said that the lack of comfort and beauty in this life motivates people to think of a restful, happy paradise that lasts forever: 'They just think this to feel better – nobody knows for sure.'

Another option for envisioning life-time beyond death is the image of a parallel universe. 'We are here, the dead are there, close by,' said a woman, illustrating closeness to her dead father by pressing the outstretched arms together. One of the wise elderly men in town expected that the living and the dead existed next to each other, separated only by a flimsy divide, 'like a curtain', and sharing the same time. 'They can see us,' he said.

The pessimistic expectation that bad features of worldly time will continue in the afterlife is available, too. In either case, good or bad as it may be, how this will work is unknowable. Most people's pragmatic presentism leads them routinely to dilute dogma with expressions such as, 'The mullahs tell us that paradise will last forever, but how do they know?' The option to dismiss descriptions of time after death by clerics and Party-of-God ideologists is gaining popularity. 'How come the *akhond* (mullah) knows more about how the dead will spend time than what his own son is doing?' a neighbour said about the alleged misbehaviour of one of a local preacher's children. Empirical evidence makes the here-and-now features of life on Earth a fact, while the images of afterlife-time need trust in theological authorities asserting them. As these assertions are not first-hand solidly 'real', one should not even talk about them, local ethicists say, relegating such speculations to 'gossip', a bad, unappealing way of talking.

The most extreme choice for imagining 'what happens afterward' I heard from women in the past. Over-burdened by chores and children, and troubled by lack of space and rest, they insisted that likely or hopefully everything ended when one died: 'No tomorrow, no paradise, no forever, no angels, nothing.' The only way ever to attain stillness was to take death as a no-time, not-being condition. Recently, this view is reportedly growing again among men and women: on a personal level, time ends with death.

Islamic theologians and scholars who discuss creationism try to place the arrow-line of evolution and scientific cosmology within the Quran. The divergent accounts of the creation of the world create the choice to take them as issues in the say-so, maybe, who knows? category or as mullahs' attempts to justify their status by claiming such knowledge without any 'proof'. Neither is a reassuring, pleasant thought. 'Look at this stone-snail,' a farmer said, showing us a fossilised shell he had found in the rocks above his field. 'A snail! And I am to believe that God put it there as a rock just some years ago?!' Even strong believers opt for the choice of dismissing the issue, saying that only God knows when and how He created the world and how it will end, the mullahs do not – they are just ordinary people. Only few local adherents to a hard-line interpretation of religious scriptures defend the literal, simple, orthodox story of the fairly recent creation of time and the world as the only possible one. For everybody else, school science and science films on the Internet make glimpses of 'deep time' popular, adding new choices for placing the present into the path of time.

Entropy
Although I heard comments on the difficulty of aligning the arrow and the circle when dealing with time, experience establishes that both are 'true': the sun comes up and goes down reliably year after year and without signs of aging; a person gets up and down every day but ages and dies in a straight time

line. The easiest and most popular choice to deal with this difficulty is to accept it as just the way it is and to adapt to the obvious earthly conditions of needs and dangers and decline. It is plain to see that everything on Earth, from rocks to bugs, from trees to people, more or less slowly withers, becomes ugly and useless, disappears. Only a fool would doubt this, a neighbour said. The sky, which never varies, provides a choice to see it as an exception to decay and lets one think that it may exist beyond time, but the option to assume that stars will 'live and die just as we do' is available in the local cosmology. When a star 'falls' a person will die, too: 'Stars and people are linked,' insisted a grandfather.

For the local realists, decline-without-return is an ever-present, undeniable, aesthetic principle, a hardship built into the laws of nature to be accepted for lack of choice. Hardly anybody in town declares it reasonable to see beauty or mystery in decay or to have a romantic interest in it: rack and ruin are bothersome and unattractive; broken tools are repaired or discarded, tattered clothes are mended or burnt, garbage is an eye-sore, a leaking roof is a bother, wooden poles in a crumbling house are re-used, ruins are hang-outs for jinn, corpses are eaten by worms. This classical, local concept of aesthetics does not endow decay with semiotic significance or philosophical insights, unlike, for example, the Japanese '*wabi-sabi*' aesthetic that values things old, worn and tinged with sadness (Kemske 2021). Such refined taste is not an available choice. The pious choice for explaining entropy is to take it as a sign of the Will of God, deplorable as it may seem. However, the ugly misery of decline provides the option to question, mildly, quietly, God's purpose in creating such a world.

There is no beauty or comfort in the knowledge that time reduces all living things to dust and dirt, but there is a link to another time-loop in remembering that God created Adam from soil, that is, from decomposed life, and that therefore God may move life in a circle. However, for the pre-ceramic realists in town mud is not attractive, and Adam was a long time ago. Now new life is made only from older life, children from a father's semen, wheat from seeds, trees from fruit-stones and nuts, all living and dying on the same time-line as people. In other words, the aesthetics of the creation myth and of people's life experiences are divided by a logical and experiential gap which God has to fill: the enigmatic shift from made-from-earth to made-from-seed ending in death is due to God's Will.

The best option for local pragmatists to deal with entropy is to keep things useful as long as needed: berries and herbs are dried, tools are mended, the dirt-roof is damped down in the rain to prevent water from seeping into mud-bricks, compost becomes fertiliser. A teacher summoned 'reason' to defend entropy: if nothing went back to dust the world would become so heavy with people and animals and stuff that it would sink like a rock in water. God did well to allot everything a certain time-limit, including people. At the death of old people mourners may say, 'Their time was up.' Most readily, though, when musing entropy and death people choose to refer to God's inscrutable Will, the catch-all, shoulder-shrug explanation that allows one to take step after step in life without the burden of doubt when things fall apart.

Past, Present and Future are Linked

Past events can be kept 'real' in story-telling – 'In the past, when . . .' – and, for the literate, in books and documents. Before widespread literacy, the unanimous assumption about writing was that anything written was heavy with truth, had permanence and was a firm proof, while what one heard was just hearsay, a floating opinion, a dimming memory. This optimistic view about writing changed when it became obvious that one can lie 'with the pen as well as the mouth', as a neighbour said about politicians, thereby shrinking the truth-value of available information on anything. 'I have three different prescriptions from three doctors,' complained a pained patient, wagging three papers at me – 'all lies!'

Interlinked as they are, past and future cast light and shadows over the present: 'The past is gone but it won't let us be,' a grandmother commented on her life, on the town, on memories and on the human scale of time. Patterns familiar from the past extend into the present in habits and memories, especially 'the very good and very bad ones', as a neighbour put it. One is well advised to forget the bad parts: 'Don't you have anything better to do?' (*ma bikāri?*) is a standard reply to complaints about old grievances, as are: 'Let it go' (*velesh kon*); 'It happened!' (*vābi, da*) – delivered with a quick up–down headshake of dismissal. Remembered events make one happy or sad, and thinking of the future easily makes one anxious, people say. The past is 'real' within memories and traditions, and the future is 'real' within borders set by expectations, potential and hopes. The past can also explain the present and endow it with emotions: 'If only one of our four sons could be a daughter, I'd have some help in the house.' 'My grandson was an A-student and is a doctor now!' Reactions to the effects of past happenings and of visions of the future suggest that God's plans (or, for less pious people, nature or evolution) have a bias that does not always promote individuals' desires and wellbeing. The pious choice is to gratefully accept and cherish whatever 'good' happens and to pass on the benefit. 'Whatever helps me and my family is good and obliges me as a Muslim to help others,' said a successful, generous, well-regarded engineer.

The past–present link pertains to the living but also, with less urgency, to the dead. Inheritance is the most tangible such link, but gardens and trees also may be seen as living testimony to the ancestor who had planted them. One of my local friends said a quick prayer for her dead grandfather whenever we entered his old apricot orchard. The trees reminded her of him, and this remembrance was 'good for me and good for him', she said, based on the popular choice to believe that the dead are 'really dead' only after nobody remembers them anymore. Visits to relatives' graves on Thursday afternoons are expected to have the same beneficial effect for the dead. Thus, past, present and future overlap.[18] On time's straight path the farther from just-now an event is in either direction, the dimmer it is remembered or foreseen. 'Time is like a fog,' said a nurse. Given that memories fade and are selectively recalled for certain purposes, they may be challenged, and all hopes and predictions for what may happen next are tentative. Dealing with past, present and future in such experience-based ways is a popular choice for making sense of time.

The future

The past cannot be changed much except by forgetting and lying, but the future can be manipulated somewhat, such as by tending fields for food in the winter, by sending children to school and thereby on a path towards economic success, by engaging relatives to find a good wife for a son, by using inoculations to prevent measles. The hoped-for or feared future is not a distant time but is just around the corner, and the assumptions and models for imagining it are familiar: to get married, to leave town, to emigrate abroad are choices that people had already several generations ago mulled over or selected for themselves and their children. As time went by, others were added, such as owning a car, climbing Kilimanjaro, visiting a brother in Sweden, while 'revolution', for example, locally is not an option. Likewise, to study, to become a contractor or merchant so as to afford a comfortable life that fits urban and global middle-class lifeways was already a desire grandparents voiced for their children, while aspiring to be a famous artist or inventor or movie star is called 'crazy'.

Only the staunchest believers declare the manipulation of the future to be a challenge for the primacy of God's Will or an attempt to subvert God's plans. Much more popular is the argument that by planning ahead one is using God-given reason. If the exertion is successful, one may see it as God's doing and be grateful, or one may be proud of oneself for the result (or both). If it is unsuccessful, one may blame oneself for not having tried hard enough or – more likely – may say that success 'was not in God's programme', as a mother declared when her son's application to a university was unsuccessful. As the future is taken to be already established by God's Will and planning but our senses are too dull to recognise it, one may opt to try to access it by interpreting dreams. Dreaming of jewellery or of snow, for example, is taken to announce an impending hardship. Such dreams are discussed with relish and some anxiety but dismissed as superstition by the supporters of government Islam and by the 'enlightened'.

Time and Space

Timed events are linked to spaces. Rituals based on the solar calendar take place outdoors in nature, such as in picnics around New Year celebrations, or at home such as in visits to relatives to greet them and admire the New Year's spread of seven mostly agricultural products.[19] Given the importance of seasonal agricultural and hunting-gathering activities in the past, the absence of events marking harvests or a successful hunt is apparent to local people. 'Has anybody ever seen a turban in the mountains or harvesting wheat?' asked a young man, tongue in cheek. Depending on their religious and political leanings people either blame or laud 'Islam' for having done away with earlier such practices.

In contrast to the nature–outdoors–agriculture theme in the solar calendar, Shia teachings link time with spaces such as mosques (for Friday prayers), prayer halls (for mourning events, for example), cemeteries (for mourning), shrines (for pilgrimages), 'holy' places connected to events in the early days of

Islam (for pilgrimages), the streets (for politico-religious demonstrations), theological seminaries (for 'teaching mullahs how to wrap their turbans around the head', as a joke among young people goes), and the battlefield (in holy wars). This means that time- and space-aesthetics of sun-calendar events and Islamic ones are 'a hundred percent different', as a man said who had difficulties planning his son's wedding because of a string of government-organised mourning events that made joyful celebrations impossible. 'Instead of dancing in the courtyard and sitting together, eating and talking and feeling well, we have to cry in the mosque,' he said.[20] Although martyrdom has become a trope in discussions of Shia theology, locally it is not a popular choice for self-understanding or for envisioning national identity; rather, criticism of the government's emphasis on death and mourning is quietly popular. 'We have to make a living today and tomorrow and for the children. Tears don't help. Death will come by itself,' said an old farmer.

In day-to-day activities, traditional time-linked work spaces are fields and orchards, niches in the courtyard such as the water tap, the fireplace, a kitchen, a grinding stone, the hen-house, barns and corrals. Rest time is passed in quiet places (except by young children who fall asleep anywhere) and at night by sleeping on bedding spread on the floor or on a raised bed indoors at night. Other than for sleep, staying in bed is taken to be a sign of severe illness or of laziness, which, given people's busy traditional work schedules, is a blemish. Even a sick person will hear, 'Get up!' frequently, 'To make him feel better and not sorry for himself,' as a wife said of her husband who was down with influenza. I heard it too when I was ill, to keep me from thinking I was seriously sick, as my friends said.

In the slow, snowy winter days and nights, any warm indoor space was a comfort spot, be it the barn with sheep and cows in the pioneer days, or near a wood-burning fireplace until cheap oil- and gas-fired heating devices became available. The flimsy winter clothes made these places a necessity for keeping well. Women spent most of their time in or near the house while men spent it outside, and without exception people connected the time–space link to propriety: as little girls grow up, their space outside the house shrinks. It still is 'not good' for a young woman to be seen outside more than is taken to be necessary, and even less appropriate when being out alone, although 'necessary' and 'proper' cover many more occasions now than just a generation ago.

At unusual times, such as at night, any person walking around outside without a known, approvable chore may be suspected to be up to no good.

The proper space for the time after death is in the grave, a dark and unappealing place, or 'in paradise or hell or wherever', as an elderly man said, but not in a house. The house above the ground is for the living, and to keep a dead body there is not a choice in house aesthetics at all. A corpse is washed and shrouded in the mortuary house right away and buried as soon as possible. Although people do not express a fear of ghosts or revenants, there is an implicit assumption that to prevent the dead from getting lost or hanging around they have to be shown the way to their new, proper house. There are stories about a dead person being seen walking alongside mourners returning from the funeral, obviously having missed the clue about the grave-house. This is not a popular theme, but it is a choice in the aesthetics of death. Some local graves have lanterns and, in the past, had small roofs over the headstone. 'It's good for them,' I was told.

In these choices for thinking and musing about time, the knowledge of beginnings and endings stands out, of time changing the look of everything and of how people think and feel, yet itself never changing and maybe not ending. Alive or dead, a person is moved by time.

4

The Flair of Kith and Kin

Introduction: People need People

The compelling aesthetic structure God and religion are said to provide for people's benefit also includes the experience that it is difficult for humans to use what the Earth offers. Indeed, God's hardship principle runs like a constant current through all life on Earth for everybody to see and feel and deal with. God's creation thus includes the contradiction between 'made for people' and 'full of hardship, pain and death'. For those who see a problem with a loving yet inexplicably uncaring God, the story of Adam brings punishment for disobedience into eschatology. But as this story is taken to be mostly hearsay it offers the choice of doubt: Adam's punishment may be just a gripping tale. Too many obvious sinners have a good life and too many blameless people face hardships to make Adam's punishment a reliable principle. More important yet is the popular insight that the idea of punishment does not help an innocent sufferer but adds guilt to the pain, guilt for maybe having committed a forgotten, unspecified sin. Indeed, hardly anybody I ever heard talk about it linked their own misery or success to punishment and reward or derived consolation from the thought that, since oneself is blameless and forgiven, it might have been the wrongdoing of an ancestor that brought about the present suffering. Only people who have a gripe sometimes use such cause and effect to explain other people's conditions.

It is much more common and a more reasonable choice to say that hurt and sick people need help, no matter what may have caused their predicament. Although God may indeed send help and healing, on the level of everyday life it is nearby people who assist each other, good, competent people. To live alone without neighbours is declared odd, uncomfortable and dangerous. Yet although people expect and insist that the company of others is important for one's wellbeing, and that there are many kind people who help when necessary, they also vehemently insist that humans' natural selfish inclinations often makes life in close proximity with others difficult. Like everything else that occurs naturally, relationships need ordering devices to make them manageable and to provide choices when dealing with others in right – and wrong – ways. This is where relatives come in.

Kin Group Aesthetics[1]

The category 'kin/relative' is the opposite of 'stranger' on the scale of closeness, with seven main terms covering categories of people accordingly. From closest to farthest, they are: *qoum-khish, aqvum*: patrilineal/bilateral relatives; *māl-e khomun*: belonging to us; patrilineal/bilateral relatives with whom one has contacts; *fāmil*: family, a new word used for nuclear family members, related housemates and close patrilineal relatives; *dust*: friend, somebody one likes and trusts, relatives and others; *āshenā, shenā*: an unrelated acquaintance; *gharib*: a stranger; and *deshmun*: an enemy, whereby relatives can be enemies, too. Boir Ahmad society is patrilineal/bilateral, androcentric and authoritarian, with all the structurally built-in advantages and hardships for men, women and children that are discussed for such societies by social scientists and by the people in town.[2]

Locally, until one or two generations ago nearly everybody took this structure to be God-given and God-ordered and therefore as to be accepted like a law, no matter how convenient or inconvenient it might be for individuals. The rules of kin terms and kin behaviour fit into this aesthetic structure. Although relatives are often felt to be a nuisance, one has little choice: kin just happens and is declared to be necessary for one's wellbeing ('Who would get a job without an uncle?' is the reasonable argument for nepotism). People insist that, by and large, having no relatives is worse than dealing with problematic ones. Staunchly orthodox believers declare that God-less people such as 'communists' or 'the Americans' neglect kindred and family which provide essential social order, and that they 'kill each other and commit incest because they don't know their kin from strangers', as a mullah's wife assured me. The uses and consequences of kin relationships with their mix of beautiful and ugly, assuring and irritating, useful and demanding are located in the matrix of good–bad, and their position on this aesthetic scale depends on circumstances and on who is judging. Over a span of two weeks a neighbour called his young paternal cousin 'a nice boy; a smart son of a dog (*pedar sag*); an idiot; a top A-student; a lazy bungler; a good worker; a spoiled loafer', each choice fitting an occasion and accompanied by predictable patterns of interaction. Each epithet carries a story about local values.

Patrilineality dictates descendance counted through males and makes male relatives on the fathers' side important in old 'tribal laws' and in property management. Thus, for example, a married man is the ruler in his house, his children belong to his kin group, and if he dies, his eldest brother by default will become the warden of his children and like a father will function as their leader in matters of authority, economy and politics. In contrast, a widow's brother has no managerial obligations towards his sister's children because they likely belong to another kin group. Instead, he is expected to be supportive and kind to his own sisters' children.

Together with individuals' habits and dispositions this structure makes for a great variety of emotions and interactions, and strongly influences how people feel about themselves and those around them. As the nuclear family became more popular, the town became more diverse, and more people were moving away, kin networks lost some practical import. Yet calamities such as the earthquake in 2021 'wake up' kin ties, as a grandfather predicted. Soon after the quake the owner of a damaged house, a young man who lived with his parents, discussed the costly repairs with his parents and his three siblings. A sister who had emigrated to Australia ended up paying most of the bills although she had not seen the brother in years and had little contact with him. 'I have no choice,' she said, 'He is my brother.'

In personal relationships kinship is bilateral, with mother's kinfolk expected to be closer to the ideal of harmony, trust and friendship than father's kin. With few exceptions, in people's talks and stories the best-liked relatives are mother, maternal grandmother, mother's sister and sister. One turns to them for help, for fun, for companionship. Paternal relatives, with many exceptions, are less close and more problematic, and in-laws even more so; co-wives are declared to be at the bottom of amicability. A mother's siblings and their children are said to be 'warm' and easy to hang out with, while the father's siblings and their offspring are more formal and distant. Seen from the position of a young man, he, his brothers and paternal cousins vie over inheritance, and, in the past, competed over wives,[3] and therefore will likely see paternal uncles and cousins as competitors over the paternal group's resources and status, while his maternal cousins are 'just guys' for him. In everyday interactions there are many exceptions to these customary relationships. They are discussed and judged, thereby proving the assumptions and the rules.

Small Group Aesthetics: Comfort and Discontent

The many strands of aesthetics among relatives are a mix of beauty and comfort on the side of ideology which insists that without kin one has nobody to turn to for support. In practice, though, competition among relatives easily crosses mutual support, subtle power-games cross the formal status hierarchy, and disagreements cross good manners and result in the need for mediators and peace-makers. Experience shows that in everyday life discontent among relatives is unavoidable, less of a choice than a given. 'My father's eldest brother stole the best of our land'; 'My paternal cousin (*kurr tāta*) and his people are lording it over us whenever they can'; 'The arrogant cousins from the great-uncle's kin group never greet me'; 'My mother's sister has not returned the meat grinder I lent her two weeks ago!' Thus, in daily encounters, ideology that stresses cooperation among relatives squares off with individuals' claims and expectations, and both sides may refer to ethics, aesthetics, religion, duty, politeness and 'being human' to bolster their claims: 'My crude cousin steals water from us, which he knows is a sin, and when we tell him off he maligns us – his whole kin clique is boorish and ugly and subhuman (*ādam nist*, not human)!'

In many ways this core condition of potential conflict remains to this day, although kin groups have weakened considerably. Control over resources such as property and people is a top concern, fought over by relatives who, if unsuccessful, have the choice to be miffed and turn 'cold': *ve qar* (avoidance) is used for this reaction among people who have had a falling-out and are not on speaking terms. Or the losers can opt to accept their inferior position as God-willed, or may decide to plot revenge, or may choose to say, 'what happened, happened, let it be', or use all options on different occasions. According to town council members, in 2015, most cases brought before the town's citizen's court involved fights among relatives, and this condition was reportedly even worse in the small villages elsewhere in the province. The explanation for a bitter, loud verbal fight in a tent-camp we visited, was: 'What do you expect? Cousins' wives!'

For explaining enmities among housemates and relatives, the fall-back choice is to blame the women. 'They sit at home all day and should know better than to fight with their relatives about everything,' a female local town council member said. About coping with kinfolk, men and women report pleasures and profits; they praise and visibly cherish even-tempered uncles and wise aunts, and deplore difficulties, bitterness and accusations in the group. An immigrant resident with no relatives in town coined a proverb: 'A small kin group has few friends and few fights.'

Bumpy intra-kin relations fit what is known from collectivist relationships in small, interdependent groups with a strong identity. In contrast to purported prevalent harmony in such groups, people say and show by their behaviour that they often feel the closeness as a burden, that they feel observed by their neighbours and in turn want to know what these are up to, and that this is bad.[4] 'In Shiraz you can wear what you want, but here everybody knows us and people will talk about your tight jeans and your hair showing!' a young woman heard from her aunt in Sisakht in 2015. Small-group members observe each other's looks and habits to learn about shifting norms, to avoid falling behind in trends and tastes, and to note breaches of etiquette, signs of one-upmanship and competition (such as over scarce irrigation water), but also for signs of crises and needs in other houses.

Poverty, for example, elicits help from others, but the need for help may also produce embarrassment in the receiver and the giver. In 2015, a neighbour recalled that occasionally in the past when there was 'nothing in the house to eat', her grandmother would put a cauldron with water on the fire as if she were cooking rice or lentils so that the neighbouring relatives would not realise that the family was hungry. A retired nurse in town quietly managed to help a near-destitute relative with food for weeks without anybody else being any the wiser (the woman's drug-impaired husband was periodically unable to earn a living, and this shameful condition added to the necessity for secrecy).

Although people do not openly discuss anxiety about the opinions and habits of others, such episodes and many remarks indicate the importance of watching neighbours and of weighing the troubles interference may cause.

Hamćeshmi (jealousy) describes the habit of measuring oneself against one's neighbours and relatives: 'It is a bother but everybody does it,' a young woman said. Noticing one's neighbours' looks and habits creates pretence and secretiveness not because people are mean-spirited but because limited resources, close proximity and identical economic and lifestyle goals produce suspicion and ill-will. 'Anything new I wear, my cousins and neighbours see and talk about,' said a high school student, explaining why she did not want to wear her new shoes to school. The resulting distrust led a local man to refuse – politely and with many excuses – to let a cousin's son and his new wife live in a room in his house: he was afraid that as a relative he could never turn them out again without creating 'bad words and deeds'.

Kin Terms: Structure, Behaviour, Emotions

The kin structure lays out norms and expectations encapsulated in kin terms that serve as markers for the identification of relatives and for obligations and conduct among them. They define the father's side and the mother's side and reflect generational difference, distance to the speaker, relative age and also modernity. But they carry meanings beyond the structure itself, and these are of aesthetic consequence in daily life – words get their meaning and their emotional weight while being used: '*bābā*' and '*bou*' both mean 'father', but the first is a term of endearment ('daddy' and 'grampa') and the second is a term of authority ('dad', 'father'). As the use of '*bābā*" for 'father' has increased over the past two generations, '*bou*' now may be a reprimand or an order: 'Father, listen to me!' Kin terms thus may be used to make points about status and relationships, about closeness and distance, about being modern or traditional; they gauge feelings and influence how one behaves, be it polished and gracious or blundering and offensive.[5]

Kinsmen likely are close neighbours, which makes the manipulation of kin terms and relationships important for one's daily wellbeing: terms may create and express security and comfort as well as confusion and discomfort. A youngster who was calling an aunt *khāle* (mother's sister, expressing informal liking), as he heard his mother addressing her, was told by grandmother that he had to call her *āme* (expressing authority) because she belonged to his father's group, but he would not hear of it: 'No,' he argued, 'Father calls her only Maryam so I call her Maryam or *khāle*, like my mother does. And I like her!' Uneasy feelings about expectations and the choices in the complicated etiquette of proper use of kin terms often make young people anxious and extra careful so as not to offend. At a formal visit of a paternal cousin and a few of his relatives from another village who were looking for a potential wife for the young man, the young woman they wanted to check out hid in a shed. She was embarrassed, she said, because she did not know them well, they were 'like strangers' to her and she was not sure how to address them properly. A few years later, at a similar scouting party, a self-confident young woman did not hide but addressed everybody with formal 'modern' titles such as Mister Engineer, Misses Doctor; or as *Hajj(i)* or *Meshedi* and *Sey(yed)*, implying they had made the Hajj or a pilgrimage to Mashhad or had ties to the Prophet.[6] With this trick she avoided any awkwardness. 'Religious titles come in handy,' she said. 'I can honour anybody by calling them "*Meshedi*", even if they have never left Sisakht.'

Political intentions colour kin terms, too. One may choose to manipulate rank by using an authority-laden, paternal-side term for addressing maternal relatives to make them more important, or by using a maternal-side term to cut down a paternal relative. 'I always call my neighbour *dada* (sister, a term carrying fondness but little authority) although she actually is my "*āme*" (father's sister, a term of authority), but I have three children and she isn't even married – *dada* will do.' The urban, modern use of titles can function similarly: a mother may refer to her son as 'Mister Doctor Alizadeh', using the academic title plus the father's last name to build up his and the family's status, and may complain about a relative who calls the young doctor simply 'Mahmud' – 'as if he were a little boy!' Generally, though, the use of generic formal titles (*agha* for men, *khānom* for women), academic titles and religious honour titles have their own range of uses and meanings and may replace kin terms. The implied status formality lessens the danger of social mishaps – formal titles are easy to learn, and nobody is miffed when a man calls an uncle '*Hajji Agha*' even if the uncle has never seen Mecca.

The following short discussion of basic kin-terms is meant to illustrate aesthetics in the interplay of emotions, practical uses of terms and consequences in daily life.

Mother and Father

The Luri terms for mother, *dei* in reference, *dāi*, *dā*, in address, and *dādi* in children's use, are heavy with positive feelings of safety, warmth and indulgence. They are being replaced by Farsi '*mādar*' and French-derived '*māman(i)*' now. This moves words and relationships into an informal, urban, 'chic' kin aesthetic and divides old-timers and 'modern' people. A man may address an older strange woman as *mādar* to put himself and her into a respectful, positive relationship (when this happened to me I often responded teknonymously,[7] answering the young stranger with 'mother, dear' and then adding kindly advice or praise or a request which he, as 'son', politely and smilingly accepted. This kin game always was successful.).

The replacement of the traditional term for father, '*bou*', carrying fatherly authority and respect more than warmth, with the term '*bābā*', an affectionate Persian term[8] used by children in Sisakht for grandfather, may either dilute traditional fatherly authority or strengthen patrilineal authority, depending on the situation. 'Father' and 'mother' are strictly genealogical terms: a stepmother is 'my father's wife' (*zan boum*) in reference as well as address unless she is a relative and retains the kin term she had before marriage. A child whose father has died is an 'orphan' (*yetim*), taken care of by his paternal uncle; a motherless child is a 'without-mother' (*bi-dei*) and is greatly pitied: no woman except, maybe, an older sister, maternal grandmother or maternal aunt is expected to provide a mother's care and affection. To be fatherless is bad but manageable; to be motherless is treated as an emotional catastrophe.

Siblings

The traditional Luri kin terms for brother (*kākā*) and sister (*dada*) were used for reference and occasionally also when addressing one's own eldest siblings and paternal cousins. To address such a cousin as '*kākā*' or '*dada*' in a dispute or when asking a favour, amounts to a gesture of respect, appeasement or submission in the speaker. In contrast, maternal cousins likely are referred to descriptively ('mother-brother's son/daughter', *kurr/duar hālu*) and are addressed with their first names, but when talking to much older cousins the speaker may elevate them to the elder generation (uncle, aunt) to show respect. As terms of address, 'brother' and 'sister' have their own range of uses and meanings along the lines of relative age and closeness. 'I call my eldest brother *kākā* when I like him,' said a ten-year-old girl, 'and when I don't like him I use his name and say, "Dirty Kerim!"' The terms carry authority as well as responsibilities. A person without a *dada* was pitied; a brother without a *kākā* was pitied but a *kākā* also could be called a 'bad nuisance', as a young man said after an argument with his eldest brother who used his authority to usurp a contested piece of land.

Big Brother and Big Sister keep their positions throughout their lives. A woman without a *kākā* is 'nothing', said a grandmother, meaning that such a woman has nobody to back her up when troubled. But the position also meant that the eldest brother and sister in a large family likely had a hard life. The eldest sister had to work as mother's helper at an age when younger siblings could just play; she was expected to watch the little siblings, and when things went wrong, eldest siblings were often used as scapegoats by overburdened adults. A successful professional man compared himself with his youngest, pampered brother: 'With all the blows I had to take for the problems my siblings caused, I learned how to work and stand pressure. But my little brother is spoiled rotten and nothing but trouble will come from him.' A first-born sister of several siblings I have known since her birth, a highly respected professional now, is the only girl in her family who had to learn to bake bread and milk goats, was badly scalded while carrying a big can of boiling water when she was five years old, often had to study by candle light and in between chores, helped raise her siblings, paid her own way through university and in her family has climbed the farthest up the status ladder. 'I can stand anything,' she now jokes. Recently, when the beloved eldest sister among five siblings died, her elderly brothers and sister were inconsolable. 'They carry on as if their mother had died!' miffed a young nephew.

Jealousies and one-upmanship among siblings occur mostly among brothers over inheritance and, especially in the past, over access to a wife. The choices are limited by the availability of women and money for the bride-price. 'Three brothers ahead of me who need a wife!' one such brother complained – 'I'll be an old man before I get one!' Procuring a wife was difficult and expensive for most fathers, handled according to the age of the sons, and with few available choices because of the high infant mortality rate for baby girls. 'There are seven boys in our kin group who need wives, and only three girls,' said a worried father. The bride-price has remained a troublesome concern in cash-strapped families. Regarding inheritance, a man whose education led to a paid job did well to watch his claim to fields and animals closely because the farmer-brothers who took care of his property could – and often did – choose to argue that his salary counted more than his field or orchard. Sisters had fewer reasons to be unhappy with each other but occasionally were pulled into relatives' hostilities. As a tea-guest, I once was caught in a heated argument among three sisters discussing a fraternal fracas over ownership and management of a wheat-mill. In the end they were miffed, but luckily they had let me just listen without pulling me into the dispute.

Uncles and Aunts

The terms used for father's brother (*tata*) and father's sister (*āme*) still carry the traditional authority vested in paternal kin and can also cover other paternal relatives who are older or more important than the speaker. A self-possessed, outspoken local woman, the eldest sister in her sibling group, was referred to and addressed as '*Āme* Maryam' by old and young in her kin group and beyond, including by me and my family. In contrast, mother's brother (*hālu*, *hal*) and mother's sister (*khāle*) have the connotation of likeable, accessible close relatives, but these terms also may be used for addressing a stranger younger or of lower status than oneself. A much appreciated member of the barber class who was helping out with tasks in many people's houses was routinely called 'uncle' followed by his first name, '*Hal Shurgela*', in reference, if not to his face. Children learn kin terms their parents use, and apply them even if they do not fit: if a mother calls her father's brother *tata*, her children will likely call him *tata* also, although he is not an uncle on their own father's side. Eventually, they will have to learn the proper terms so as to avoid a faux pas.

Husband and Wife

At present in Iran there is a great deal of experimenting with marriage, cohabitation and male–female relationships, and the terminology expresses the underlying, often confusing, options. (Afary and Faust 2021). Locally, the traditional terms for husband (*mirei*) and wife (*zan*) are used in reference, but 'husband' refers only to the husband of a particular woman ('*mirei* Fatemeh'), while '*zan*' is a generic term for a married (or widowed, divorced) woman. A man will likely refer to his wife as 'my woman' (*zanom*), and will address her by her given name as he would address a child, or with her name followed by '*khānom,* madam' ('Fatemeh *khānom*'). For women it is more complicated. A traditional local woman will likely avoid addressing her husband at all and will use 'thou' to get his attention ('*to, zi biou*' – thou, come quickly). Referring to him, she may stress his status as father: 'Father of Ahmed' (*bou* Ahmed) or, most modern, use the Farsi term 'my husband' (*shouharam*). In the shifting, progress-oriented aesthetics of 'modern' husband–wife relationships, she also has the choice to use the husband's last name or a professional or religious title to address him or refer to him. For a wife to use her husband's first name is considered chic among young urban people, and rather daring; in the cases with which I am familiar it implies closer, less formal and more intimate ties than were expressed in the parental generation.

The terms used for addressing one's spouse indicate that the status and power hierarchy which puts a man in charge of his wife has always created some confusion. The unsettled etiquette in husband–wife interaction is mitigated by new choices for address and reference, but is not resolved. In order to avoid offence or an impropriety, formal courtesy is said to be the safest choice. Recently, a local young woman, engaged to a familiar but unrelated local man of similar age and status, identified him to me over the telephone with his first and last name, followed by 'a grandson of Mr X', to place him for me – I know old Mr X well. She said she addresses him as 'Mr Engineer', and he calls her 'Maryam *khānom*'. How they would address each other after the wedding she did not know: 'We'll see how we'll get along,' she giggled. Intimacy, 'liking' and other emotions are features that become important in new marital aesthetics.

In-laws

Unless in-laws are also one's relatives with proper kin terms, the norm and prudent choice is to address them with their formal last names or a title, and to refer to them descriptively: my wife's brother; my uncle's wife. Only mother-in-law has a well-used title, *khassi*, used in reference by a husband and a wife. Especially young people avoid addressing in-laws directly so as not to offend. Formality and closeness, age, genealogical position or strangeness may be manipulated in the terms one chooses for in-laws, but one rule is clear: an in-law is either 'one of us' – uncle, aunt, cousin – or a non-relative, a 'stranger', with a formal title such as Mister, Misses, no matter how much or little I have to do with him or her and how much or little esteem exists between us.

The use of the terms *dumā* (groom, son-in-law), and *aris* (bride, daughter-in-law) is a bit more complicated. These words include the option to count the respective person as an in-law to the spouse's whole kin group (*bonku*): 'Ahmad is the son-in-law of my uncle' means that Ahmad is married to my uncle's daughter but also may mean that Ahmad is the groom of a daughter of any one of uncle's close patrilineal relatives, that he is a 'son-in-law' for the uncle's kin group. The same counts for 'bride': Maryam is 'their' bride, whereby 'their' refers to her husband's kin group. The terms carry expectations: a son-in-law is obliged to help his wife's father if called upon. 'The bride-price alone can't cover a father's troubles of raising a daughter for the benefit of her husband's family,' explained a neighbour watching his son-in-law stack firewood for him. Indeed, a husband is indebted to his wife's father 'forever' no matter where he lives. 'Tell my son-in-law to send a water melon back with you for us,' said a landless craftsman when we set out to drive to the provincial capital, where his married daughter lived.

By all accounts and remarks, for a daughter-in-law locality is of great importance. In the past any daughter-in-law living in a traditional, patrilocal family was the servant for everybody in the house, 'from granny to the chickens', as a young man said who was feeling sorry for the new bride in his uncle's house. 'But then,' he said, 'They paid the bride-price for her, they bought her, that's it.' Recently, a young woman repudiated an offer of marriage with, 'No way will I marry into *that* kin group – his mother wants a maid for the six people in the house!' The expected servitude decreases or ceases altogether when a son establishes a separate household. The wife of the youngest son in a family remains the designated caretaker of the husband's aging parents 'forever' because her husband inherits the house and is expected to live there. Thus, while the demands of a bride's father on the son-in-law mean that a 'groom' cannot ever fully repay his debt to his wife's father, the bride's maid service is explained and justified by the same argument: bride-price: it paid for all her services, forever. 'Ha, that's how it is!' said a young married teacher, and then changed it to, 'No, it used to be so – it is better now.'

In-laws, furthermore, may be accused of meddling in issues of inheritance or in competitions for status in either family or by actively supporting a daughter in disputes with her husband's people. Here, again, opting for polite formality 'makes everything go more smoothly', said a neighbour, who was in good spirits after a talk with his daughter-in-law's father about a disputed matter of irrigation water. Obligations and demands set women up for difficulties on every level of life, with few choices for solving them, and the problems daughters-in-law have with managing tensions and expectations are well known and freely discussed in town. Women whose daughters-in-law were 'happy' (*khoshhāl*, literally, of good health), or at least 'satisfied, in agreement' (*rāzi*) are praised by everybody. In 'these modern times' when young women are granted input in the marriage contract, a demand for neo-locality has become a choice amounting to 'a matter of course for girls so as to be away from the old folks and their demands', explained a matron.

It is 'good' for many reasons to have sons-in-law and daughters-in-law – good for status, for helping with chores, for potential political advantages, for enlarging one's kin group's sphere of influence, for enhancing resources and possibilities, for good company in the house; people talk about many positive effects. But how domestic relationships develop depends largely on the personalities involved. A son-in-law, for example, proverbially may turn out to be 'better than a son' or 'a good man' or 'a donkey's fart'.

Kin and Gender

The emotional side of kin includes gender expectations. At both ends of the pleasure–pain spectrum in a house, women who live with their husbands' kinfolk feel the varying moods strongest. As newcomers in the house they have an uphill struggle to create enough power to assert themselves vis-à-vis the other women in the household.[9] While until recently married men could expect to stay near their father's kin group all their lives, women upon marriage had to move to the in-laws' compound and had to cope with new housemates and with mixed loyalties: controversies between their own kin group and that of the husband's left many in difficult spots without good choices. Neo-locality made things easier for everybody. 'I am alone a lot but I like it,' said a young wife in a new, small apartment, in 2015.

Furthermore, some young women in a traditional compound were likely strangers to each other, and although each couple had a 'room and fire' (*tu o tash*), women had to share work and resources. The range of moods could go from peace and pleasure to the worst hostilities. 'My washed skirts are in the dirt! Guess who did this!' complained a furious woman about her sister-in-law. In the herding outposts, men liked to choose cooperative arrangements that let their wives share the dairy work with their own sisters because sisters got along much better than did brothers' unrelated wives, and everybody profited emotionally and economically from the peace. Animosity in the house made men suffer, too, but if work assignments, competition and bad words among brothers and cousins became too stressful for a man, especially a young, unmarried one, he could opt to leave and find work elsewhere. Older people remember two young men who killed themselves over family issues in the past but tell of several young men who 'fled' the village, at odds with their elders. Some returned eventually but a few were never heard of again.

In contrast, women in loud, unhappy houses or compounds were stuck there, quite literally, with death the only way out of intense pressures for some. Until a generation ago, Boir Ahmad had a very high rate of women's suicides and attempted suicides (likely also including camouflaged honour killings like elsewhere in Iran; Parsa 2021). Unanimously, suicide was called 'sinful and ugly' and the dead woman was abused for committing it and for leaving her children motherless, although those around her understood her motives very well and pitied her and her circumstances as much as they scolded her. Aesthetically and ethically, the situation was 'very bad' for the whole province, said the town mayor in 2000. By then the provincial governor, an urban man, had taken steps to learn about the bad domestic situations of local women, as he said, and found that women suffered from over-work in over-crowded houses and from 'violent husbands'. A fair-minded man, he had paid for a study of the issue – it agreed with what women themselves had said all along. There was no easy solution, he said.

The most benign – and most popular – local explanation for female suicide attempts was women's purported weakness of mind and body, a lack of intellect and stamina to withstand the hassles of life and the whispers of the devil. Weak women are known to succumb easily to brooding, to 'falling into thoughts' (*ru fekr oftādan*), to being troubled (*narāhat*), sad (*ghamghin*) and weary (*kesel*). Girls learned this language early: 'Mother, I can't help you today, I am weary!' a seven-year-old girl explained, to the mother's amusement about this clever excuse. 'I'm going to kill myself,' was a much-used, matter-of-fact expression of discontent of women and girls.

The suicide rate has been falling since about 1990. People ascribe this to literacy, that is, to the ongoing individuation process brought about by schools; to the lightening of the workload when agriculture and herding declined; to indoor plumbing, kitchen appliances and more living space apart from in-laws. 'Thanks be to God for progress!' women say.

Sharia law helped, too, women point out, by adding the choice to demand favourable conditions in the marriage contract, such as the stipulation of neo-locality. In 2006, a story made the rounds of another legal help, when a married teacher persuaded a judge, a cleric, to limit her husband's many visitors because she had no help with the hospitality chores. Recently, the wife of a youngest son in his family stirred up emotions when she disregarded the local firm custom that allots a youngest son his father's house together with the duty to care for the parents, and persuaded him to move to Mashhad with her, 'a thousand kilometres away', leaving the old people to fend for themselves. Such stories rattle local aesthetic sensibilities and make people question their assumptions about 'how women and the world work', as an elderly farmer said.

The Ambient of Marriage: Necessity and Emotions

Monogamy and Polygyny

'Good marriages' were monogamous by tradition, by reason and because of economic limits. However, rich, powerful men could choose a different aesthetic frame. Islamic law allows a man four wives simultaneously, and divorce and temporary marriage being easy for men, only economy and social controls set a limit. Some well-off khans validated and increased their status by having several wives, either beautiful women who had caught the khan's fancy or elegant women of powerful families who were aesthetic assets on several counts: their polished manners enchanted the khan and his guests, their high status added value to the khan as a host to important people, and their own fathers' fame and the khan's socio-political aims were mutually supportive. 'They had a very good and comfortable (*khub va rāhat*) life,' an old retired nanny assured me, 'except for the jealousies among themselves, huh, huh!'¹⁰ Some infamous chiefs had 'many' additional consorts they demanded, bought or stole from local people. Owning women was a hallmark of sovereign power for them and a 'very bad sin' in the eyes of most people. 'When we girls heard that the khans were coming up to the village we hid in the orchards so they wouldn't see us,' old women remember. Over his lifetime, the most famous and powerful chief of Sisakht had thirteen wives and fathered thirty-three children. Mostly, the set-up was criticised for the implied exploitation of tribal people and their resources, including women, that made the khans' ostentatious status displays possible: the aesthetics of power combined admiration for such men's lifestyles with envy and criticism.

For the last two generations, wealthy urban men supporting a second wife in style, a 'love-wife', are talked about in a similar way. The arrangement is legal and thus has to be accepted on principle if the first wife agrees to it,¹¹ yet also may be condemned because a man cannot treat two wives equally as stipulated by religion, and because experience shows that co-wives do not get along unless they have separate houses and are provided for equally well. As these stipulations are hard to fulfil, polygyny is called 'ugly'; it should not happen, at least not among ordinary, reasonable people. When it became known that a local married man secretly had another wife elsewhere, the judge, a mullah, granted both women the divorce they requested because the man had not elicited their consent (Sharia judges in Boir Ahmad frequently take a woman's side when ruling against tribal law marriage traditions). A little while back the man would have had no legal problem and the women would have had to make do.

The choice to condemn polygyny remains popular but one may also envy a pretty young nurse or secretary who secures an easy life in a chic apartment as the second wife of a rich man. For a married man who wants to marry a new, young wife it is easier to keep his first, aging wife and the children in the old house with a budget large enough that she cannot legally complain, than to pay divorce settlements and find childcare he is legally responsible for, elsewhere. Unless the wife agrees to losing her children in a divorce, she has no choice but to agree to a co-wife 'in a separate house, if she is lucky'. With the first wife and children settled and quiet, he can 'enjoy himself with his second wife in a nice apartment and travel with her wherever he likes', as a local student summed up the case of her university professor in a northern city in Iran. Such stories are known locally, spreading unease.

A commoner likely had two wives only when levirate obliged him to take responsibility for a brother's widow and children in addition to his own family. This had nothing to do with sexual gratification or high status but was considered a good custom, a duty, a good deed and a sensible solution because the children belonged to their father's patrilineage and thus to the paternal uncle anyway, and because their widowed mother had no good place elsewhere to live. 'What one has to do often is right and good but very difficult,' said the father of a son who struggled with this responsibility. Levirate was a proper choice but marred by the man's increased economic burden and by the likelihood that the two wives would not get along, would pass their enmity on to their children and would cause unrest in the house. A noisy house is 'hell' for those living there and 'ugly' for everybody else in the vicinity. Here, too, the aesthetics of ideology and everyday practice collide over 'good' and 'bad': both wives 'get a place to stay and a piece of bread', as people say, which is important and good, and they can assist each other, too, but any conflicts that are built into the domestic structure are declared to be due to their faulty characters and to show that women in general are troublemakers. In such cases, gender ideology provides the main assumption underlying the choices for evaluating domestic unrest.

Furthermore, in such levirate cases inheritance can also become an issue if the husband de facto adds his dead brother's property to his own because he is taking care of the brother's children and the land. 'This happens more often than you may think,' said a middle-aged woman telling me of a case about cousins in a neighbouring village. An alert, reasonable second wife will watch her children's father's property carefully to forestall disputes later, but this watching may also cause discord.

In town, polygyny is not a burning practical issue in the aesthetics of marriage. I will single out three other topics for a look at the qualitative, emotional impact they have on many people: love and bridal consent, weddings and inheritance. These get little attention in the social science literature on Iran although they have far-reaching consequences for everybody concerned.

Love's Problems[12]

Women talk quite openly about having few rights in traditional 'laws' and about rarely being allowed to use those they do have. 'They won't let us . . .' (*nilenmun*), women say, whereby 'they' encapsulates the powers vested in the elders (men and women) as well as in rigid customs enforced by social control mechanisms such as gossip. Law-like, sturdy customs allowed few choices in marriage arrangements, and feelings, let alone romantic love, were rarely an issue in marriage. Indeed, there is no term for 'love' in use, and young people now choose the English word when talking about affection. Even so-called love songs have few terms for emotions (Friedl 2018a). 'Passion' (*eshq*) implies an unsettling feeling, even a danger to order and peace – the danger of uncontrolled passion in young people, especially young men, was given as a good reason for arranging child marriages.[13] 'In the time of the khans' the danger coming from passion indeed was great: there were a few infamous, high-ranking men who counted it as a privilege of their status to take any villager's beautiful daughter or wife they fancied. The women's fathers and husbands did not have the power to prevent what in their eyes was an outrage. 'Only ugly women were safe!' remembered a grandmother, with a curse on 'these men'.

There are milder words than passion, and they provide more popular choices for talking about affection. The way 'wanting' (*khāstan*) as used in this context suggests liking, such as when a mother tells a child, '*ikhāmet*', literally, 'I want you'; '*Ikhāmet – nikhāmet*' (I want/like you, I don't want/don't like you) is a counting game one may play with a toddler; 'I am pleased, I am happy' (*khoshom iyā*) may be used for anything that elicits a good feeling, be it a beautiful face or music or seeing a beloved aunt. It is a strong term for 'liking', the opposite of 'detest, not liking' (*beyom iyā*). 'To agree' (*qabul kardan*; *pasandān*), when describing a feeling means that, all things considered, a person (such as a suitor) or thing (such as a skirt) passes muster, is not offensive, is '*o-ke*'. The word '*dust*' (friend, ally, consort) has become popular, and means to like a person or thing, but its emotional content is rather muted, as in 'I like apples', for example, even when strengthened with 'very much' (*kheili*). Used for a potential spouse, it implies that the two young people know and talk to each other freely and are at ease with each other. In the times of arranged marriages, positive emotion-heavy words were, if at all, deemed appropriate for married people, connoting devotion and peaceful togetherness. *Yār*, 'lover, beloved', is known as a poetic expression but is not a vernacular choice.

Until about two generations ago young people's feelings were rarely the main reason for a marriage arrangement. Since then emotions have become a bit more important for match-makers, especially negative ones. When a father suggested a certain cousin as a potential wife for his son, the son's answer, 'I don't want her, she is ugly' (*nikhāmesh, zeshte*) settled it as 'no'. At a similar inquiry by an aunt of her seventeen-year-old niece's suitor, the niece burst into tears: 'No, no,' she cried, 'I detest him, leave me alone,' and the aunt desisted. Local marriage aesthetics make people expect that a man and a woman will find each other tolerable when they get married, eventually will come to respect and like each other or even fall passionately in love, but for a successful marriage feelings were much less important than fulfilling the obligations that the new status and the interdependence created. 'My brother and his wife really *laaf* each other,' said an astonished, bemused sister, in 2006. When their parents were married some thirty years earlier the suggestion that they had felt 'anything' for each other produced giggles and no-no signs. A high school principal had met her 'very good' husband in college but almost did not even talk to him because, she said, she expected that like in the movies, love would have to strike her first, and she had felt 'no such thing'. But later she came to 'laaf him good', she said, in English and a bit embarrassed, with sideways glances at her little nephews sitting with us and listening closely.

'In these modern days,' according to a mother of several daughters, the young ones use Persian words for liking, such as *mehr, mohabat* (liking, affection) *aleqe dāshtan* (to have affection, to be inclined towards . . .). Thus, 'school language' provides more choices now in the local emotive vocabulary among the young and educated.

Romantic love and mutual attraction not being serious issues in marital arrangements, parallel- and cross-cousin marriages, considered 'the best' in the past, still are attractive, whereby 'cousin' is a generous category spanning generations and including relatives living in other areas. One of the purported benefits of marriages arranged within a kin group was that a young (or very young) bride would be living with close relatives and thus would be well cared for, no matter how much or little she felt for her husband. In large kin groups, though, some brides had to move far away to live with relatives they might never have seen before. For them, getting married implied several upsetting re-adjustments. 'Why is Maryam crying so much?' asked a little girl about the new bride in the house her brother had brought from a village about three hours away. Talking about the past, no woman said the transition to a new place had been easy or 'happy-making' for her. Rather, their lack of choices made them use the popular expression that their fate was 'written on their forehead'.

Bridal Consent

Religion and tradition demanded that a bride give her consent to a marriage proposal and to the contractual stipulations in the marriage contract,[14] although she might not know the content of the contract nor her future husband, and might be too young to comprehend what 'marriage' implied. In a discussion with some middle-aged women of what 'marriage' had meant for them when they had to consent to it, there appeared few choices: 'a wedding feast with music' was a prominent expectation, as were 'getting a necklace and new clothes', all delivered with giggles; 'going to live with my aunt, playing with the children and taking care of babies in the aunt's house'; 'being rid of my eldest brother's blows'; 'having children', all high on the aesthetic scale of pretty, wellbeing and social order. An elderly woman friend in town, spoken for to an adolescent son of a paternal aunt when she was an infant, and transferred to her in-laws house when she was 'six or eight' years old (meaning, before menarche), said, in a flat voice and blank face that she had no idea what marriage meant other than that she would get nice clothes and there would be a party with music and dancing but she would not be allowed to dance because brides could not dance at their weddings, and that she would go to live with her paternal aunt and help her as she had helped her own mother. She had not expected any 'pain' from her husband in bed. People explained child betrothal as 'normal' in the past, as mostly due to the prevailing shortage of women on account of the high mortality rate of girl infants (Friedl 2017). This, people know very well, was a consequence of 'benign neglect' of girls that also led to great age differences between child brides and grooms. It was not 'good' in any sense, just a fact of local life which women summed up as 'God's Will'.[15]

Given these circumstances, a young bride's murmur of consent was not her choice but simply part of the marriage ritual and was rewarded with a gift from the groom or his people. That a child bride obviously was unable to judge the merits of a proposal and a marriage contract made it entirely reasonable for her elders to make the choice in her name and demand her consent to it. I know of only one young woman who refused consent successfully, two generations ago. She was about fourteen years old then and was beaten up for her disobedience by her father and his brother. The ruckus caused ill feelings throughout the village for years. If a suitor who was a close relative was passed over in favour of one who was richer, more powerful or of economic and political use to the girl's father, he and his miffed relatives could turn 'cold' and interactions become strained (a ditty sung at weddings speaks to this: 'Oh God, come closer – do you see the old man's hand play on the girl's navel?!'). A less offensive way to discourage a proposal was for the girl's father to demand a very high bride price, but even this polite way of saying 'no' left the rejected family with the options to accept it quietly or else to retaliate with noise and enmity. Fights and bad words among relatives in the courtyards have no aesthetic merit whatsoever and were blamed on the women who, as stay-at-home people, had to cope with the discontents in daily encounters 'with everybody'.

Instead, beauty lay in the two parties' negotiating skills and a satisfactory marriage deal, sealed with the formality of the bride's consent. If marriage talks ended with good feelings in both parties and a quiet, cooperative bride, an orderly transfer of generational obligations was secured to the benefit of everybody who counted; the new couple was put on the narrow path of economic and procreational activities, and a pleasing or at least inoffensive picture of well-managed social life was secured to general approval: 'All went well,' in the laconic words of the father of a newly wedded twelve-year-old bride. And: 'We agree and they agree and the young ones want each other, too,' in the words of the happy mother of a twenty-year-old bride, in 2022. Her mother had been spoken for when she was 'six' and had to fight to be allowed to finish elementary school before getting married.

Left outside the aesthetic frame of marriage arrangements were the side-effects of girl-children's traumas and injuries resulting from forceful separation from mother and family and from forced sex and marital rape, as well as a groom's inability to perform on command with a panicking bride. People rarely talk about such memories, and neither did women comment on their part in 'helping a groom with his bride' by calming her or restraining her on the bed. Rather, they move all the pleasant and hurtful circumstances of a wedding to a woman's lot designed by the Will of God. 'Women here side with those in power, and God is the most powerful,' a local woman teacher put it in 2015. However, in a traditional, bawdy all-women's party before a wedding, women often alluded and described such painful wedding scenes as jokes. Mothers of very young brides furthermore could choose to insist on postponing a wedding to defer the sexual part of it because they felt 'pity' (*delsuz*, a 'burning heart') with the daughter, or else to buy a weakness spell for the groom's penis, but few did so because it was known as 'a very bad sin'. Nevertheless, if a groom was unable to perform his duty of defloration, the next best explanation was black magic, and murmurs to this effect easily led to friction between the two sides.

Choices and Expectations

All this is mostly tradition and memory, though. Consent has become much more than a formality, and its implications for marriage are debated. With rising marriage age, decline in marriages, ample pornography on the Internet and more choices for how couples may form, the earlier hardships and aesthetic conundrums dimmed. A mother joked about her son's wedding night in 2020: 'The youngsters who get married now know everything better than I ever did. They learn it from internet movies.' Elderly women tend to find scenes in pornographic movies more hilarious than shocking. 'Look what she is doing with her legs!' tittered a grandmother, and the women around her were overcome with mirth while watching a lively sex-scene on the Internet. However, shrinking marriage and birth rates have become problems in Iran generally, and to counter the trend, child marriage is allowed and on the rise again. 'Fathers sell their daughters to make good money,' said a disgusted local administrator recently, and a teacher furnished the example of a middle-school student from another village who was being 'married off out of the classroom' when her father needed money for his son's bride-price.

Some marriages are still arranged in Boir Ahmad, including for children and without bridal consent ('nobody asked her!'). In Sisakht they are called 'backward' and are unpopular. But sticky situations may arise when a poor outsider of religious or political prominence, such as a Seyed or a Revolutionary Guard asks for a girl in a well-off, esteemed local kin group. Such an unattractive pauper or politically dangerous man cannot be denied easily because of his status, and young women and their parents say they fear such suitors. In one case, the young woman's father quickly arranged a bogus match with a far-away nephew to discourage the unwanted suitor, a penniless Seyed with no land and a low-level government job, and 'ugly' to boot in the girl's opinion. In the past there were several such marriages in town, and the wives to this day blame their fate and their own fathers who forced them to agree to the mis-match. More recently, a denied consent highlighted the opposite problem, that is, a refusal of an upscale marriage by a low-status woman: the famously attractive daughter of a poor, landless family caught the eye of one of the former khan's relatives, a well-off, 'good' man, but she refused her consent. 'No matter what my own people said about such a good match, I did not agree. It was clear to me that in any quarrel between me and his people later, the in-laws would hold my background against me. "No", I said.'

Choices for spouse selection have increased 'in these modern days'. To make dating and marriage easier for young people, the government is providing dating advice on the Internet in the '*hamdam*' app.[16] 'I tried the internet twice,' reported a local twenty-something friend recently, 'but one guy was an arrogant show-off (a "big-neck") and the other was on drugs, as I learned by making inquiries.' Then I found a good husband myself with the help of a co-worker. People insist that gathering intelligence about potential spouses, especially suitors, has become necessary now that matches have declined between close kin well known to everybody concerned. 'My aunt's husband's sister's son who is a student in Shiraz found out through a classmate that the man who wanted to date me is only a student, not a physician as he had said, and so I said, "no",' reported a young local woman, adding that she was equally disappointed by the man's lie as by not getting a physician suitor. 'It didn't happen' (*navābi*) is the dry, final shoulder-shrug comment on such experiences.

It also is more likely now than only two generations ago that close relatives steer a young man or woman towards approving ('agree to' and 'like' are used) a distant relative as a spouse. If this does not work because of a lack of appropriate potential candidates, or blemishes such as a drug problem found on the potential groom, or of lack of attraction in either party, a young man's well-meaning relatives may discreetly look at girls in unrelated, socially compatible families. Several times over the years I faced the diplomatic challenge of evaluating the compatibility of certain young women with young men in a family who 'needed a bride'. Young men are notorious for trying to arrange marriages between their sisters and their friends. 'I am staying at my grandfather's until my big brother's friends leave our house again,' said a sixteen-year-old high school student in 2006. Later her brother hit and berated her for embarrassing him because he had promised the two friends a look at her.

Such semi-arranged matches are usually consensual, though, and thus a girl's official consent has much more meaning now. Recently, a local eighteen-year-old high school graduate said about an insistent suitor who together with his people had come for her so often that she was embarrassed and annoyed, 'I don't like his looks and how he mumbles and averts his eyes, and I know his brothers are bossing him.' No approval, no consent. Her parents shook their heads at this. 'These are good people but we can't force her to quit saying "no" and we can't tell them to quit coming,' said the father. Insistence, though, a skill learned in childhood as an effective tool for persuasion in any situation, is still the often successful strategy of choice in such cases. 'They tried and tried until I got tired and said yes,' a middle-aged teacher explained her 'dry, quiet' (boring) marriage.

The new freedom of choice in spouse selection, good as it is said to be in principle, together with the penniless existence of many young men leads to worries. Local young men without jobs, money or a good economic future are unable to find 'beautiful, good girls' who will consent to marry them, they say. With the bitter joke of, 'We all are boys here', a neighbour's son introduced his three friends to me, all unmarried in their late twenties and more or less jobless: without a wife a male is not a trusted, responsible man (*merd*) but just a 'boy'. A young woman's dismissal of such a suitor with, 'He is old and has nothing and can't find a job and ogles women,' sums up the problem.

Some young men find wives in the city where they work or study, with the consequence of a shrinking pool of attractive local available men. Unspoken-for in their mid-twenties, the local girls are called 'old maids' (*duar pir*). This was very bad in the past and continues to be seen as not good at all. It may prompt one or the other to consent to a man deemed unattractive or poor, to a 'strange outsider' or to a widower with children, especially so if they feel they have overstayed their welcome in their father's house after the youngest brother and his wife have taken over the management. Other 'old maids' choose to make the care of aging parents their purpose in life, although there are no customary choices for a proper life after their parents are dead. 'We'll see what God wants later,' said one of them, chuckling and shaking her shoulders. By taking on their brothers' traditional filial duty and diverting some of the brothers' authority to themselves they also change family dynamics. This, however, in practice often is more of a relief than a bother because the brother's wife is thereby spared the obligation to take care of her husband's old parents.

Aside of this advantage, to stay 'at home' is odd as it makes the daughter who is the care-taker dependent on her father's means, on the good will and financial support of the brother who is responsible for the parents, and, later, on the eldest (or financially most able) brother who is responsible for her, unmarried as she is. This position of dependence on father and brothers as an adult woman is talked about and said to be difficult, but for the elderly to have a daughter to see to their needs is said to be much more comfortable than having to rely for care on a youngest son's wife. Indeed, there are 'old maids' in town who are so well integrated in the household of their elderly parents and their youngest brother (the heir), that even after a parent's death they stay on as a matter of course. One, an exceptionally assertive and competent woman was the 'shah' in her younger brother's house, running the household, tending to her old, frail mother, arguing with her brother as only an elder sister may, caring for his ailing wife and raising his three sons. 'Where would we be without her!' said her relatives.

Unattractive potential suitors and looming singleness place the acquisition of money-making skills for women more firmly into gender aesthetics now. In practice, though, the bad economy and the traditional ideology of proper gender relations that makes women financially dependent on men make this choice problematic. 'We are at the nurse-or-teacher stage now,' a teacher summed up women's realistic career choices.[17]

Difficulty in spouse selection and job acceptance is linked to a tenacious expectation by women of any level of means and education that husbands ought to – and will – take care of them as in the past but will also provide the perks of a modern lifestyle such as a good living space, appliances and travels. This is a strong, popular aesthetic factor in marital relations, a much-discussed topic in families, and largely ignored in the literature on Iran. The groom's family may criticise a potential bride's family for being greedy in their demands, and at the same time, as bride-giver it may deplore the stinginess of their own daughter's groom. 'My brother has to come up with a good house for his bride and we expect an even better house for my sister from her groom!' said a young man, finding such deals 'dumb and expensive'.

Expectations take many forms. The employed wife of a local under-employed man refused to contribute financially to the support of her in-laws'/husband's house, where she lived, and instead demanded that her in-laws give their son an allowance so he could take 'better care' of her (she expected a car, she said). A college-educated local woman married to an Iranian professional man in a small town in Canada was appalled at having to 'sit at home and look out the window at corn fields', as she said, because her husband 'refused' (that is, did not have the time) to take her places. 'I could as well have married my cousin at home,' she said. A young, poor nurses' aide said she liked her job but would 'of course' quit once she was married. However, when she did get married to an under-employed man with no hope for a better future, she chose to become a registered nurse and managed to turn her small income into domestic power as the de facto manager 'of everything'. I heard many positive comments about her, including from young women who said they wanted to be like her, but her father and some others were visibly uncomfortable with this change in customary husband–wife interdependence.

Adults see young men's, and especially young women's, increasing independence in marital matters, and daughters' insistence on taking consent seriously as very progressive (and, as such, 'good'), but also as a zero-sum power game because it weakens parental authority and erodes parental privilege. Yet parents also have the choice to see it as lightening the heavy parental obligation to provide spouses for their children and to take responsibility for an unsatisfactory marriage. This is appreciated. A mother summed it up: 'I cried at the wedding because I knew that my daughter made a mistake giving consent to this good-for-nothing guy, but now that she sees it herself, at least she cannot blame me – I warned her!' For her, the daughter's headstrong decision had saved arguments and peace in her own house (the daughter, though, was getting 'very tired' of hearing how right mother had been).

Weddings: Pros and Cons

Unanimously, weddings used to be called the most beautiful, happy-making events. Weddings could heal frictions in kin groups by bringing relatives together dressed in their finest and intent on being agreeable, on having a pleasant time and performing well as hosts and guests in dances, at meals, in keeping up with news. They are high up on several aesthetic scales. On the economic side, though, the costs of getting married were always high, especially for the groom's people who had to pay the bride-price and most of the festivities' expenses. 'Four headaches', a father called his duty to facilitate marriages for his four sons. The urge to keep up with neighbours, increasing familiarity with urban practices, videos of expatriates' extravagant weddings, and steeply rising demands by brides and their parents have turned weddings into expensive, debt-laden rituals. These expenses and hefty severance payments women may demand now in marriage contracts[18] make young men shrink from committing to a marriage, they say, the more so as 'in these modern times' they no longer can count on financial assistance from father and brothers. Although there are stories of brides who demand 'only a Quran' or a similar token in the contract, everybody can tell of men bankrupted 'forever' by contractual divorce payments – television movies are fond of them. 'Money can make weddings and wives ugly,' said the mother of an unmarried son who was at the age when his own father already had two children.[19] To her, to her son, and to most others this was not right and proper, but cheaper new alternatives to a traditional wedding are problematic, too.

In order to avoid the high costs, a couple may choose to sign the legal marriage contract, the *aqd*, quietly, without a feast, and postpone the wedding. Locally this is declared a religiously acceptable licence to have sexual relations ('they can travel together now', as the mother of such a couple said), but also as too strange and colourless a choice to replace a proper wedding. Other cohabitation choices that bypass weddings, expenses and official blessings altogether are increasingly popular in the urban middle classes but locally mostly are said to be not right, to be immoral and 'bad' especially for a woman who is not protected financially by a contractual money clause in case the couple split. The most casual option, simply 'living together', is seen as a convenient, modern way of skirting expenses, but also as running afoul of cherished local tradition and Islamic law, and as a refutation of the prime goal of sex, that is, of producing children. A habit of urban young people, in town the idea lacks social comfort and any beauty.[20]

The ever-increasing ('bad, devastating, troublesome, debt-creating') costs of getting married, and the danger of complications with government agencies over traditional weddings celebrated with music and men and women dancing in public leave few satisfactory choices. People are still happy about a wedding but the aesthetics of getting married have changed towards urban tastes with white brides and parties in hotels. 'Debts are bad, police is bad', said a groom recently about his planned wedding party in a new wedding hall on the outskirts of town.

Inheritance: Traditions, Ethics and Modernity

Last, but not least, kin relations play out in inheritance rules. Traditional inheritance rules in Lur communities are as binding as laws and are meant to provide firm aesthetic boundaries regarding any kind of ownership after an owner's death. They are simple and straightforward, indeed, but their application often is short on comfort nevertheless and easily and frequently turns ugly by creating conflicts among close relatives. The aesthetics of inheritance are weighed with problems.

Ultimogeniture and Eldercare

In accordance with local custom and religion, sons inherit equally. But local custom ('tribal law') accords one additional share and the parental home to the youngest son because he has to care for his aging parents. This has worked well for generations, people say: eldercare was built into inheritance, and old people could stay in their house and be taken care of more or less cheerfully by their youngest daughter-in-law.

The 'modern days of the children' made this arrangement problematic because there are few sons in a family and these few may leave. A middle-aged woman said she was running herself ragged with taking care of her in-laws with whom she, her two children, her husband and his unmarried youngest brother were living, and in addition to helping her own elderly parents in their house because their only son had left town. Not only does the absence of sons make eldercare an issue, but so does ultimogeniture that gives the youngest son the parents' house. What happens when he leaves? is a looming question in families. In 2014, when such a youngest son decided to move away, his parents did not need care yet and all went well until an accident damaged the roof of the old house and it became clear that the absent youngest son would not repair it. The parents moved to a relative. This was 'not quite good' but got worse when their son tried to oblige his siblings to repair 'his house', arguing that otherwise his inheritance was worthless. To escape the arguments, an elder sibling decided to build a small house next to his house for the parents in his own name and with his own money, arguing that he would have to take care of the parents in his brother's obviously permanent absence anyway. This new choice created discussions.

The Islamic rule of equal inheritance for brothers and the local rule of ultimogeniture for men continue to be a structural given. In the few local cases of a man with only a daughter, marriage to a paternal cousin made especially good sense to people because the daughter's husband was of the same patrilineage and thus land and animals stayed in the family; he became his paternal uncle's heir and, eventually, his caretaker. In many other cases, though, the application and the consequences of the seemingly just and simple inheritance rule are neither good nor easy. The division of fields of different soil condition, location and size posed problems and resulted in ever-smaller, dispersed plots that after a few generations of such dividing could no longer sustain families. Furthermore, the equal-share rule caused worries and fraternal conflicts when large age differences among brothers led to differences in social status, authority and access to resources. An elder brother may be accused of getting – or usurping – the better parts of the inheritance because he had worked the land longer alongside father than the younger brothers and could invoke a kind of usufruct right and past practice. The younger ones also may argue that elder brothers got some of their inheritance when they got married in order to set them up economically, leaving less property to divide among the younger brothers later. Younger brothers and fatherless boys are at a disadvantage, people say. There is the story of Kerim, whose well-off, salaried father died when Kerim was young. The paternal grandfather was still alive, and all his land was managed by Kerim's uncle. To make sure Kerim would not be overlooked as an heir to his dead father's inheritance, his mother sent him to his grandfather's house 'every day to make sure I wouldn't put the fields in my pocket and run away with them,' as the grandfather said. Tired of these inheritance talks, grandmother told Kerim to visit less often because he was stirring up troubles 'instead of helping and entertaining us'. The ensuing rumbles were widely audible for a while.

Although accusations rarely can be proven, they often cause resentment, especially in cases where a man and his paternal nephew are close in age, which confounds status and inheritance claims associated with age and generational position. Misgivings may increase further when a younger brother received an education and got a job: education and salary may be counted as part of the inheritance, and the other brothers may choose to balk at sharing fields and orchards with the 'rich' brother, especially if he let a local brother manage a field in his absence. Thereby they weigh the value of resources of different kinds and insist on equitable inheritance rather than on 'equal' inheritance. For this, though, no hard-and-fast rules exist.

After about 2000, fields and orchards no longer were simply places for growing wheat and apples, but were becoming valuable real estate. Dissent among brothers over management spills over to sisters, wives and children, and ensuing bad feelings may burden families and the community for years.

There is always the choice for the heir who feels injured to forget and forgive, to accept the status quo without further enmities. This keeps the peace and honours the forgiving man. Such gracious wisdom is appreciated and serves as example of 'good' conduct, although it may be a bit tinged with 'weakness'.

Women as Heirs

In Boir Ahmad (and elsewhere) women did not inherit at all in the past and thus there were no inheritance issues. This tradition was in defiance of the Islamic inheritance law that allows a daughter half the share of her brother's inheritance, and was justified with the argument that a wife is cared for by her husband while a husband needs every bit of help to care for his wife and children. A more convincing but less popular choice uses the structural position of women in patrilineages: anything a daughter gets from her father de facto will become the property of her husband, who might be from another patrilineage. Women thus potentially alienate property from their paternal descent group. Both reasons made sense to people, although women, especially wives with overly controlling husbands, complain(ed) about their lack of means such as a 'little inheritance' would provide to make some decisions themselves. 'I don't have a single coin in my pocket,' grumbled a mother when her little boy asked for money to buy 'a pen and an ice cream'. Women call tight-fisted husbands 'khan' and 'shah' because they behave like autocrats. Such 'dictator' husbands are frowned upon and gossiped about, and found mostly where a salaried husband is the sole supporter of his wife and children while his wife has 'nothing to do' in the new, non-agricultural economy: 'I don't even have a pot of yoghurt to sell,' said the wife of a postmaster. Already decades ago women said that only by controlling their own resources, from egg-money to a salary, by having 'their hands in their own pockets' could they gain the clout necessary to handle their own affairs at least 'a little bit'. Likewise, it was clear to men that women's access to money and property, however gained, was a threat to the control many men deem necessary for their stewardship. Words and signs of discontent and anxiety accompany commentaries on the issue on both sides.

When a woman got married, the father, honouring tradition, gave her a bride wealth in the form of some animals and household utensils in the past and furniture or even a modern kitchen now, which he could buy with money and goods he had received from the groom's people for her. This bride-price bought the bride, people say. With it, the groom's father reimbursed the bride's father for the trouble of raising her for the labour and reproductive benefit of the groom and his people. But the father was not obliged to match the bride wealth with the bride-price. In quarrels between a husband and wife or between 'his people' and 'her people' accusations of stinginess and greed often referred to these financial matters, such as in a mother-in-law's complaint to her son's wife: 'Your father got so much bride-price money from us and all he gave you was a cooking pot and a flimsy old rug!' There is a fine line between 'good and proper' and 'bad and insulting' involved in all marriage finances. The bride's father can, for example, without words claim or bolster superior social status over the groom's people by spending much more on the bride wealth for his daughter than what the bride-price was worth.

In any case, though, brothers could choose to count their sisters' bride wealth as a kind of inheritance because it made their own inheritance smaller (they could also – and several did – decide to help a sister whose husband had no property by giving her a field or a piece of land for a house. This showed a brother's generosity and regard for his sister but had nothing to do with inheritance rules.). The aesthetics of inheritance economics 'have many dark spots', said a member of the town council. A bride also got gifts from relatives. It was understood and expected that any valuables she got would support her husband and children should the need arise. 'My gold is in the new roof,' said a woman neighbour when I asked about the pretty necklace, a wedding gift from her husband's uncle I had seen during an earlier visit.

The traditional no-inheritance rule for women changed in the Islamic Republic. Sharia law gives women the right to half of a brother's share, and thereby pitches an important local custom against the government's religious law. One cannot argue against religion but it nevertheless took many years until the first local woman claimed her part of her father's inheritance. She belonged to the former local khan's family, was in danger of losing the house she lived in as a widow and decided to go to court to claim it. This caused consternation in town for many people, because what counted as an important, reliable and sensible tradition in the eyes of those who lost – brothers and men in general – had been undermined by religious authority.

Now a sister has two choices: she may either generously renounce her inheritance for the benefit of her brothers (and thereby risk reprimands from her own children and her 'greedy' husband) or else she may claim the inheritance so as to 'help my husband and the children', potentially angering her brothers. Neither choice harms local men seriously, but the new rule causes some discontent nevertheless. 'One doesn't know what is good and what is not good any more,' said a widow, watching her four grown children argue about a contested field near a road that two daughters wanted for a building site. For the increasing number of unmarried women, though, the inheritance, however small it may be, is a 'God-sent help' that allows them a little buying power or at least gives them some clout as co-owner of a property that may be managed by a brother or a nephew. 'It makes all the difference,' said a single woman with a toss of her head, obviously pleased that she was able to help her nephew, a student, with the rent she collected for half of a small apartment she had inherited.

Inheritance of Widows and Widowers

In tribal custom widows did not inherit either: a man's property belonged to his sons, and adult sons had the duty to care for the widowed mother unless she remarried. An adult woman fitted into the social order well only if she was married; being single – be this never-married (*duar pir*, old virgin/maid), widowed (*bivezan*) or divorced (*talaqi*) – was an anomaly that provoked comment and pity as it was straining the aesthetic fabric of the quietly humming social group. A widow had no proper place, she was 'nowhere', as one said, unless she remarried. A dead man's children belonged to his patrilineage, and they and their mother were best taken care of if one of the dead man's brothers married the widow and managed his nephews' fatherly inheritance. A young, childless widow had no claim to her dead husband's property and no choice for living other than back at her father's house. Her relatives took pains to get her remarried quickly.

In contrast to traditional local custom, the Islamic Republic's laws give widows the right to a share of the dead husband's property and to remain in the husband's house. 'This is good', they say. Problems arise, though, if she wants to sell the house, given that local ultimogeniture makes it the youngest son's property. This has consequences for eldercare, too: 'Why should I be my mother-in-law's caretaker if tomorrow she decides to sell the house?' argued a disgruntled young woman when she was criticised for trying to persuade her husband to move away. Such stories show how vulnerable elderly people have become in Iran generally: not only are there no longer enough children available as caretakers but neo-local residence and inheritance regulations, too, work against traditional eldercare (see Hegland, Sarraf and Shahbazi 2007).

Other arrangements are more problematic for elderly widows who rank low on any aesthetic scale anyway. A widow may dismiss the choice to move in with a married daughter because the son-in-law's house for her is a stranger's house, a place she hesitates to visit, let alone live in, even if he is a relative and invites her. 'She sits alone in the cold house, she is grouchy, people gossip, and it is bad for everyone,' a frustrated man said about his mother-in-law's refusal to move to his house. The choice to move away to live with a son in a city is proper but without nearby relatives it elicits the fear of loneliness. In most cases, elderly widows choose to fight for the little independence that living in the old house affords them, even if a caretaker is not always available. They prefer being 'a little cold' and 'sometimes a little hungry' to 'being dragged to the kitchen of my son's wife', as one of them explained, dismissing tradition. 'Most of the time I listen to the radio and all is well,' another one said, sitting in the kitchen of her quiet, empty house. But everybody agrees that the elderly are vulnerable, a potential headache for neighbours and nearby relatives, and this is not good. Few, if any, have valuable possessions, and it is generally accepted as reasonable that the men who take responsibility for her get her belongings when she dies.

Ugliness about possessions and money arise only when one or the other son becomes greedy or shirks filial responsibilities, or when grandma plays one son against another, carrying gossip, little gifts and misgivings back and forth among the houses. Talks about cases of 'stubborn' old women being blamed for inter-family discontent show that people, especially women, understand very well that some elderly women's manipulative behaviour is motivated by their attempts to hold on to some power, influence and independence. 'My mother-in-law likes to hear her eldest son's wife thank her for the watermelon or the cookies she takes to them from my larder,' said a woman with empathy in her face and a dismissive gesture of her hands. Such behaviour feeds the popular assumption that women more often than men turn cantankerous, headstrong and unpleasant with old age.

A widower may be sad when his wife dies, even inconsolable, lonesome and despondent, and likely will be inconvenienced by lack of her services, but inheritance is no issue: whatever she owned belongs to him – old tribal custom is no different from religious law in this case. A widower will stay in his house and will be taken care of by his daughter-in-law with much less friction and 'bad words' than a widow would have with a daughter-in-law. Unlike a widow, who may find a suitor only if she is still young, a widower may get married again at almost any age, and inheritance ties into such marriage in a serious quality-of-life way: a widower's daughters usually support his wish to remarry much more readily than his sons. Daughters say that they feel sorry for the lonely man and also that they are glad to be relieved of providing more or less occasional care for him 'out of the goodness of their heart'. But the sons are not happy – they are afraid that should father have more children the inheritance would have to be divided further; that should he die, they would have to take care of his widow and children; and that people could think and say that the old man wanted a wife because he was not treated well in his youngest son's house. 'Not just not good but bad, bad, ugly,' said a man about such a predicament in a cousin's family.

I emphasised here the importance of structures and habits over individual people's inclinations and personalities. Indeed, character and disposition can avoid, mitigate or enhance potential conflicts caused by structural conditions. There are many cases of peaceful and contented kinship relations, of peaceful and orderly transitions of property, but they are formed often despite the limitations set by rules. 'What will they do in Uncle Ali's house now that he is dead?' was the anxiety-driven comment I heard several times after the death of a well-regarded, just and by all reports capable man who had managed his large family and kin group without creating animosity and upheavals. He was successful despite the normative assumptions, difficult rules and expectations that make many men autocrats in their houses, and despite 'the habit of humans to be loud and demanding', as one of his cousins said, wiping his eyes.

5

The Aesthetics of Needs

Introduction: The Logic of Life

Local choices regarding ethics extend the purported human natural inclination towards aggressive behaviour to everything alive. This popular view of life is based on the observation that all living things go by a similar playbook, with the rule that in order to live one is forced (*majbur*) to intrude on other beings' lives while adapting to what is given and trying to stay alive and avoid harm.

Majbur is a key concept in the local art of living, covering the choices available to acknowledge the necessity to work competently as well as the necessity to employ strategic behaviours such as dissimulation, flattery, corruption in order to hold one's own or to get ahead. People argue that God must have willed it all – why else would it be like this? But in contrast to plants and animals, people, especially men, have big brains and the ability and duty to discern between good and bad, and therefore they should do better than birds of prey and wolves. This is 'obvious to anybody with eyes and ears'. God demands from people that they to do good, and doing good furthermore is for people's own benefit: 'If you feed your dog it will not bite you, and if you weed and water your lentils they will grow well, and if you are friendly with your wife's mother she won't badmouth you,' a farmer said. This ethic is beautiful and simple to understand yet hard to act upon, people say, a difficult choice because people are weak-minded by nature and in the old times they also were tired and often hungry and sick.

The insight furthermore creates conflicts. For an old hunter to shoot game, for a woman to kill a chicken for a guest, and for the local butcher to slaughter an ox are seen as a necessity yet also as an unavoidable sin. 'Everything we kill and cook and eat would rather live,' said a host while turning meat on a spit over a fire, and a woman shooing hens from wheat drying in the sun spun it further: 'Worms eat wheat, chickens eat worms and wheat, and we roast chickens and cook wheat and poison bugs or keep them away with prayer amulets. This is how the world works!' There may be a vestige of animism here, the belief that everything alive has a life-soul more or less endowed with the main aesthetics of life in needs and wants, fears and likings. People casually make such remarks, revealing a sort of self-evident base assumption about life on Earth. Only few people, though, speculate why nature is lovely as well as dangerous, useable as well as destructive – it is what it is, with necessity (*majburi*) as a principal mover in the behaviour of anything alive, animals and people alike.

Animals

On the basis of observation and experience, people take it for granted that different kinds of animals have different habits and personalities. The negative qualities in animals' aesthetics are voiced freely when angry people call somebody behind their back a dumb ass or a dirty dog, a slow sheep or a horny donkey, a voracious wolf, a secretive cat, a dangerous snake. But in contrast to people, animals and plants are said to be neither good nor bad – they do what they do without moral connotations. Obviously all animals have some kind of reasoning power for finding food and avoiding dangers, and an old herder put it in words: 'Nobody needs to tell bears and wolves how to find water or to take care of their young, they just know it and do it.' But it is just as obvious that they cannot discern good from bad in an ethical sense, and their will and resulting responsibilities are, at best, rudimentary.

Wildlife

Wildlife easily counts as nuisance based on people's experiences with flies, flees, lice, rodents, scorpions; or as dangerous competitors among themselves and of people over food resources, such as boars, wolves and bears. These animals had little aesthetic value aside of belonging to nature, and one avoided to see them or be seen by them. It was commonplace to say that their behaviour was God-given, that they had to struggle to survive and bring up their young 'just as we do'. To this day people express a quiet awe when they are 'out there' in the oak woods and pastures. Old-timers tell stories of *periun* (fairies, mostly in the form of human-shaped women) as the masters of the realm of woods and wildlife. The last master-hunter in Sisakht explained the contradiction between respect for fairy-masters of (game) animals and hunters killing these animals by insisting that a hunter could only shoot what a fairy-owner sent in front of his gun, as a present.[1] With noises from tourists, cars and machines the woods fell silent and fairies with their animals slid into a sad memory for some people and are taken as a sure sign of better modern times for critics of 'superstition'.

Given the Islamic food taboos, only a few wild animals are useful as food for people, and these are called 'beautiful', such as wild sheep and partridges (bees are valued highly, too – honey is an expensive, 'healthy' delicacy to this day). Game is nearly extinct and hunting without a licence is illegal now, with poaching a somewhat dangerous choice. Other animals did not fare any better, though. By the middle of the twentieth century men had killed bears, boars, wolves, hyenas, ungulates, mountain lions, snakes, foxes to near extinction, with 'good riddance' as the common comment. Self-defence, protecting one's crops and herds and the need for food brought the killing of wild animals into the 'no choice' (*majburi*) category for the hunters and balanced the potential sin of the killing. Successful hunters were heroes sung about in wedding songs; 'master-hunter' (*mirshekāl*) was a title of honour. 'A man wasn't a man unless he was a hunter, a fighter and a thief,' said an old woman who had lost a son in an inter-tribal fight a long time ago. To this day some men like to pose with a rifle, recalling the excitement in the aesthetic of guns and hunting.

Domesticated Animals

Goats and sheep, cows and oxen, donkeys, poultry and herd dogs depend on people to survive and to fulfil their purpose, which by general agreement is to support their owners. 'The animals are our servants', said a farmer, 'and therefore we have to feed and protect them'.

There are no pets in town. Cats live outdoors as mice hunters and are not fed. Mistrusted as food thieves and potential jinn and shape shifters, they are shooed wherever they appear. Dogs lived outdoors, protecting herds in the pastures from wolves and people in the settlements from enemies. They were fed minimally and were dangerous for strangers. Their barking at any unusual movement around them and a low-pitched, quiet howling ahead of an impending earthquake were familiar background noises in the village. At best, cats and dogs were ignored when scrounging for food. Keeping dogs inside the house is considered a modern city habit, an abomination on religious grounds (dogs are declared *harum*, polluting) and a dirty health hazard among hygiene-oriented progressives.[2] They were treated like outcasts, and by 2020, when dangers from enemies and control of herds were no longer issues, there was not a single dog in town. Stoning cats, birds and dogs was a favourite pastime of boys with slingshots, and young birds and kittens were play-things for children and soon dead in their hands. Adults scolded youngsters for this cruelty but only half-heartedly so on the assumption that children have an underdeveloped moral compass and thus are innocent, and that they would grow out of this habit as their reasoning power increased. Hens have the run of the neighbourhood, return home at dusk to get fed little balls of bread-dough, and to crowd into their hen-houses for the night, that is, into baskets and, earlier, small, barrel-shaped vessels of dried mud made by women.

Most animals were in poor health, undernourished and plagued by parasites. Poultry was regularly decimated by epidemics, and chicken dishes and eggs were rare delicacies until they appeared from 'chicken factories' for sale in the bazaar. Keeping one's animals alive through the cold, snowy winters was a challenge, a source of anxiety and also of satisfaction: donkeys' loads of dried fragrant grass (*jāshir*) in the barn remain a reassuring testimony to competent stewardship. Animal noises and noises people made to control chickens, cats, dogs, birds, and to summon stray herd animals were a constant, reassuring din in the old village, a 'good noise'.

What domesticated animals learn beyond their natural habits depends on the skills of their human masters who teach them, using punishment and few rewards, and by using sounds the animals understand, as the farmers say. These skills are part of the aesthetics of good husbandry. When our daughter Kati, a veterinary student then, and a veterinarian in Michigan found a herd of cows they had to inoculate widely dispersed in a pasture, the frustrated veterinarian wanted to leave but Kati called the animals with the sounds she had learned in Sisakht, and the cows came. Shepherds of the neighbouring Qashqa'i are admired in Sisakht for getting sheep and goats to line up for milking by themselves, while in Boir Ahmad helpers have to fetch each milk animal from the bunched-up herd. Identifying animals by their colour markings, faces and voices belongs to the aesthetics of the skills of husbandry, too. 'Our sheep and goats are as different as the faces of my neighbours,' said a young girl, helping her mother at milking time, in 2006.

There is little choice in attitudes towards animals. The way they are treated suggests that their value comes from being of use to people. Unlike humans, who have ideas about how they fit into God's universe, animals likely do not have such thoughts, people say. Their habits do not show morals or good manners, and they depend on humans 'to think and care for them'. Rarely does one show attachment or kindly interaction with a cow, for example, or a donkey. Although shepherds clearly appreciated the dogs helping them control and protect the herd, and although all barn animals were familiar to their masters, they were treated with little empathy. Lambs and kids were deprived of milk because milk was a cash crop. Unwanted young cats and dogs were buried alive. Barely enough young animals survived the regular spring-time diarrhoeas to keep herd sizes stable. The healthiest animals were donkeys, thriving on thistles while roaming the poorest pastures.

People insist that as God's creatures animals deserve decent treatment and it is a sin to make 'hapless creatures' suffer but that the owners are unable to treat them better. 'We are hungry and the dog is hungry,' said a herder in the 1960s, when the herds of the fast-rising population had depleted the earlier verdant pastures around the growing village. Additional fodder was expensive; epidemics 'came and went', killing the under-fed, sickly animals; home remedies were of little use, and touching '*harum*' animals such as dogs made touch-based treatments cumbersome. Even in nostalgia-tinged hindsight husbandry had been difficult then. The few herd animals left now are herded in cooperative arrangements and the owners add fodder and administer inoculations and medicines they buy in the city. 'It is much better now', said one of the few full-time herders in Sisakht, looking at the sheep and goats in his corral, 'but it is expensive'.

Considering that just a few short generations ago people and their animals 'lived together in barns', as a local physician rightly said in 2006, the lack of insight into animals' needs and the lack of effective traditional medicine for animals astonished him, a farmer's son. By then herding was a minor enterprise and for reasons of public health a town ordinance prohibited animals in town. With their rare appearance in daily life, with nature films on television and the adoption of the urban disdain for 'dirty' farm work, the attitude towards animals is changing, too. 'I like cows in pictures and on television because they remind me of my grandfather's house, but those on television are so clean and pretty,' said a young neighbour. Thus, the farming and herding past is being taken out of the aesthetics of work and dirt now and placed into the aesthetics of nostalgia: hearing a herd's bells in the evening, eating a fresh, 'natural' egg, putting a load of fragrant hay on the donkey, listening to the swish-swish sounds that milk makes in a milking woman's pail, feeding little dough-balls to the chickens, shooing a cat, sloshing yoghurt in a goat-hide bag to make butter in the small, cool hours before sunrise – in this mood, all these tasks belong to a kind of lost beauty, while the toil and pain of the way of life behind this beauty are played down. 'Sometimes I miss the old ways, and rarely do I think of what we didn't like,' said a neighbour, and then came up with a long list of half-forgotten hardships.

Humans

Compared with animals, humans are not much more perfect – not as a species and not as individuals, people say. The nearly unanimous insistence that most human beings' flawed judgements and reasoning very often dominate their good intentions and qualities is based on the idealistic assumption that people ought to be good, rational and competent. Islam and theologians elevate the assumption to a mandate: 'ought' becomes 'should' and 'must'. The local realists, though, insist that observation and common sense demonstrate that the basis of morality, of virtues and vices, is an innate disposition that is only a little bit malleable and controllable by people's own will.[3] Choices to explain morality shift easily between God's Will and people's reason, upbringing and wilfulness. What 'ought to be' is the ideal aesthetic frame, anchored in the practice-based insight that requirements for collectivist coexistence include cooperation and tolerance, trust and good conduct. Islam demands this, too, but insight, longing and demands do not agree with people's experiences of how most everybody actually behaves. The way people talk about their behavioural choices is guided foremost by how they satisfy human needs.

Needs

Humans' bodily needs for food and sex link people to most animals. Both and the need for shelter and warmth in winter are taken to be obviously

God-willed and have to be satisfied in an orderly way so as to sustain life and good habits, and to prevent death, crime and immorality. This is taken as a given, beyond doubt and beyond choice. But how the needs are fulfilled lies within the aesthetic frame of morality: the choice of seeing virtues and vices as under a person's control makes especially food and sex also matters of moral decisions. It is further taken as a self-evident fact that God assigned men the management of food and shelter, and gave them the right to satisfy their need for sex. A man's wish for a wife is taken to be an obvious requirement for a normal, healthy life rather than a choice. In 2015, a young man argued about his father's hesitancy to 'buy' him a wife: 'Everybody needs food!' the young man said, counting food and sex as equally strong needs. But while eating is a matter of survival and an open daily routine with overtones of religious merits (such as in hospitality or feeding the poor), sex is a topic for talk only in jokes and rowdy company, and its fulfilment has no religious merit.

Need for Food

The need for food is satisfied with gender-complementary skills and duties, with men producing raw food items and women turning them into edibles.[4] This is a firm aesthetic structure with few choices. Being a woman obliged even me, the 'foreign lady', to take over a kitchen for seven people for a day, and, especially funny, to milk goats for a herder whose wife was sick. I had learned this skill in Austria as a child but he took it for granted that I had it simply because I was a woman.

The interdependence is judged by individuals' efforts: one can be a good or bad provider or a good or bad cook, be hardworking or lazy, with major consequences for everybody's wellbeing. Depending on satisfaction with the partner's performance, the interdependence can create harmony as well as arguments in the house. When a married man complains that he only gets 'bread and yoghurt' for supper or that he has to boil his own water for tea he is saying that he feels neglected by his wife. In the past a wife may have complained that she had to get a log from her father to make a fire because her husband had not seen to his wood stack,[5] or that 'the peas dried on the vines' because her husband had not irrigated the fields on time. Now she may lament her husband's failure to go shopping for the house or arrange for a plumber to repair a tap, as he ought to do, but she also may choose to be proud of taking over such chores. Women are responsible for feeding everybody in the house, which makes shortcomings in the larder especially worrisome and galling for them. Shopping, however, seems to be more of a problem for women in cities than in Sisakht where shopkeepers and their customers may be related and where therefore requirements of modesty and prompt payment are relaxed. Few local women make shopping an issue of proper modesty, but will stress occasionally that they were obliged (*majbur*) to go to the bazaar.

The modern economy made the gender division in food matters more marked and rigid – men and women comment on this. The demise of women's labour-intensive chores in the home-economy such as processing milk, churning butter, lugging water and spinning yarn, and the increase in household gadgets and indoor plumbing turned women from being economic assets to consumers. New choices for women's activities link women to expenses, such as travel for visiting relatives, home-making projects, cell phone use or shopping. Television and urban relatives model how one ought to live, including what to eat. Any of these choices, including getting foodstuff in the bazaar, require money which, in most cases, men control. A wife might complain about owing a shopkeeper for a can of tomato paste or about having to beg her sister for the use of a mixer because there was 'no such necessary thing' in her house. The new '*normál*' home comfort includes a sharp increase in food needs and more than ever keeps women dependent on husbands' and fathers' willingness to provide 'every grain of salt and every drop of cooking oil', as a wife summed it up. 'Bread was from my dough and eggs from my hens but now I have to wait for the old man to bring them from the bazaar,' said a grandmother. Controlling men argue that women let money 'drip away' for nonsense such as sweets for children, and women with a salary complain that husbands use the salary to buy land instead of 'making a good life' for the family.[6] This causes hardships and arguments. More than ever, women say, it depends on a man's character to keep his house in good spirits.

Mostly, though, with few children, few chores, ready tap-water, more food available and easy cooking on gas-ranges, local women are no longer 'hungry and tired all the time', and this is 'very good'. Now they make fun of their leisure condition: 'My bones ache from being lazy,' joked the wife of a school principal. 'Come sit with us – we count sugar cubes and watch our tea-glasses,' was the mirthful greeting from some women sitting together on a porch. Indeed, physicians and women themselves blame the noticeable rise in body weight and related ailments on house-bound women's inactivity. Hiking with other women has become an acceptable choice, with a catch: 'Strolling in the gardens is very good but it also makes us hungry!' said a retired teacher after an afternoon 'out in the pleasant open air'. Good food combined with lack of exercise also has created issues for desk-bound men. When a well-nourished neighbour returned from the doctor with the advice to lose weight and walk more, his cousin made a rhyme on the spot: 'What earlier was pain from an empty stomach (*kom pati*), now is pain from full pots, sweets and sitting on the fat fanny (*kn gyepu*)'.

Sex and Passion

It is taken as a fact established by experience and medical authorities that sex is a strong health-need for men that is difficult to control. There is no choice in this: normal men have the urgency for sex just as they have loud voices, a young man said. Men who are denied sex are said to be in danger of becoming sick because the dammed-up semen might cause problems 'like anything that is clogged', as a nurse explained. Indeed, when we first visited, even a blind and a lame man had a wife despite their dim economic prospects. In some rare men the sex urge is low enough that they do not need a wife, but such men are likely called 'sister' (*dada*) behind their backs. The short monthly rest during women's (polluting) menstruation is no issue for men, but with giggles and frowns women occasionally remarked on the forty days of post-partum abstinence as a problem for some husbands. In the past women saw the sex pause as helpful for preventing being pregnant 'all the time, like cows', and many added the wish for a longer rest period. Men and women readily accepted birth control devices when they became available in the 1970s (see A. Loeffler and Friedl 2014).

The unmarried young adult men who live in town now blame the bad economy together with rising lifestyle expectations of young women for keeping them out of the marriage market (and thus out of legal access to sex). This means that the marriage age for women is rising and some local girls get no husband. Lack of access to sex is one reason given for why this singleness is 'bad': nearly everybody declares it to be 'not *normál*', not good at all because it leaves needs unfulfilled and complicates social life.

Homosexuality, called '*baće-bāzi*' (boy-play), is known as an 'ugly, stupid habit' of adolescent boys, is punishable by death in Iran's legal code and not is an issue locally. This may change when marriages decline further, a physician predicted. Prostitution is not an issue locally either, but there are rumours about a few women in the province who are 'friends' with men, and of husbands who pimp their wives for good money. It is loudly declared to be scandalous and sinful by just about everybody, but the outrage is tempered by sotto voce remarks about the difficulty of living well when one has to rely on lawful, ordinary means to procure an income.

The natural need – and therefore desire – for sex is said to be weaker in women than in men: 'Men want sex because they need it, women want it to get children,' is the popular opinion. This difference makes women more 'heavy, grounded' (*sangin*), which enables and thus obliges them to avoid arousing men other than their husbands. The need for such modesty is accepted as a fact established by experience and supported by custom and religion, or else, as a choice for staunchly orthodox believers, as established by God and religion. There are few doubters of this 'fact' and no good alternative choices. An 'immodest, light-weight' (*saboq*) woman risks her own good reputation and that of the men who react to her by turning 'ugly' or 'crazy'. Over the years several young men are remembered to have left town because they were infatuated with local young women they could not have, mostly for socio-economic and status reasons. A famous, sad stanza in a wedding song bemoans this: 'In my camp a blossom has opened; neither can I reach it nor does it fall.' Rumour has it that two young men – students far away from home – tried to commit suicide over such a denial. 'Sex and girls make the boys crazy,' said a grandfather.

Such love-sickness was called 'drunk, crazy' (*mas, kyelu*) and to be due to passion (*eshq*), indicating a loss of reason and control in the suffering men.[7] Although alcohol, a widely used illegal drug in Iran, is not an issue locally, the idea that alcohol causes men to lose control over their sex drive and then commit incest is widespread and asserted strongly by pious people. The young women who cause men's love-derangements are criticised and cursed for their lack of reserve and modesty, and the young men are scolded to their face and abused behind their backs for the foolishness of letting an infatuation get the better of their mind. The idea of a woman losing her senses over a man other than her fiancée or husband was taken to be absurd. Listeners giggled and shook their heads when a student told them a sad love-story of a young woman at her university. If it happened at all locally, it would 'stay hidden in the kitchen', as a mother said. In a case from a neighbouring village, a young woman 'liked' her married cousin 'very much' and the two left town together, causing a stir first and then silence. Other than this story, I heard of no love-crazed, sad young women, while the motif of forlorn, depressed, love-sick men is a popular poetic motif.

The way people talk about sexual matters suggests that men naturally like sex but women have to learn to like it. Husbands and wives who 'like to be with each other', who 'joke and play' with each other find general approval expressed in giggles and smiles. (In a gender-context 'joking' and 'playing', have sexual overtones. Young widows have the reputation of missing 'play[ing] with their husbands' and thus ought to get remarried soon so as to prevent flirts and gossip.) But very many women, traumatised by early-age sex, 'never really like it', women say, with a dismissive toss of their heads. The Islamic legal marriage age of eight or nine years (that is, for sex) for girls may be taken as a reasonable rule to prevent immoral premarital sex but may also be declared – and is so by most everybody, again based on experience – as a mistake, an ugly habit, a backwardness.

Given the purported gender differences in sexual matters, it was considered reasonable for a wife to have 'a pillow ready' or have 'her skirts gathered' when her husband came home from work, but it was not right for a wife to demand sex from him. However, a husband is obliged to attend to his wife's sexual urges and purported longing for children, and a husband's sexual neglect of his wife is a legally acceptable reason for a wife to ask for divorce. Locally, people took the 'neglect' idea as a joke, at least for young men. Young married women used to complain that mothers-in-law acted as guardians of their sons' sexual rights and admonished their daughters-in-law to be attentive to their husbands' desires. 'According to men, the only thing women ought to like is having children,' said an elderly woman, dismissing men's expectations yet also accepting them as reasonable for orderly life. The traditional link of sex and many children is weakening nearly everywhere in Iran and is affecting the gender philosophy regarding sex locally, too.[8]

Elderly, post-menopausal women talk about sex – if at all – as a burden, and men complain about this attitude in little asides and jokes about the advantages of polygyny. Women, in turn, mention two benefits of polygyny, half-jokingly: a young co-wife sees to the husband's sexual needs and – hopefully – helps with housework. For women, sex often appears in asides and short comments as a domestic chore in the aesthetics of married life. An old funny anecdote about a man with two wives who ends up sleeping alone in the mosque got an update recently: 'The man's first wife, his cousin in the village, sends him 'for a bed' to his chic second wife in the city, who promptly sends him back, telling him not to bother her all the time, and he falls asleep on the bus.' The religious–legal allowance of four wives and easy divorce for a man is justified with the purported sex needs of men by supporters of the law, but is disparaged and condemned more loudly by critics (men and women) quoting the equally important religious mandate for a just and peaceful home life, which, in practice, is deemed near impossible with polygyny.

Any kind of sexual activity outside marriage is declared sinful '*harumkārī*' (unlawful) and locally condemned mostly because it is disruptive in the community. Women may quickly decide to nip unseemly attractions between neighbours and relatives in the bud and to settle such affairs as quietly as possible so as to prevent gossip, upheaval and violence. When a young man had once too often visited his beautiful, married cousin in the next compound, her husband had a 'loud word' with his wife, and the young man's eldest sister had 'many words' with the young man, and this stopped his visits. Gossip about a 'flirty, light-weight girl' or about a man with 'dirty, crooked eyes' is put to good use as a warning for everybody to guard their behaviour. The behaviour as well as the gossip are ugly, and the danger of a loss of face and respect for some is a deterrent for any gestures that could be seen as unseemly interest in a person of the opposite sex. After a well-regarded local man's outgoing street behaviour caused comment because he greeted everybody, including women neighbours, he choose to keep his eyes firmly on his feet when outside. 'He'd rather bump into walls than look at anybody now,' said his sister, shaking her head and lifting her eyebrows to indicate that he had over-reacted to the talk.

In 2015, a story circulated about an attractive young woman in a nearby village whose flirtatious behaviour irritated people and kept 'good', well-off suitors away, as they explained. Eventually, her father 'bought' her a husband from elsewhere by giving him a house. It is not important to verify the story; people found it believable and variously lauded the father, pitied him and were angry at him for setting a bad example and causing confusion because by pardoning the usual bride-price and instead rewarding the groom, the father forfeited the customary subservience of a son-in-law and upset the flow of authority. In dealing with my husband and myself, however, people choose to discard strict modesty requirements. We talked with most men and women alike, anywhere, and they responded without ado. When I discussed this with one of our neighbours, he said that people knew we were 'different', that we would not turn familiarity into anything 'ugly'. Here, too, rules within the aesthetics of modesty appear as choices ranging from strict avoidance to familiar closeness, and people fit their choices to their own judgement of the circumstances.

Given the rapidly easing sexual mores in Iran, basic assumptions about sex and gender are changing, too, but locally the gravitas of local young women, especially unmarried ones, remains a concern. Except for *hizbollah*-oriented women who try to follow mullahs' modesty demands to the letter, young local women more or less emphatically choose to resent the stress of modesty as a curtailment of their freedom (*āzādi*). 'Freedom' has become a popular word with many meanings and provides a handy choice in arguments against any form of authority, as the anti-government demonstrations in Iran showed in 2022/23. They started with women: the curtailment of their 'freedom' within their families 'never ends', as a young wife in Sisakht declared. Many young men joined them, implicitly protesting the rule of old men (*qānun piremerd*) who, in the words of a fifteen-year-old local boy, 'own' them. In Sisakht, for the past decade the word 'freedom' has created important political and lifestyle choices especially in its use by young people.

Shelter

People remember that their ancestors used to live in caves like many animals and demons, or else close to their own domestic animals in makeshift dwellings while on the move, and that these shelters were often cosy but generally 'not good'. The verdict implies that the more elaborate, solid, 'good' and well-appointed a dwelling is, the more 'human' are the people who have the skills, the knowledge and the wherewithal to build them. A family's house and social status were connected in the aesthetic frame of living. Whenever we said that we had no jacuzzi in our house in the United States, no 'salon' and not even wall-to-wall carpeting or a rose garden, people were incredulous – it did not fit our status as university professors to live in a small house without such amenities. However, one also may hear a critic say about somebody, 'Such a good house, and he is a wild animal!'

Dwellings developed over time from branch huts and tents to stone-and-mud buildings and bigger ones made of dried mud-brick, both with flat dirt roofs on wooden beams, to two-storey buildings – a mud-brick one for people on top of one of stones that sheltered the animals.[9] Built next to each other in closed courtyards, they offered security and all the advantages and disadvantages of tight living spaces. After outside dangers diminished, people opted for 'modern', free-standing buildings in small yards, made of cement blocks or even burnt bricks (both city imports), and, more recently still, of houses with cement walls reinforced by steel-rods to withstand earthquakes. The older buildings were cheap, made with readily available materials by the owners and their helpers. Every man knew how to get beams, make mud-bricks and stack them properly, but the small houses were unstable in earthquakes.[10] A severe earthquake in 1971 did much damage, as did the strong one in 2021, including to new houses that had been built with reinforced steel rods as per government ordinance. People blame corruption for this destruction because to save money, builders welded the iron rods together instead of screwing and bolting them. It might not be the only or main cause for the collapse but this explanation makes people visibly uneasy and angry.

People point out that each new architectural development increased privacy, comfort and distance from the dirt outside. They retained the customary porch or veranda in front or on a side that 'good' houses always had, places where strangers state their business and casual, familiar visitors can come and go without much ado. Footwear stays outside the house or right at the door inside. Men and women visitors will separate unless they are close relatives, and will be offered tea, fruits, cucumbers or store-bought sweets. This mix of hospitality, friendly interaction, neighbourliness, order and getting one's business done is called 'very good', a useful pleasure with few exceptions, such as of untimely or unwelcome visitors. Since around 2000, new houses have been modelled after urban one-family homes with two storeys, and to build them one needs professional builders, craftsmen and 'a lot of money'.[11] Neo-locality increases the pressure on housing in the area; there are several apartment blocks in town now, and for some, renting out apartments and houses is a lucrative business.

Character and Personality

How needs are fulfilled depends on customs as well as on people's personalities and character. Islamic ethics of 'doing onto others only what you do to yourself', the Golden Rule, differ little from the Persian ethos of 'being human' (*ensānyat*), and of what local people claim always to have held dear and called good, proper behaviour of well-ordered human beings. 'He/she is not a human being, not a person' (*ādam nist, ensān nist*) is a telling verdict on people who lack understanding and manners, whose preference for dissimulation and manipulative strategies makes them greedy and unreliable or whose quick temper (*tondrou*) makes them 'ugly'. Yet these qualities, too, are 'deep' in people. An astute elderly farmer summarised the most popular choices for thinking what makes people human and different from anything else alive: God-given reason (*aql*), inherited traits (*ersi*), family traits (*neshād*) and discipline (*tarbiat*), learned at home, in school and from other people. In practice, on the level of everyday interactions, 'being human' shows in people's many kind and generous dealings with others, in attention to other people's needs, readiness to help and being meticulously hospitable. The two extremes – dishonesty/aggression and reliability/empathy – are seen as two sides of the same coin and used when and where deemed necessary, advantageous or simply feeling right. This basic model of social aesthetics covers everybody, explains differences in personalities and provides choices for interactions.

The terms used locally for a person's character and personality, *ākhlāq* (morality, ethics), and *raftār* (behaviour) place them into the aesthetic realm of morality and ethics (the Farsi term used routinely for character, *shakhsiat*, means personality, temperament, and is a descriptive term light on ethics). Mullahs and their followers explain that God put at least four forces into each human being, all good and useful as long as a person uses the first, reason (*aql*), to rein-in the others to prevent excesses in rage and violence (*zurguï, ghazab*; *tondrou*); in desire (*shahvat, hers*) for food, women and status; and in greed (*tama*) and brutal power (*qodrat, zurguï*).

Listening to people's arguments, reason emerges as the most important human control feature, an aesthetic pinnacle of human abilities. Although it is not totally reliable, pious people stress the divine wisdom in putting reason into humans' minds. Just about everybody takes reason as 'real', as a given based on experience, and as necessary for living. But there also is the choice to take it either as not specific enough to explain the wide range of people's personalities and behaviours or else to modify it by the 'strand/line'-theory (R. Loeffler 2022) that sees various inclinations and forces as strands or lines (*reg*) in the body that change in response to 'the happenings of the day', as a usually quiet woman explained after yelling at her son in a fit of impatience. Nobody is always all good or all bad, all beautiful or all ugly, all wise or dumb. Rather, individuals combine moods and behaviours, leaning more to one or the other side of the possibilities as circumstances vary. A father can be a violent 'khan' for his sons when in the mood of order and obedience, and also their staunch supporter against critics; he can be strict towards his brothers' sons and a kind uncle for his sisters' sons. Choosing among the 'lines' allows people to adapt and react to conditions of the moment in ways that seem inconsistent when compared with other occasions.

Beyond assuming God's Will behind this system – implying that the system has to be accepted as is – the most popular general verdict about human nature is pessimistic: people claim that observation and experience show that humans lean towards 'bad' qualities, that despite their reasoning power they have a hard time in controlling their *nafs* (ego, passion). 'Violent and competitive', a retired teacher said after a lifetime of observing boys' peer groups; 'Destructive little devils', adults say about children; 'Jealous and arrogant', said a pious student about fellow students. With 'rotten to the core', a disappointed householder summed up his wife's relatives, and a tired woman called all her sons' wives 'lazy spendthrifts'.' Dozens of Luri and Farsi standard terms are in use for 'bad, ugly' character qualities, from arrogant and dictatorial to wild, dirty, stingy and bad-mouthed, and when provoked, people come up with more colourful ones on the spot. Most of these terms place the 'bad' person on the side of arrogance, aggression and violence, of causing irritation, pain or danger for others.

For the much shorter list of good character qualities, from truthful and reliable to patient and kind, the opposite prevails, that is, the words laud a person who is self-possessed, polite, wise, contented and guarding his or her reputation, with the potential to err on the meek and mute side. Often a sad face, a hint of pity accompany judgements such as 'locked-tongue' (*zounbaste*), implying shy and unable to defend oneself; or 'luckless, without recourse' (*badbakht, bićare*) as a comment on an unassuming, quiet person who is struggling with the vagaries of life. A pious, outspoken veteran woman teacher stressed the choice to see these attributes as dividing men (on the aggressive side) from women (on the good but meek side) and it was beyond her to even guess why God wanted it this way. 'Women can do absolutely everything men can do', she (and others) said, 'and they do it without commotion and yelling.' Humourists have fun with the idea that God is learning from the shortcomings of humans so as to make better beings when creating the next world.

Goodness

Most appreciated are men and women who choose – and manage – to control ever-present bad inclinations successfully: kind neighbours, supportive brothers, patient mothers-in-law, generous hosts, reliable workers, attentive wives, obedient children; incorrupt, straight (instead of 'crooked') officials, caring physicians, entertaining jokers, skilled craftsmen and parents who quietly do right by their families. These rank highest on any aesthetic scale. 'Never have I heard a bad noise out of the neighbour's courtyard,' said a woman with approval and wonder about his ability to keep his wife and four children always at ease. A mention of the first physician in town, a young man from Tabriz who fulfilled his draft obligation in – for him – the wild Zagros mountains in the early 1960s with good sense, skills and empathy, brings smiles to people who had never even seen him. Equally good are people who are self-possessed and reliable in their opinions and actions, keep their cool under stress, are governed by good reasoning and humour: they are the wise (*fahmide*) ones other people look up to and listen to. Such people have *abru*, a mix of gravitas, modesty, dignity, honour and authority, and take care not to diminish it by their own or their family members' offensive behaviour.[12]

Wisdom and reason also suggest being polite and kind (*merabun*) if for no other purpose than to encourage others to respond in kind. The short phrase, 'your own goodness' (*khubië to*) as an answer to a thank-you remark or a praise means that 'If you find me likeable it is because I respond to your kindness'. Politeness is valued highly, is said to minimise hostility, to build cooperation and to make life bearable and often enjoyable. It is 'good' and beneficial for everybody. To explain pleasant personalities one can point to the Will of God: the exemplary, good householder reportedly was unusually 'mellow and reasonable' already as a boy although he was growing up in a rowdy family. One also may point to a 'good' person's learned ability to control bad impulses; to guidance by elders and leaders ('my grandmother taught us good manners'); to inheritance of character traits from parents (*neshād, ers*: 'his father was like this, too'); to father's lawful or unlawful semen (*tokhm halāl* or *tokhm harum*) – 'son of a dog' is a curse for a scoundrel – and to mother's lawful or unlawful milk (a father or mother's grave sin is expected to turn semen and milk unlawful). In addition, water, air and soil (*ou, havā o khāk*) provide a choice for explaining health and behaviour of people who note that they influence human beings just as they influence the growth and taste of plants. 'We are lucky to be from Sisakht! Our air-and-soil makes good wheat and good people,' said a farmer.

Of all people, mothers come closest to being called 'all good' at least by and for their own children. But remembering their youth, adults talk less about mothers and goodness than about pain and embarrassments suffered from parents, accidentally and in corporal punishments, usually meted out by an irate father or elder brother. Indeed, in stories, proverbs and anecdotes, fathers are much more likely to vex or harm their children than are mothers. They are more ill-tempered on account of being male, which makes temper a gender-specific inclination, but one may also choose to point out that they are overburdened with their responsibilities 'for everything' and thus are on the lookout for others' mistakes, as the wife of an irascible man explained when he lost his temper over a son's disobedience.

Despite verbal orders 'to be good, polite, helpful', many fathers model short temper and aggression, and boys' peer groups used to reinforce them (with organised sports and schools, especially high schools, aggressive peer group behaviour is declining, parents say). 'How can he learn to be patient and kind with such a father!' said an angry mother about her young son after a fight in the family. A young woman remembered that when she and her siblings begged their father to take them in his new car to a cousin's wedding in another village, he did not want to go and got kind of angry (*ouqatesh tal ābi*, he got 'bitter'). In the end he loaded wife and children into the car, drove there, stopped within sight and sound of the festivities, ordered them to take a good look and listen, and drove straight home again. Such father stories fill a book, whereas bad memories about mothers are rare. When a wife complains to her husband about his mother making her life miserable, he is expected to take his mother's side: the very woman his wife suffers under, for him cannot do wrong.

There is a shadow side to goodness, though. People like to point out that even the best customs, behaviours and character qualities may have dark consequences. A man's generosity towards a relative, good in terms of ethics, may irk the man's heirs and his wife who all may – as a reasonable choice – see it as cheating his children out of part of their future inheritance. My story of charitable largesse by rich people in the United States created confusion because to give money away for no benefit to oneself or one's family does not make sense locally because it will anger the heirs, people said. Such generosity is appropriate within a religious frame, such as in fulfilment of a vow or when providing food at a religious ceremony or even by building a mosque – it benefits the poor and the faithful but also heaps merits for the afterlife on the benefactor. When people discuss such altruism, the choice to see its political benefit becomes obvious: a businessman's wealth kindles unwelcome interest and attention in governmental or religious officials, and one is well-advised to keep such interest 'healthy' with public religious generosities. 'One is forced (*majbur*) to be generous,' a well-off merchant shrugged.

Hospitality and Reciprocity

For all its much-touted merits, hospitality's aesthetic aura too is clouded. As understood locally, hospitality's moral base is to protect travellers in need and to demonstrate mutual good will and reciprocal appreciation among one's fellow human beings. It is not a choice, people say, but a pillar of Persian ethics as well as a Muslim's duty. A guest, furthermore, honours the host, and a gracious, generous host, a *meimandust* (guest-lover) is praised 'by the people and the angels'. There is the choice to quote Zoroaster who famously advised hosts to make visitors welcome so as to be welcomed in paradise later. On this lofty plane of ideal conduct, hospitality has no limits or conditions, and includes the offer of safety, food and comfort to anybody at any occasion, from popular rituals such as wedding feasts and mourning parties down to the simplest *sofreh* (tablecloth, food-spread) in a house. It is an aesthetic foundation of social life.[13]

Yet for decades people in Sisakht talked with anger about the misuse of hospitality by the last paramount khan of Boir Ahmad who invited his half-brother to his house and ordered his assassination there. A local friend warned at one of our visits that the only person hostile to our presence in town, a *hizbollah* (Party of God) official from a city, was 'hiding his enmity under the tablecloth' when he invited my husband with punctilious politeness to a family dinner in his house. Indeed, every stranger coming to the door may be seen as a potential danger especially for women in the house. There are stories about mendicant dervishes who swindle and misuse their hosts, guests who vex their hosts with unreasonable demands and strange habits, visitors who overstay their welcome or covet their host's belongings or take advantage of the host (people joked that we obviously were not Lurs because we were 'innocent' in a host's house and did not have the evil eye either, meaning that we could freely admire the house, which always pleased the host). Once, when a stranger came to the house where I happened to visit, he was welcomed politely and offered tea but somehow created unease around us. When he left, the host spread his fingers after him in a dismissive, good-riddance gesture. 'You can't trust them,' he said.

Furthermore, no matter how welcome a guest is on principle, hospitality is a burden for the women who have to provide the additional work and for the host who has to cope with the implicit expectations of obligations and demands of reciprocity that easily may turn into fierce status performances. The host–guest etiquette allows the choice of subtle evaluations of relative status, of power games, a play-of-mirrors scrutiny of the performance of host and guest, which includes noting 'everything' so as to be able to reciprocate as deemed necessary to stay even, to do better and to keep one's dignity (*abru*): hospitality invites competition.[14] Pre-empting a hostess' disparaging routine formula about her 'humble, tasteless food' at the end of a wonderful meal, I invented a guest formula: 'Dear lady, your food was too little, too salty and overcooked, and I couldn't eat anything.' This cracked everybody up every time I used it; the women realised very well that their exaggerated, self-deprecatory host formulas are good drama, and appreciated my joking appreciation of their impeccable hospitality performance.

Connected to the do-ut-des principle, hospitality entered the folklore of wry humour in an unclouded appraisal of human follies and the Lur culture, such as in this story: 'When Ali the poor cobbler learned that a well-off hunter had bagged a wild goat, he sent his little son to him with a bowl of dried curd-balls (a staple for making buttermilk in the winter), hoping to get a generous piece of meat in return. The kid came back empty handed, but in the evening the hunter personally came to Ali's house with thanks and a bowl of dried blackberries. Now Ali had not only exchanged his good cheese-balls for a handful of berries but also had to be a good host, entertaining the hunter and serving him dinner he could ill afford.'

The importance of reciprocal deals is expressed in the versatile, much-used saying, 'Nothing comes from nothing' (*bi hić, hić*) and applies to buying and selling, to acts of gratitude or revenge, to dealing with gossip, to creating and honouring obligations, to offering gifts in exchange for a favour. It fuels bribes, nepotism and a myriad of corrupt practices, and truly everybody openly and generally deplores these although they might feel 'forced' to resort to them when 'needed'. The urge of reciprocity also motivates people in need of help to visit saints at their shrines, bearing a gift. The visitor is honouring the saint with the visit, and with this act of deference expects to oblige the saint to listen to his plea. When a boy's right arm was badly injured in an accident, one explanation was that the saint who had been asked to protect the boy at birth and had received a votive gift from the parents, obviously had not lived up to expectations. Either the gift had not been sufficiently large or else it had never reached the saint, said the mother. Later, as a young professional man, the 'boy' choose to remember the accident as 'lack of caution and reason', while his father, a bit tongue-in-cheek, commented that 'boys are wild and saints are busy, eh!'

Control and Competence

Given the popularity of declaring many innate human qualities to be problematic, firm proscriptions and criteria for judging one's own and others' actions are deemed necessary for an orderly life. This necessity has no choices; only the kinds of control vary. Religious texts as well as old traditional Persian customs provide models for good conduct and for controlling bad impulses. Indeed, people who follow good advice are liked and lauded and make life comfortable for everybody. However, it is equally obvious to most that despite all wisdom, all guidance and efforts, human nature as such is not much improving over the generations. No matter how good and reasonable parents are, their young child, lacking reasoning power and respect, is 'wild' by nature, destructive, demanding and often violent, and 'has to learn to be human' with firm, nurturing discipline (*tarbiat*), good examples (which, in practice, are hard to come by), loving advice (*rānemā*) – and, if good words fail, with corporal punishment ('*izanemet*!'; I'll beat you!).

Religion declares children's misbehaviour to be free of sin, but experience shows that children will turn into 'wild boars' and sinners unless they develop control, compassion and reason inside themselves, people say, and unless outside control from other people guides them in this development. This control, guided by reason, experience and force, is a prominent feature in the aesthetics of social life. Indeed, there is near total consensus that external control is necessary to instil and enforce proper behaviour. But there also is agreement that a punished child, a reprimanded wife, an anti-government demonstrator arrested by the police, or anybody at the receiving end of criticism or restraint will likely resent this control and may meet it with bitter thoughts of revenge. These are facts of life. 'Don't try to tell me that this is different in Europe!' a farmer argued with me.

The key concept for wielding control is said to be *tars*, a combination of respect and fear, and thus presuming an authority. It ranges from respect for and fear of God to respect for old age to fear of punishment, fear of an accident or loss of face. Although often disparaged, authorities demanding obedience are accepted as useful, necessary enforcers of laws, of customs, of good conduct, as part of a God-ordained order. This claim keeps ideas of revolution at bay with the same argument many elderly people use to sum up their fear and resentment of the chiefs: 'Nobody liked the khans but we needed them to keep order'. A family without *tars*, that is, without respect in the form of obedience to those with authority, has a chaotic house with unruly children and violence. A neighbour put his annoyance over the ruckus in the next house into a verse: 'Noise in a house drives peace and comfort away, and without a dog and a shepherd, sheep are food for the wolf.' Lack of respectful fear is the choice explanation for present-day problems with uppity (*por-ri*), worthless (*biorze*), rude (*bitarbiat*) children who often disregard, vex and thus shame their elders.

People's ready assurance that fear of revenge and retribution makes one respect others' rights and thus prevents many a theft and insult, makes the efficacy of 'fear' a generally shared assumption. Fear of embarrassment (*sharm*) and shame (*khejālat*) make women pull their headscarves and veils half across the face to hide behind in potentially awkward social situations. Fear of loss of face makes one pay attention to what others think and say about oneself and also deters gossip and violence in oneself so as not to get a bad reputation. It appears as a positive factor in people's talks. Another aspect of control lies in the verb 'to speak' (*goftan*): 'Talk about what's good, speak well of others' (*khubsha begu*) is a popular advice; 'Speak up; don't say this; tell him that . . .'; 'Be quiet' (*nagu*; *kuft*) – all encourage propriety. Idle, loose talk (*goftegu, ve vel*), is worthless rumour. A person who argues and scolds with abandon is said to have 'a long tongue' (*zoun drās*), which is no compliment, while one who speaks well and convincingly has a 'sweet tongue'. It is always wise to talk and think 'quietly inside oneself' and to think before speaking up so as to avoid being offensive or known as a gossip. Only people who do not care about the blemish of having a 'thick skin' ignore such advice.

Common to all these concepts is the wish to be valued, to keep face, to bolster one's status. A good reputation makes one feel good, people tell children. Protection of one's 'face' (*abru*) can be tricky, though. When the brother of a high-school aged girl had seen a young man hanging out near the house in the evening, a discussion inside about what to do produced two choices, the girl told me: the brother who had seen the offensive guy offered to beat him up, and the eldest brother offered to have a word with the boy's elder brother, for the same effect. Both actions would keep the boy away, but father and grandfather vetoed them because they would embarrass the boy's family and – most important – would embarrass themselves as well by creating unwholesome attention. The third choice, suggested by the mother, was for the girl to stay with her grandmother and for the father to catch the boy and have a quiet talk with him in the dark. This succeeded and ended the story without loss of face (reportedly, though, a few days later the girl's brother with the big fist beat up the brazen boy anyway just to make sure he got the point, but this happened outside the domain of domestic aesthetics).

The father's talk with the boy was a competent solution, and competence counts as gratifying and 'very good' and is highly valued. Taken partly as a given quality like a beautiful face, as a grandmother said, it nevertheless can be strengthened. Incompetence in any form is seen as a blemish (*eib*), be it dishevelled clothes or a girl's come-hither look or a loud house or a bungled chore and lack of success. 'Auntie was the best weaver. The straightest lines in her rugs and never a wrinkle in the warp,' said a niece at auntie's funeral, lifting auntie's skills so high up in the aesthetics of weaving to merit a reward in the afterlife. One may choose to take incompetence as lack of respect, as laziness or else as a kind of social disability that prompts kind bystanders to help out ('I'll shoo away her chickens while she is spreading the wheat to dry'; 'Hold the log for grandfather or else he'll hurt himself again with the hammer'). Competent people are capable. They do not need *tars* to keep good order and make progress, and do not need much help either – they give help. A capable mother rarely needs to yell at her children; a wise, well-respected father does not need to beat them up; a skilful woman who knows her duties does not need to fear criticism; children who 'listen to reason' (instead of being saucy and headstrong) will be careful and will not have to be afraid of making occasional mistakes.

A competent, reliable person makes everybody around feel good and safe, our host insisted, be the person rich or poor, a man or a woman. The two young sons in a neighbour's house were 'not much good for anything but their books', their grandfather said, but the daughter was 'a born engineer', handy with tools, and as competent repairing a leak on the roof as mending a water tap or baking bread or doing school work. 'Let's ask Karima' solved many baffling problems. One readily listens to a competent neighbour and discards demands by a bungler. 'Why should I defer to cousin Ali, who smokes opium, sleeps half the day and lets his orchard go to waste?' argued a young man in a dispute. A wizened elderly farmer summed up the human condition that includes competence as well as the need for control, saying, 'People are not equal in their abilities. Some do well because they apply themselves and learn, and the others ought to listen to them. But nowadays scoundrels and people with loud mouths are everywhere. Yet one has to try to behave well to avoid being like a dumb, wild animal.'

At the most basic, ethics and the ability to discern and follow best practice and best advice are intimately linked to reason.

6

Reason, Logic and the Good Life

Introduction: What Ought To Be and What Is

Of the thirty explanations for why bad things happen to people that an elderly illiterate farmer rattled off to my husband's question as if he had learned them by heart, fifteen are of a person's own doing (such as ignorance and lack of reason, idle talk, envy, laziness but also shame, fear, urge to do good, duty); six are 'natural' (genetic, age, birthplace, parents' conditions, forceful circumstances (*majburi*)); four are God's doing (will, fate, punishment, justice); three are due to extra-human powers (jinn, chance or luck; evil eye); three more are due to outside control (official authorities, unwise people, enforcers of prayer).[1] Exceptionally astute as he was, he summarised the available choices open to all people when making sense of what is happening around them. The over-arching concept for him then (and in town generally to this day) for 'making sense' is reason (*aql, hush*). Locally, what is taken as the established, empirically 'proven fact', namely, that human beings tend to be led by moods, prejudices and aspirations, and thus often are irrational and floundering, which is bad, is based on the assumption that to be truly human, people ought to be rational and competent. The difference between what is and what ought to be creates an aesthetic conundrum for the pious, for doubters in God's wisdom, and also for the 'enlightened' who try to summon science when confronting problems.

Reason and Intellect[2]

In Sisakht, mind or reason (*aql*) and intellect (*hush*) figure as key features in being human. They are taken to be located in the head and a bit also in the solar plexus (*del*, the seat of emotions), and even, as a lesser choice, in the whole body, as in: 'Hands and feet know what they ought to do'. There is overwhelming consensus that it is not a choice to 'believe' in the power of reason but an undeniable fact established by experience. Reason is treated as the best tool for figuring out problems, for looking behind the obvious, for making sense of things. 'Don't you have any intelligence?' (*Ma aql na'āri?*) is a handy, much used challenge, meaning, 'Don't you have enough of a mind to avoid this blunder?' 'Good mind' (*hush khub*) and 'sharp mind' (*tizhush*) are words of praise.³ Reason thus is an ever-present, quintessential authority. Next to life itself, it is universally declared to be the highest power God bestowed on people. A reasonable, sensible person gets approval. 'If everybody would use his mind and mouth the way Meshedi Einullah does, nobody would complain about anything,' said a woman about one of the highly esteemed, pious men in town.⁴

The opposite paints a bleak picture: little or no reason (*kam-aql, kam-hush, bi-aql, bi-hush*) makes one unable to learn, to discern and judge, to apply common sense, to deal with the problems of daily life without 'getting one's feet entangled' (*pāpici*), that is, without getting stuck in contradictory rules and demands. Weak-minded persons acting 'like sheep' can be hoodwinked easily and talked into believing nonsense and swindlers. They may be called crazy (*kyelu*), dumb (*ahmaq*) or else a bad sort (*badjens*) with a bad character (*badākhlāq*), and thus expected to be congenitally prone to mishaps, discontent, sullenness, anger and violence, and making bad decisions. Lack of progress is seen as a form and function of lack of reasoning power, and may be used to belittle bungling people as well as an unsuccessful government. This means that intelligence is measured not only by competence but also by the skills and wits necessary to adapt to circumstances and by aptness for cognitive tinkering – quick and dirty heuristics often win the day: smart scoundrels live better, and dissimulation is a fine skill, people say.

Reason is said to grow from birth with use and help from admonition, and by imitating others until old age weakens it and makes old people childish again. Parents, the household and the peer group are named as powerful moulders of personality and reason. However, like other bodily features, reason also has a component inherited from ancestors and from parents via the father's semen and mother's blood in the womb as well as from her milk. In arguments, one may choose one or the other model or combine them, such as in: 'Our whole kin group has had good minds for generations, they were honest, pious people'; or 'The guy next door has a good mother but he is a scoundrel because his father was a thief and robber which made the semen unlawful.' The siblings of a bright but lackadaisical youngest brother argued that the parents had spoiled him (*nāzelish kerden*, 'darling-ed' him) by neglecting discipline. The parents in turn insisted that he had been 'like this' from the beginning and choose two features of inheritance to explain it: the mother pointed to her 'difficult, crazy' father-in law, that is, to a genetic component, and the father thought his wife had been negligent during pregnancy either by eating the 'wrong' food or by being hit by a jinn. Beyond these causes, the elders declared the boy's faults to be due to the Will of God but this was more a resignation than an explanation.

Taken to be a pan-human necessity for progress, reason is a *sine qua non* for making good in this world. It turns the pursuit of the best life into a reasonable, common-sensical, 'normal' ambition for everybody. Experience and tradition make it obvious and beyond any doubt that people who think well are better off than slower, dimmer ones. Lack of ambition in anybody is deplored and begs explanation.[5] Reason-driven ambition had inspired people in Sisakht 'since ever' to do better, to apply themselves. This led to high value being placed on enlightenment values and education: literate, knowledgeable (*roshan*, enlightened) people managed life better than uneducated ones, and therefore the pursuit of knowledge was 'very good'. Literate men and women got the honour title '*mulla*' – Mulla Ahmad, Mulla Maryam – and scholars, teachers, writers quite generally were appreciated for their knowledge, even if they were not rich.

The aesthetics of knowledge changed fast, though. By the 1960s it was a truism to say that only with formal secular education could one make 'real' progress, earn a salary and climb the status ladder by becoming a government teacher, for example. 'How are you doing in school?' was a standard greeting of adults to boys and girls then, and parents boasted about their successful A-student children ('Every child in town is an A-student,' quipped a teacher). By the 1970s there was great pressure especially on boys to get high enough grades on the nationwide university entrance examination to be admitted to medical school or an engineering programme. Acceptance promised a good salary later, high social status and a boost to the family's self-esteem.

By 2000, however, a still higher value on money in the aesthetics of wealth put a good income at the top of parents' wishes for their children. By then a degree in medicine was deemed less lucrative than one in pharmacy and therefore a less desirable choice, and medical students evaluated the specialties according to income. And soon after, when it became clear that the 'real money' was in business – 'in honeypots you have to find and quickly put your hands in', as a young entrepreneur put it – and that for business ventures one needs skills different from traditional learning, enlightenment values weakened. While before the revolution local intellectuals (such as, for example, Taheri 2009) liked to discuss the European enlightenment and its values for Persians, by 2010 talk was popular about the declining value of education and culture (*farhang*), of science and academic knowledge (*elm*) and about the rising value of the ability to catch opportunities, compete with others and attach oneself to 'spigots of money', in a contractor's words. A sociology graduate retooled herself as an accountant. It was boring work, she said, but one had to be reasonable because 'to handle money is always profitable'. And a young man without a profession turned his inheritance and some relatives' savings into rental apartments in the next city, making a handsome profit 'for us all', as his grandmother said proudly. These are the modern models of success.

One may argue that such globally widespread scenarios[6] are simply part of the local culture now, that they create their own aesthetic measures, with choices for lifestyles modelled by lifestyles of the rich on top of the scale. However, people show in many ways that they are bothered by the shift in ethics and life philosophy, and are worried by the slippery ethical basis for 'running after money' that makes one abandon traditional ethical and moral principles when choosing one's actions. 'Whoever is poor is either dumb or lazy, or else God doesn't approve of him' is one extreme choice for cognitively handling the increasing difference between rich and poor. This explanation is uncomfortable for most people. Traditional values have not disappeared, but people claim that it has become difficult to attain the new good life while honouring old ethics. To choose a life based on old virtues and habits likely means remaining poor and falling behind (*aqab oftādan*), and it is difficult to find value or beauty in this.

Some local young male paupers choose to present themselves in a dervish (*darvish*) mode.[7] This is a traditional but ambiguous status based on piety and on forsaking worldly pleasures by living outside the hustle and bustle of normal adult male existence. The few local *darvish* are unmarried and reject the 'idle pursuits' of their likewise jobless, unmarried, penniless peers by choosing to stay quietly with – and living off – their parents 'forever', as an unhappy man described his brother: 'His only goal in life is to get wise by reading religious books'. But not only these few young people with no future criticise modern life by dropping out, so to speak; even people who are successful with the aspirational ideology voice regret that for the aesthetics of everyday life the embrace of money is harmful, creating discontent and anxieties. 'Everybody who has money now is a swindler,' said a neighbour in 2015. A young physician evaluating his choices for employment concluded that it was easy to make good money among the many ailing local people. And the mother of a wealthy professional son said, with a frown and a shrug, 'I don't ask him how he makes his money. It is good that he has an easy life, but I am sad.'

The opinion that reason alone cannot easily change the path of discontent and worry has become a truism.

Common Sense

Reason and common sense within a cultural system rich in contradictory values and choices can easily produce explanations and justifications for good behaviour as well as for selfish, even violent, 'not good' conduct. Common sense will motivate a man to be hospitable to a stranger because hospitality is a virtue and a stranger brings news and might be an important person, yet also to hide his wife and daughters from him; it will let one be punctiliously polite with relatives, with government agents and powerful people, but also will let one choose to curse them behind their backs or to look for ways to profit from them. Common sense dictates to guard against jinn as well as to deny their existence when a 'better' explanation for certain mishaps is at hand or when challenged by a socially superior authority. Parents who dismiss a daughter's well-off but arrogant (*gardan koloft*, 'thick-necked') suitor may be called wise for preventing their daughter's future unhappiness as well as criticised for dismissing a rich man. For unambitious, 'quiet' people, keeping peace with relatives and in-laws, avoiding conflicts with government agents, catching occasional opportunities for a better life and employing good manners are understood to be the smartest choices for living.

They also make one a good Muslim, people insist, because God values good interpersonal relations above the performance of rituals such as prayers and fasting, not to speak of wasting time by shouting slogans in pro-government demonstrations. If a person chooses to pray at home instead of publicly, it is taken as their business; but how people deal with others will be judged.[8] A mourner at the funeral of a local young physician renowned for his caring, impartial services who was killed in a car crash in 2018, said, 'He had the biggest funeral we have ever seen.' She documented it with photographs, implying that the size of the crowd indicated the doctor's goodness. Nobody asked about his praying. Rather, pious believers take such esteem as common-sensical guarantee for a 'good place' in the other world because the transcendental authorities deciding a person's fate after death accept the good opinion of peers and relatives as testimony to the deceased's merits.

People are well aware that peaceful co-existence in the small, interlaced groups of their town relies on what members share: habits, values, expectations, peace. It is common-sensical to laud peace-makers, to value people who always have something enjoyable to say or who can calm unhappy, dissenting, disengaged troublemakers. But it makes as much common sense to learn about shifting norms, to keep up with neighbours, retain approval, guard one's social position and avoid 'sticking out'. With few exceptions, persons who stood out in the community as opinion leaders and role models in the past belonged to the local upper social strata and were thus expected to be outspoken and more daring and enterprising than others: the first man with a terminal university degree was from the chief's kin group, as were the first ophthalmologist and pharmacist, the only high-ranking Islamic scholar with his own circle of followers, and the first two salaried women in Sisakht, teachers both.[9] They became models for self-presentation and aspirations for many young people in town.

In contrast, and just as common-sensical and important in the aesthetics of small places, guarding one's good graces in a group with little difference in social standing requires the balancing of aspirations and social ties. Mutual observation often feels nosey and invasive, and encourages secrecy, pretence and steady use of polite assurances of devotion and appreciation. It is a popular, reasonable choice to be suspicious of a neighbour's fast rise in status that may lead to one-upmanship games as well as to distrust demonstrative courtesy (*ta'arof*) and other forms of 'heavy' politeness because they may hide a manipulative strategy. A local psychologist and a psychiatrist from Boir Ahmad blamed the over-use of such insincere habits of adults for obsessive-compulsive disorders and insecurity-motivated behaviours they observed in local children.[10]

Under certain circumstances reason and common sense dictate the decision to be 'smart'. It is reasonable for teachers to participate in politico-religious events because the authorities demand it, one's colleagues attend them, and boycotting them might cost one's job. Common sense honed by tradition makes a man control his family by any means necessary and will make a wise woman choose to 'keep her mouth shut' and defer to her husband's mother. It is eminently more promising of success for a householder to send his strong teenaged son to fight with his cousins over irrigation water than to go himself and risk losing face in a fistfight with a young nephew. And a medical student contemplating emigration, said, 'There are many ways to take advantage of sick people anywhere in the world – and why not?' Good reasoning also points to ways for circumventing authority and laws, for dodging orders and punishment, and for lying well, that is, convincingly and not too much. A father in need of a marriage permit for an underage daughter will not hesitate to present her elder sister's documents to the authorities. A man everybody knew to have rustled (and eaten) a sheep in a neighbouring village got away with it by telling the gendarme that, in the words of a local joker, 'he had never seen a sheep in his life'. Whoever wants to avoid discomfort, blame or danger better learn to create plenty of social wriggle-room.

People who have these skills are called alert, smart (*vāred*) and may be admired, while a shy (*kamri*), naive, simple-minded (*sādelu*), 'mute' (*zounbaste*) or weak (*zalil, zaif*) person may be both 'good' and pitied. Children who are quick to learn when to duck, when to obey and when to be sassy are called 'devils' (*sheitun*) and are scolded and admired. They get the message that 'good' and 'bad' are relative and negotiable, and that what really counts when praise and punishment are done is the success. When one evening a boy was hastily staggering by our veranda with two watermelons under his arms, the neighbours I was sitting with assumed he had stolen them. They abused his parents for their lack of moral guidance but also quoted the proverb, 'Stolen food tastes better,' and giggled at the idea that the boy's people had a surprise treat that night. Nobody challenged him.

Religion does not encourage these behaviours but it provides arguments that can be used to condone such kinds of common sense. An infamously violent former local chief turned his misdeeds into merits with the explanation that it was his duty to force people to work hard in order to develop the village, which otherwise would be a mud-pit today rather than the renowned, successful town it is.[11] An irate father beating a child may declare his attack to be for the child's own good and thereby will make it a sensible and morally defensible act. A racket in a neighbour's courtyard turned out to be caused by a young man home on a visit from work in Kuwait where he had become a chain smoker. He had caught his young brother with a cigarette, beat him up, and argued that the memory of the blows would make the kid withstand the urge to acquire a bad, sinful habit that would ruin his health. Violence used as a deterrent, punishment and retribution, although socially 'ugly' and defying the ethics of peace and cooperation, may be turned into 'good reason' furthermore with a reference to God: God's perfection must be assumed in the creation of reason and how it works, including judgements on when to choose violence. Although condoning injury and stretching the aesthetic boundaries of what is good and proper, this argument turns violence into common sense and an integral choice in the local authoritarian playbook.

The use of Islam in such cases can be seen as a sinful misuse as well as honouring God's gift of guidance in navigating life. Smart people pursuing their ambitions may turn features in Islamic scriptures to support their own versions of 'reason' or, conversely, may insist that lack of adherence to religious values are the cause of problems. Both choices are popular. An example from the past is the khans' claim that the oppression of their tribesmen supported God-willed order. Recently, people ascribe the behaviour of what they call disobedient, obstinate children 'in this modern era of the children' quite unanimously as an unintended but foreseeable consequence of the lack of God-ordered, reasonable parental discipline that fathers started to neglect when permissive educational models became fashionable. Outspoken local young women claim that insistence on male authority means that men bend religion to support the domination of women 'in order to get cheap maids'.[12] Indeed, a much-used argument in town asserts that Islam is getting a bad name because of incompetent, unreasonable men running the Islamic government, cleverly combining their brand of religion with their powers of office and self-serving reasoning to enrich themselves. This opens the choice to call such leaders illegitimate with the circle of justice argument popular among critics of leaders since pre-Islamic times: leaders are legitimate if their people are well and prospering; if the people are poor and discontent, the leaders are illegitimate.[13]

Beyond the use of religion to justify 'bad' behaviour, a popular choice for quick minds is to turn morally questionable actions into sensible, acceptable, adaptive strategies with the claim of being forced by circumstances: 'I have no other way' (*rāhi na'rom*), 'I am forced, have no choice' (*majburom*), and 'they prevent me' (*nilenom*). The pan-human penchant for turning explanation into excuse is a way to balance any wrong locally, too. Defending herself against her mother-in-law's accusation of negligence, the mother of a toddler who fell off the open veranda said, 'I did not know he was playing outside,' and the elder woman just nodded. One's needs of the moment and the ability to deal with adverse circumstances and powers take top priority when combined with 'duty' and the purported human inclination towards bending ethics.[14] A herder looking for a lost lamb cannot possibly take time out for prayer, people argue, and neither is a mother of young children rarely ritually clean enough to pray on time: in local ethics of the everyday, mundane duty needs top religious proscriptions (*hoqm*). From a father beating a disobedient child to a khan ordering a theft, from raiding a village for revenge or for loot to feed one's children to bribing a teacher for a good test grade that facilitates a university education – most forms of swindle and corruption can be explained and excused with the 'having no choice but . . .' argument.

Parents of all shades of piety and progress-orientation express concern about the dim future of children whose common sense is weak, who ignore opportunities for their own advancement or are shy, risk-aversive and 'excessively truthful', as a troubled mother said. All these shortcomings prevent them from using their God-given reasoning power to advantage.

Truths and Lies

Truth and lies are both called 'difficult'. The much-used term *duru*, lie, comes from *druj*, an old Persian dangerous monster that over time turned into the antithesis of truth and knowledge. As used now the word covers any unreal story (such as stories in books), a puffed-up story (such as news on television), gossip and a deliberate untruth told to hoodwink somebody or to get out of a sticky situation. These are expected, reasonable lies, and no smart person will fall for them. A person who often uses lies *ve vel*, 'for nothing', as a mere bad habit or to press an advantage, gets the epithet *durugu*, liar, untrustworthy babbler. Reading people's intentions behind their talk and grasping the ad hoc meaning of words is an art children learn early. Parents say that the brighter the kids are, the better they will manipulate words and the more options they will have to make good in a world full of pitfalls. 'I never know how much of what she is telling me is a lie,' said a mother with disgust, pride and chuckles when her fifteen-year-old daughter with a straight face told us a funny tall tale about one of her class mates. Folk tales used to be called 'lies' simply because they were made-up rather than 'true and real'. However, the protagonist in such tales is a hero no matter how many lies he tells to produce his success. An irreverent young man made a self-deprecatory joke of the double-edged skill when he declared, stony-faced, that a Lur who did not tell at least one good lie every day would get a stomach ache.

By standards of correct piety, though, any untruth is sinful or at least a sign of a bad habit. Teachers see lies as a function of childrearing ('the fault of the parents'), but also as fulfilling a need for self-preservation in the face of general insecurity. Taken as a necessity, lies are uppermost in the choices one has available to cope in tight situations. And when lies turn 'white' and become a tool for avoiding harm to others (by smothering bad news such as an unexpected death or a troublesome event) they cross an ethical divide: as a tool to prevent shock, sadness and troubles they become 'good lies'. Physicians say they are caught in the truth dilemma when deciding to withhold bad health news from patients and caretakers so as not to do 'more harm' by creating anxiety. This easily casts doubt on what doctors say: 'The doctor said but I don't know . . .' is a routine remark in health stories.

Under these circumstances truth (*haqiqat*) and being truthful, right (*rāsi, sahih, dorost, sedāqat, rāstegu* – the last two also are family names) are highly praised, called a beautiful pinnacle of ethics, a religious obligation – and hard to come by. Moreover, truth's aesthetic merit is often disconcerting. We were known for not haggling over prices with shopkeepers, and with this eccentricity 'forced the bazaar to be excessively truthful', as a trader joked with a sour face. The extreme choice of epistemological scepticism, of questioning the sheer possibility of 'true knowledge' in this world, is not popular but is available: 'Nobody knows anything anytime (*hićkes hićvaqt hić noune*) may be the end note to an argument or a commentary to a murky, disquieting story. Furthermore, considering that unmitigated truth can also be dangerous, cruel and hurtful, it can be used as a weapon in arguments. It has to be handled with care. Swearing to the truth, although declared sinful by Islamists, remains popular: one may swear by God (*bā khodā qāsam*), by a saint (*bā hezrate Ali*), by the Quran as well as on the head of important relatives.[15] It carries the danger of causing a mishap, and with its overload of sincerity is not worth much on the trust scale. Children, especially girls, use it 'a lot, all the time', as an eight-year-old girl assured me, knowing how little such an oath was worth to convince others of a 'truth' (the local school psychologist called this habit a misbehaviour and ascribed it to girls' low social status making their opinions inaudible. 'The girls try to assert themselves,' she said.).

Truth, then, hinges on authority. Of all sources of authority, personal experience such as, 'I have seen it with my own eyes' or 'I have tried it myself' are the most convincing and trump doctrine and hearsay. This is followed by what a witness says who is known to be trustworthy. Good authorities are the Quran and the scriptures, followed by what is written down (a doctor's prescription, a book, a legal document), and, last but not least, anybody who has the power to enforce his or her own claims on truth. Anything else is hearsay, just talk, and its acceptance is a doubt-laden choice. 'They say that . . .' (*igon ke . . .*) puts what is said into the frame of 'maybe, possible, interesting but unverified by an authority'. A popular choice for handling descriptions of the afterlife and of the end of the world is to put them into this category of 'it is said that . . .', thereby implicitly questioning an important feature of religious doctrine. Observations such as 'people and the mullahs say one thing and then another – we'll know only when we get there', emphasise the authority of first-hand knowledge and defer talk about afterlife and eschatology, of punishment of sins and rewards for good behaviour to a time when one will witness it.

In the challenges one faces between morning and evening, lies and truths are entangled: 'truth' is knowledge but uncertainty (*namalum*) is prevalent, and fibs and lies are tools for living. All are to be handled with circumspection and with arguments that make sense to oneself and others. These arguments work best when they can be linked to 'reason', and this kind of reason is based not on the logic of science but on home-spun, vernacular logic.

Vernacular Logic

Popular opinion maintains that over time traditions and one's own experiences turn into knowledge about patterns and causalities that one can choose to use or discard today. Contained in memories, anecdotes, stories and emotions, such experience-based knowledge may be used for predictions, explanations and judgements, for the construction of aesthetics and ethics, and for the logic that holds all together. This is the logic of cognitive maps that let one deal promptly with issues in time, space and memories.

I call this thinking 'vernacular logic'. It is a home-made, practical logic that allows one to quickly deal with what one sees as the requirements of one's existential situation.[16] Formed and used in daily routines and practices, it functions well as a kind of shared language among like-minded people. For example, in 1981, the explanation for a little boy's fall from a high porch, namely, that likely a jinn had pushed him, was perfectly sensible to everybody around, based on the shared assumption of malevolent jinn-agents interfering with people. The boy's aunt, a teacher, in a minority opinion blamed the accident on the lack of a guard-rail. Eventually, the 'jinn'-choice receded in town and guard-rails became popular based on the shared realisation that toddlers were inexperienced and wobbly, naturally so, and prone to fall. People had known this in the past, too, but then the 'jinn' explanation had been handier and cheaper.

For scientists, vernacular logic is a problem (except when they use it themselves). For anybody else with strong agendas such as theologians and politicians, it is a handy tool for manipulating people ('Candidate X is rich – vote for him and you'll get rich, too'). Ethnocentricity makes people use derogatory terms such as 'illogic', 'irrational', 'superstition', or even 'folklore' and 'folk-religion' for the vernacular logic of others, implying a lack of brainpower and education in those who disagree with them. Such judgements are a tactic of self-preservation. 'Superstition' (*khorāfāt*) is a handy example. In 2018, a pious urban Iranian social scientist assured me that 'the superstitions of poor people in backward provinces' would disappear as soon as people everywhere knew enough Arabic to read the Quran; at about the same time a leftist-leaning intellectual in Iran assured me that the Quran was 'full of superstitions'; and in Sisakht one of the options to deal with religion is to say that the Quran is absolutely right but what the mullahs make of it is 'full of their own superstitions'. I argue that anthropologists' recent shift towards studying positivist aspects of societies may in part be due to the dilemma that vernacular logic and contradictory opinions pose for remaining 'objective' and for trying to generalise 'culture'.

Paying attention to how people use vernacular logic with all its so-called logical fallacies to support their beliefs, their ethics and actions is a way out of the dilemma. 'Logic' thereby is acknowledged as a cultural system and an integral part of any group's aesthetics, a universal feature of thinking and a key to understanding what motivates people, what makes them 'tick' and how they manage their affairs.

Psychologists postulate the universality of cognitive biases in decision-making especially in cases where one is pinched or challenged. Wishful thinking, over-confidence in oneself and under-estimation of others' opinions reflect biases and assumptions that affect judgement and performance systemically. When a woman complained, 'The doctor gave me vitamin C – these white, sour pills! Sour! Silly young man!'[17] her sister nodded. 'We all are dumb sometimes, not only you,' she said. Her negative reaction has merits only if one assumes that people ought to be rational. Judging by people's discussions of so-called faulty decisions, their main appeal for use in mundane situations of every life is the quick protection of one's interests, self-worth, and ethical and aesthetic schemata at as little cost as possible. To take cognitive bias as a systematic error in thinking is appropriate when judged against scientific logic, but these 'dumb errors' have not prevented humans from being successful and cultures from progressing, as a local history student said in an argument with his teacher-uncle.

Triggers for cognitive shortcuts often are questions that prompt a quick answer. The traditional custom of burning the seeds of wild rue (*dinesht*) to ward off or dispel harmful powers furnishes a good example. Wild rue seeds (*peganum harmala*) and smoke from burning them are widely used in North Africa and the Middle East for their purported apotropaic properties. 'This is our *antibiotik*', a neighbour said, wafting a tray of smouldering seeds around the room. The small, roundish seeds also are strung together to make decorative wall hangings for this purpose, blending function into visual aesthetics.

Why? What for? (*si će?*) point to a purpose: What for do you burn wild rue? 'To drive away jinn.'

Why? (*ćera?*) elicits a cause: Why are you burning *dinesht*? 'Because we had a visitor who has bad vibes.' Or: 'Because this was the second day that my yoghurt didn't jell properly.'

How? How come? (*ćetur?*) points to a process: 'I have been out of wild rue for quite a while, and yesterday gypsies came by who had some for sale.' Or: 'For two nights the baby was really restless and now I think maybe somebody with the salt-eye (evil eye) is around here somewhere.' Or: 'Just to be sure – I was worried about my sick sister, and it gives me an easy mind.'

Don't you know?! (*ma nouni?*) is a standard, popular rhetorical question, indicating lack of knowledge: 'Don't you know that the smoke of *dinesht* is good for a house?'

When? (*ke?*) also points to a cause: 'Whenever I feel the house needs it' (for protection against unhealthy influences). Or: 'When I wear my chic new jacket' (which may stir up jealousy or gossip or invite the evil eye).

All answers stay within vernacular logic. Although based on logical shortcuts and unverified unstated assumptions such as the existence of dangerous and beneficial extra-human powers, they allow the speakers to trust their own efforts to set things right and to rely on their traditions. 'I always have *dinesht* in the house, like my mother, and we always had a good house,' said a grandmother. 'If our ancestors had found the wild rue harmful, people would no longer use it,' a self-declared enlightened young man said. A young woman used a popular saying, 'Maybe it has no benefits but it surely does no harm either, and it is pretty and smells good,' while uniting beauty and health by stringing wild rue seeds and tiny dried rose buds for a wall hanging to replace a dried-out old one in her grandmother's kitchen.

So-called logical errors are ubiquitous and differ only in the culture-specific shapes they take. To brush them away as pre-rational, irrational, superstitious forms of thinking will not make them disappear nor aid in understanding people's lifeways and aesthetics either.[18] The following examples illustrate the most popular choices local people have available for explaining and justifying actions. Taking cognitive theory into ethnography, the eight I have selected shed light on how cognitive shortcuts work as reasonable choices that people see within their everyday aesthetics. All are within the general pool of cognitive shortcuts any human brain is wont to take and therefore I put them into standard psychological categories.

Eight cognitive shortcuts
Availability bias: one uses the next best or easily available information to explain one's action, bolster one's claim or make a decision.

> 'I ought to take the bus to Shiraz today but I don't feel like it, and anyway, it's Saturday.'
>
> This excuse makes good sense on the common assumption that Saturday is unlucky for starting new endeavours such as a travel. Indeed, the speaker 'did not feel like going' because it was Saturday.
>
> 'I am sick because I ate an orange and a pickled cucumber yesterday.'
>
> In the ubiquitous Galenic medical system acidic, 'cold' food is taken to disbalance the body's warm/cold equilibrium. This assumption also motivates physicians and endures, as one of them explained, because 'it is true', it fits the common view of how the body works and it does no harm when Vitamin C products are available in the pharmacy if needed.
>
> 'While he was repairing the barn, a jinn hit him and he lost his voice for a week.'
>
> Jinn are said to stay around barns and ruins and thus were a much more familiar and more reasonable explanation than 'bacteria-caused laryngitis' would have been. The jinn scare also works as control by scaring the children away from the dangers of climbing ruins, said a father.
>
> 'The rice burned on the stove when my odd old uncle was walking by the house.'
>
> Some people are said to have a negative power, 'bad vibes' as it were, that makes others uneasy and causes things to go awry. Here, the bad-vibe reason for the mishap 'is much better for me than to say that I didn't pay attention to the rice,' explained the speaker with a giggle and a shoulder shrug.

'Her miscarriage is due to a child-stone.'
Until about a generation ago, a certain mineral bead on a woman's necklace was said to harm pregnant women unless they also carried one, which, in turn, would endanger other unprotected pregnant women. It was an ethically difficult but quick, familiar explanation for pregnancy problems. As more reasons for a miscarriage and more choices to prevent one became available, the child-stone explanation lost popularity, said one of the elderly women healers who knew everything about beads.

'I already know that my aunt died – last night I dreamed of crows!'
Dream interpretations are familiar and based on the common assumption that dreams afford access to places and events that are beyond one's alert senses. Black crows may be taken to be harbingers of serious mishaps or may even be suspected of causing them. Knowing about happenings through a dream or other forebodings will not change what is supposed to happen but allows one to prepare for it.

Dissonance reduction: one interprets new, disturbing information in a way that justifies an original belief.

'I failed the exam because the teachers in my school are corrupt.'
With the claim that some teachers, like other officials, are exchanging favours for 'gifts' not only is the failure explained but is turned into a 'proof' of the initial assumption about teachers. Corruption in Iran is seen as a sin and bad behaviour, but also as an economic norm, a way for getting things done. The country is high on the global list of corruption.

'The doctor calls my cough a bad bronchitis but that's just another name for the *ćeimun* going around in town.'
Ćeimun is taken to be a vaguely personified, extra-human power in the form of a disease. In this case it means that, based on experience, sooner or later the malaise will leave by itself, thus validating the *ćeimun*'s purported transience.

'The Mullah, late for the Friday prayer, ran out of the house, and when his billowing mantle touched a passing dog, he murmured, "God willing, it was a cat," and hurried on.'

Unlike cats, dogs are declared religiously unlawful (*harum*), and therefore the polluted mullah ought to have returned home to change his coat. This is a popular witty anecdote indicating that people are quite aware of the often absurd ways and means they – including learned mullahs – use to reduce dissonance.

'The mudslide swept away two houses. One cannot prevent anything that God wills.'

The ultimate, psychologically powerful dealing with dissonance is to resign, at least for the moment, to the purported Will of God. In this case, house-owners also decided to build farther away from the path of the mudslide and, with help from the government, to dig a channel for it. 'God gave us a mind to figure out how the world works'! said a local builder.

'Just as well that nothing came of the marriage proposal. The girl is short and fat and has a sharp tongue.'

This combines a beauty judgement with the 'fox with the sour grapes' argument popular in Persian literature. It turns the disappointment into a critique that makes the failure look like a good thing. In terms of aesthetics, it also underlines the importance given to beauty, especially to women's looks, in marriage decisions.

Confirmation bias: usually a consequence of arguing deductively from a principle or from a 'false' premise, making one favour information that supports one's belief and lets one ignore contrary evidence.

'Nothing comes from nothing (*bi hič, hič*).'

Ex nihilo nisi fit is turned into the logical basis for the belief in a creator-God, and is used to explain anything. But it also is used as a motivation to look for beginnings and for reasons, such as a 'good' reason for illness. Only if a convenient, 'reasonable' reason for an event cannot be determined, does God's Will becomes the best available answer.

'When I was visiting the shrines in Iraq, I saw the blood of Hezrat-e Husein under a glass cover. My brother says that this is impossible because blood quickly goes bad, but I say that the fact that it was red and fresh is proof of the power of the saint.'

> The speaker does not deny that spilled blood changes appearance quickly but uses this proven fact to explain and bolster assumptions about sainthood.

'It is so difficult to see fairies (*periun*) nowadays because they don't like artificial light and noises from cars and radios, and now hide out in the woods.'

> The premise of fairies' need for quiet nature allows one to deduce that they shun city-life rather than to doubt their existence.

'Whatever happens has to happen – nobody can change the Will of God.'

> In this mix of dissonance reduction – because attempts to prevent or mitigate a trouble had failed – and confirmation bias, God's Will is declared to be the cause of the mishap, and the mishap is turned into the proof of God's Will.

This bias leads to information bubbles that keep those who are inside the bubble safe from challenges because the insiders support and encourage each other in their opinions.

'We all are good Muslims here.'

> This assertion may imply that we do not have to listen to arguments that shed doubt on the power of the mullahs, for example.

'My son's wife is not related to us at all but her father and I are cantors at the mosque.'

> This implies that the men likely share views and habits and therefore, as in-laws, they will be able to solve problematic issues between them amicably. On this basis a local man supported his son-in-law in a fight between the young man and his wife, the man's own daughter.

'Our neighbours are well off and all their children are attractive students – son, you have to stay close to them at university!'

> The young man is advised to attach himself to the circle of prosperous people, to copy their habits and gain their support so as to become equally attractive and successful, an insider.

'Only the BBC and my cousins in California are telling me what is really going on in the world.'

> The speaker feels trapped in Iran in a bubble of useless misinformation about the world outside. With access to the Internet and increasing numbers of Persians living abroad and sending news, this bubble-mentality is waning.

Staying in such bubble-circles makes it easy to accuse those who disagree of bad faith, stupidity or scheming. The biggest such circles are around religion and politics.

> 'America is the brother of Satan and the BBC is full of lies.'
> 'Communists and liberals are godless – stay away from them!'
> '*Hizbollah* people are dangerous. Don't tell them anything.'
> 'Everybody knows that the mullahs are using religion to make a good life for themselves.'

Post hoc ergo propter hoc: because event Y happened after event X, X must have been the cause of Y.

> 'Last year was a good year for us because the first person I saw in the street on New Year's day was my neighbour's son – he always has this effect.'
>> Just as some people are said to have a bad influence on others, others are said to emanate comfort and wellbeing (in addition, the speaker added that if one is on good terms with neighbours one finds ways to praise them).
>
> 'The headache I had yesterday is gone today. I took a bowl of rice to our shrine last evening and the saint cured my headache.'
>> Saints are expected to have the power to help people in difficulties when approached properly, and especially when the petition is fortified with a gift to the shrine keeper or the poor in the saint's name. 'Our shrine' refers to one's own purported patrilineal descendance from the saint buried at the shrine. There are few such families with genealogical shrine connections in Boir Ahmad, but saints are said to help also non-related people, especially those who visit them often. 'Imamzadeh Mahmud knows me – I visit him every week.'

'I was held up today by unexpected visitors because my little grandson was playing with the broom in the morning.'

It is assumed that a child sweeping the floor with a broom signals or attracts a guest. Women will quickly take a broom away from a toddler even against the youngster's loud protest so as to be spared an untimely visitor.

'I told him not to go to Sheruni alone – he did anyway and now he is spooked.'

Sheruni, the southern rim of the Sisakht plateau, is said to have jinn who make people 'weird'.

'When our old shrine was renovated, the first man who broke the old wall sure enough died three days later.'

A common assumption holds that the man who deals the first blow to a shrine will die soon. When nobody died in one such case of a recent demolition, the authorities used a confirmation bias, declaring the lack of death to be proof that the razed building was not a legitimate shrine, that is, had no proven link to the Prophet.

Invincible ignorance fallacy: one ignores evidence that one's own opinion is wrong, or else one refuses to listen to a counter-argument. This protects from the need to change, bolsters prejudice and is connected to over-confidence, to believing that one knows more than one actually does, and to disregarding other ideas.

'Don't listen to the BBC – it spreads lies as a tool of unbelievers.'

This we heard mostly from hard-line functionaries.

'Never mind what geologists say about earthquakes. The Zagros mountains are so heavy that the earth can't buckle underneath.'

This opinion comes from a man from a neighbouring town who had studied law in France. Despite his education-based authority local people dismissed his claim on the basis of their own experiences with frequent rumbles and quakes.

'Evolution is wrong because the Quran says that God made the universe 2000 years ago.'

In this choice to deal with a scientific 'fact', a choice popular with the pious and many government functionaries, the Quran as a scripture of unassailable authority weighs much more than the assertions of scientists who are mere people and anonymous at that.

'It can't be that all people come from Adam because if we did, we all would speak the same language.'
Some educated local people try to argue against evolution as well as the Quranic story of Adam.

Appeal to ignorance: lack of proof for an assertion is turned to bolster the original assertion.

'There is no proof that jinn don't exist, therefore jinn exist.'
'Nobody can show me that goat-meat is the same as mutton, and that shows that mutton is better.'
Goat meat, a 'cold' food in the Galenic medical system, is said to make arthritis worse, while mutton is 'warm' and therefore assumed to be healthier. It is also more expensive.
'The doctor said I should show him the wind in my sore shoulder, and when I said you cannot see wind outside the window either, he was quiet.'
'Wind' (*bād*) is universally taken to be an invisible agent able to enter the body and move around inside, causing aches and pains. It is one of the most popular explanations for pain that is not caused by obvious injuries.

Teleological arguments: things exist or happen for an ultimate purpose.

'Lentils grow so that we have something to eat.'
Function is turned into reason for existence. Lentils have been a staple in the area since the Neolithic era.
'Nobody knows why wild boars exist – they are *harum* (ritually polluting) and destroy our fields!'
The presumed lack of legitimate, beneficial purpose affords the farmer the justification to kill them.
'The fact that plants exist at all and are of use to us shows that God made them for our benefit.'

> The teleological assumption that God intended plants and animals to benefit people is turned into a proof of God's benevolent creative power.

The end justifies the means: any means may be validated by success, regardless of ethical merits.

> 'I talked my old, half-deaf uncle into selling me the cow at a good price. His heirs are furious, but so what? I have the cow!'
> 'People say that shooting birds is sinful. But now that I have shot the bee-robber-birds I have saved the beehives.'
>> The man, one of the few in town with a gun licence, eliminated an entire flock of birds that were hunting his bees.
> 'Yes, I know, my children accuse me of being a hard father – but look at them now! They are doing well; two even have cars!'
>> The father had great ambitions for his four children and forced them by strict discipline to 'study hard'. As adults they accused him of cruelty but he brushed them off: they had good incomes and ought to be grateful to him.
> 'I have a piece of land in the next town. My neighbour there bribed the land assessor to mis-measure it and make it bigger. Now the neighbour's new house there is half done – my loss and his gain, I say, this is it, and protesting is useless (*feida na'are*).'
>> Although bribing an official is considered a breach of good conduct, a sin and a crime, if it brings the wished-for result it is not much of an ethical issue for winners, while the losers wisely lump their anger or, less wisely, think of getting even eventually.

Such consequentialist arguments provide ready choices for many questionable behaviours that promise success or benefits. Philosophers of ethics debate this, but in Sisakht such popular arguments are taken to be issues of common sense. Winners evaluate the (mis)deeds on the practical plane and may dismiss the anger of losers; bystanders declare them to be reasonable and may pity the losers or call them slow-witted. 'What happened, happened' (*vābi, da*) is both a shoulder-shrug reaction to such episodes and an admonition to let bygones be bygone. As a survival strategy the benefits seem to outweigh the costs, at least momentarily.

Acknowledging that by using the justification argument sins are committed often, anger is stirred and the common good as well as trust and security will diminish, is popular when people discuss such incidents, but the feeling of being forced into questionable behaviour by circumstances outweighs ethical considerations. Pious pragmatists argue that because of basic human faults and deficits (*taqsir, eib*) that cause bad behaviour, human beings need firm guidelines for correct, God-pleasing living, and these are best found in religion.

7

Useful Religion (*din*)

Introduction: Local Islam and Canonical Authority

Despite puritan religious authorities' attempts to curtail choices for traditional beliefs and practices, these continue to be popular and people include them in the term used for any religion, *din*. Moreover, structural frameworks for Muslims' religiosity vary with tradition and place, and although such variations in Islam are well-known, ethnographically they are difficult to document for Iran without touching the boundaries of what authorities claim to be the 'right' Islam.[1] Beyond Mernissi's 1977 pioneering work and Betteridge's 2001 classical discussion of women's pilgrimages, most literary accounts consist of ethnographic hints, brief episodes and general remarks – valuable all but hidden behind other topics.[2] I know of no ethnography of the ways pious Muslims shape orthodox, 'official' Islam in the wake of modernity in Iran. This is in contrast to discussions of this issue in Russia (Poliakov 1992; Bekkin 2020), in central Europe (Kolb and Yildiz 2019) and for 'neo-Islamic' changes in general (Wright 2015).

When religious authorities denigrate local customs to ignorance (*jahiliyya*), idolatry (*shirk*) and superstition (*khorāfāt*) they follow an old political programme of discrediting competitors. In Iran, guardians of a puritan Shia Islam belittle traditional, syncretistic rituals and ideas deemed detrimental to the Islamic-political programme of the state no matter how attached people are to them and how well they fit their circumstances, and promote rituals that further their own goals. I emphasise this point because I doubt Van Bruinessen's (2008: 1) suggestion that 'popular' Islam in general was formulated as 'cultural resistance to Arabo-centric "high" Islam'. Rather, I suggest that people keep traditions because they find in them a shared wisdom that provides helpful, 'proven' ways and means for coping with life, while 'high' Islam does not adequately address such concerns. Furthermore, local people point out that what proponents of Shia Islam call 'superstition' includes features that religious authorities themselves had propagated or condoned earlier, such as amulets for health and prayers that make stolen, unlawful goods lawful (*halāl*). Many rituals and pieties are part of a reportedly resurgent Sufism in the mainstream Muslim World, from amulets to shrines and saints' powers, yet Sufi-lore was often denounced by mullahs in the past.[3]

Historians and social scientists prefer to describe and discuss mostly the official canonical structures, thereby either overlooking choices for religious expressions such as syncretised and so-called 'popular' features in lived religion or else pushing them aside as belonging to the marginalised, the uneducated, to women.[4] Until pilgrimages became big religious business in the Islamic Republic, the shrine complex together with apotropaic and healing activities was treated widely as 'women's religion'.[5] In contrast to shared popular Islam that engages men and women, mosque attendance was – and still is – dominated by men. In discussions about the small number of women in mosques in Sisakht, men and women reasoned that women 'don't feel welcome' in the mosque, that the mosque was 'not a woman's place', and that women have 'no time' to participate. In practice, these points define the mosque as a men's space. By 2020, local women's religious activities outside the mosque, such as participating in women-only prayer circles popular in cities and watching sermons on television had little impact locally.[6]

Robert and Elizabeth Fernea deplored our ignorance of the many aesthetic and ethic parameters of 'popular theology' among Muslims that make up 'a cosmological outlook in which formal Islam plays an important but by no means exclusive role' (1972: 391). Fifty years later not much has changed in anthropologists' dealings with Islam in the Middle East. Yet lowly 'folk-religion' is durable, resilient and everywhere, demonstrating how deeply embedded it is in the aesthetics of religion and of local life.[7]

Religion is Good

Just about everybody in Sisakht and elsewhere in Boir Ahmad who talks about *din* (any) religion, declares it to be beautiful and good on principle. Even devout local Shia Muslims suggest that one does not need specifically

Islam to be 'good', that many religions provide firm guidance for the kind of behaviour that graces well-brought-up, educated, responsible, kind human beings, thereby making an orderly, well-supervised world possible.[8] 'If people everywhere followed their religion we would have paradise on earth,' we often heard. By this criterion the many war-like hostilities in Muslim countries and the Iranian Islamic government's emphasis on demonstrative piety in Iran and support of violence elsewhere, locally is not a popular choice for how to understand what Islam is all about. Therefore, on the level of lived religion one may choose to doubt, dislike or dismiss assertions made by religious authorities. Words get their meanings while being used: religious language in Iran has become a largely private language ('mullah talk') rather than one that speaks to people's ethics in the 'reality of the everyday', which is, according to their words and actions, the most popular ingredient in people's religiosity.[9]

In addition, so-called liberal, cosmopolitan critics of hegemonic Islam say they feel persecuted and abused by governmental authorities and their orthodox supporters, which is ugly, while supporters of so-called government Islam complain that they are criticised and belittled by modern urbanites and secular, Western-oriented intellectuals. Nobody sees beauty in alienation.[10] Instead, local people, including critics of government Islam, emphasise that Shia Islam provides a strong identity for everybody and a bulwark against a world out there that, dazzling and alluring as it may be, is often painfully hostile and immoral.

Local philosophies and cosmologies reflect customs and routines of the past, of Shia Islam as learned from elders and from religious authorities, and of features of modernity labelled 'progress' (*pishraft*), 'nowadays' (*i ruzal*) and 'the time of science' (*doure elm*). Together these form a dynamic feedback loop: tradition informs local Shia Islam; modernity infuses tradition, and Shia Islam bends to modernity and in turn is bent by people's routines and life experiences. In Sisakht the result is 'a hodgepodge of ideas', as a local merchant said, but whatever individual people may accept or reject in this mix, as a community they see themselves as 'good Muslims' and as better than others in the area, watched over by a creator-God who variously appears in their talks as remote, kind, personal, generous, powerful, inscrutable, revengeful and close.

God Must Exist

The loudest, most emphatic theological argument is that God must exist. It is based on the properly basic logical assumption that nothing can come from nothing, '*bi hič, hič*', and is a popular choice in discussions of happenings as well as a reasonable, convincing argument for creation myths and the working of the universe. 'How else would the stars know how to move in the sky without bumping into each other?' asked a matron, and a medical doctor declared that 'there could not have been a Big Bang without God making it'. From the further assumption that God filled the world with everything people need, it is only a small step to reason that God made the world for human beings. No other choice seems reasonable, not even for sceptics and critics of 'government theology'. This line of cosmological arguments has no end and encourages the quick use of 'God's Will' for explaining calamities and any other kind of happening. The preferred phrase used for God's Will is *meil-e khodā*, whereby *meil*, meaning 'wish' and 'want', points to a potentially whimsical reason for God's Will (Friedl 2020). (This has theological implications quite different from *taqdir*, destiny, predetermination, often used by Persian speakers.)

Spontaneous 'Will of God' reactions to taxing events are not always reassuring and comforting, though, and in Sisakht are often challenged by popular human-agency arguments such as a woman used while berating her husband: 'The thieves took the sheep because you did not lock the barn! Do you think God is your watchman?' Farmers routinely argue, 'If I don't irrigate my grapes I can't blame God for my laziness when the vines wilt.' And a mother told her son that he was right to thank God for his good grades but that grades depended on studying, and studying was a student's duty.

The very obvious need for human agency causes further problems when people are confronted with the often quoted demand to obey God's orders. How do people's willpower and their (and animals') ability to reason and to figure out how to stay alive in this difficult world align with God's wishes? Theodicy looms large. The most vexing questions about God-willed suffering in the world and the order to submit to it, have no emotionally satisfactory answer – even pious believers shake their head in a 'so what can we do about it?' gesture. For people who like to 'think about life' the intersection of God's purported intentions and humans' agency and judgements of praise and blame are an ethical and aesthetic conundrum.

A fairly new choice for dealing with the Will-of-God argument popular especially among young professionals, is to see it as a stopgap explanation, a bridge across doubt and ignorance that makes sense only because Muslims are told to take God to be the creator of every second, every event, unquestionably so. This reasoning pushes God aside automatically whenever religious explanations fade in the course of increasing scientific and technological insights into how the world works. Indeed, a local student of physics concluded that soon it will lead people like him to see God either as a vague spirit everywhere, 'in every bug and every invention', or nowhere at all. Neither option is seen as 'good' in Sisakht on account of the strong assumption that ethical behaviour which makes community life possible is based on accepting God's commands and God's oversight. Agnostics keep quiet so as not to stir up emotions and be bothered by the authorities, but the choice to explain the world without invoking God at every turn is increasingly popular.[11] 'I don't need God to explain why cars move,' said a high school student; 'Vaccines prevent God sending measles that kill children,' said a young mother at the health clinic, just stating what to her was a fact. For a pious engineer, the easy choice to make God responsible for everything that happens, including for people's own ignorance and failures, was 'frivolous and disrespectful of God'. An elderly, illiterate woman who liked to ponder such thoughts said that it was a mistake to call anything that we do not understand 'God's Will'. Rather, we should thank God for what we do know and then learn more.

Such ideas were around already before post-revolutionary theology dominated discourses about God's Will. In 1971, a middle-aged, illiterate weaver explained life to me with the river image: it flows downhill and never returns; and a neighbour said at a vexing moment that God was the 'shah for all people', but that religion was made by men and for men and had many problems because 'men don't know any better'. Such remarks are quite common among the local empiricists. However, as long as there are unanswered questions such as, 'What was before the Big Bang?' (asked by a group of high school students); 'What will come after the universe ends?' (an illiterate mother and a medical assistant); and 'Why is life on earth so often aggressive and competitive?' (a farmer, among many others), the reassuring answer is to say that only

God knows. This saves the aesthetic frame in which God reigns. However, the supreme ruler becomes a Gap-God and the rich assortment of local philosophies offers the choice to think that God's realm is shrinking. Aside from changing the aesthetic parameters, people declare such theological reasoning to be a danger for religious authorities.

Yet, after all doubts are aired, the logic of final cause is convincing except for a few contrarians: God must exist as creator-deity or else there would not be anything. Beyond this argument, the most popular choice to deal with theological questions is not to ask them or else not to let one be bothered by them. 'God knows what He is doing even if I don't,' said a neighbour, depressed over his wife's infertility. The question of why good and bad things happen is tenacious, though.

Why Things Happen

Beyond the generic Will-of-God answer to 'Why –?' questions, there are several other options for reacting to happenings. All nine I list here include people's agency, are available to everybody and popular, and are often used by the same person, in the same breath.

1. Anything good one experiences may be – and usually is – ascribed to God's benevolence. For bad happenings, a nearly just as spontaneous choice reaction is 'God's punishment of a sin' (*mukāfāt*, a 'fitting reward'), especially the sin of harming other people. Among pious people it is a popular concept. The punishment may take any form, from failure and accident to a long, drawn-out, painful death. But it is unsettling, too: mourners close to a beloved relative who is dying a slow death often despair over the punishment idea: 'Grandmother is punished for what? After a life of hard work and doing so much good?' Discussions of the economic and status downfall of the last, oppressive and disliked local chief inevitably bring the satisfactory verdict of 'God's punishment', but as not all misdeeds and miscreants are punished, one cannot count on such justice in this world.

Connected to justice–injustice and theodicy is the unquestionable duty to acknowledge that God is good and that no matter what hardships one suffers, God must be thanked for them. Ingratitude (*nashokri*) pulls more hardship, people may warn when somebody is losing their cool over a bad turn in life.

2. Fate, destiny (*qesmat, taqdir*) are used occasionally for explaining one's lot in the grand arc of life that is part of God's purported Will. By definition an inescapable programme 'written on the forehead' (*pishuni neveshte*) at birth, it is chosen mostly to explain a woman's treatment in her husband's house, or to ponder why somebody is hale or hurt after an accident. Beyond this use, 'fate' – in contrast to God's Will – is not a popular concept and is often used jokingly: after having killed a chicken, a woman said, 'The poor thing's *qesmat* is that it will be eaten today.'

3. Malevolent or indifferent powers such as jinn or demons, fairies or even diseases are taken to be part of God's creation and to act on their own powers similar to dangerous animals. Belief in these powers has faded. A mother's curse, 'May *Yāl* hit you!' no longer carries the spectre of the dangerous demon *Yāl* but simply airs the mother's vexation with her child's behaviour. One can guard against such powers and thus both the danger and its deflection are manageable.

4. The evil eye (*tië shur*, 'salt-eye'), continues to be taken as a harmful, involuntary power emitted under certain circumstances in the gaze of some people. It is a popular but rather inconsequential choice to explain mishaps – anybody can prevent the evil eye striking by wearing a blue bead, for example. Most people insist that the danger from eyes is validated by experience, but rarely – if ever – is a particular person named, let alone accused, of having the evil eye.

A likewise involuntary quality validated by experience is ascribed to a few individuals who are said to have a beneficial or else unsettling effect on others, a kind of 'vibe' that makes some people who meet them perk up or else become depressed or even sick. A grandfather made sense of his granddaughter's limp arm by insisting that a relative known for his dangerous aura had visited shortly before the calamity happened, twenty years earlier (regarding choices in this case, the doctor called it an effect of an uncontrolled high fever, and an elder brother insisted that somebody had dropped her when she was a baby). One is happy to meet beneficial persons and tries to avoid the dangerous ones. 'Be quick!' a host whispered, pulling me into her courtyard to prevent a man with this reputation from seeing us.

5. Chance (*shans*, luck; *badshans*, bad luck), is a popular choice to explain a condition that appears so sudden and without reasonable cause (such as punishment or the evil eye would be) that it may be personified. One such

image is that of an alter ego who, alert or asleep, causes a person to be lucky or unlucky. 'My luck is asleep' (*shansom ve khou-e*) means that nothing goes well for me right now. There is little, if anything, that those who 'believe' in it can do about luck.

6. A period of well-being, a string of successes as well as a general malaise may be taken to mean that God does – or does not – look at me or at us or at the whole country. 'God is looking at us,' said a young man who found a job and was getting married to a 'very good' woman. The economic plight in the Islamic Republic may be explained by God having averted his eyes from Iran and having 'closed his ears' to people's pleas. 'So', asked an angry, elderly woman, 'after all our prayers, why is God ignoring us and not telling the mullahs to stay in the mosques?'

7. People's gossip and any loose talk is judged to be inherently dangerous even if no harm is intended. It is declared a much-proven fact that the smallest unguarded word can grow quickly into a big, bad rumour. While it is sinful to malign others, it is also potentially harmful to admire or envy others, to brag or to be jealous. Curses, too, are a form of talk-danger, and ought to be used with caution. These dangers are put entirely under the control of the talkers, and idle talk thus is sinful. 'Gossipy women will be hung from their tongues in the other world,' a grandfather assured me, and with, 'Your curses will hit you back one day!' a woman warned her cantankerous cousin.

8. Sometimes inanimate things hurt people unintentionally. Unintended effects of innocent causes are tragic, such as when an ordinary shovel, a lifeless, powerless thing, killed a man in a quarrel over a water issue: 'Yes, it was his nephew who hit him, but it was the shovel who killed him!' said a neighbour. Likewise, when a child got a severe stomach ache after licking a spoon that had been used for mixing insecticide, the spoon was cursed. Misunderstandings fall into this category, too, as do many car accidents. When a 'very good' local man was killed by a car door the driver had thrown open quickly, nobody talked of guilt and God's punishment. Rather, the widow and her adolescent children pardoned the driver because he had not intended any harm – the door had caused it. Mishaps are hard to avoid.

9. Most persuasive of all, and most popular, is the concept of being forced by circumstances (*majburi*) to act regardless of consequences for others. Thereby

any perceived need for self-preservation and for fulfilling one's duties turns into a compelling force: one has no choice but to work hard to care for one's dependants, to lie to get a promotion, to skip prayers while ploughing a field or driving a bus, to steal a cousin's irrigation water for one's wilting wheat.

Thus, in local theology, 'God's Will' is put into the aesthetic frame of experience and common sense. God orders the universe, but on the small, local scale of human events, the forces of nature, of extra-human powers and of 'chance' may interfere with life at any moment for better or worse: earthquakes (*selsele*), accidents, a plague (*qossa*) killing children, a bumper crop, a well-paid job, a good bride – all simply may happen. For the pious, they prove God's omnipotence but leave out God's motivations, and this creates insecurity: 'I can't predict what God has in store for us,' said a groom, discussing his impending marriage. 'If we will have children, we thank God, and if we don't, we also have to thank God. It is up to God.'

Thus, the necessity of acting within the given, God-created parameters for making a living here and now limits choices. At times, it forces one to handle the vagaries of life as well as one can, ignoring how one should behave when managing chores and family obligations or the exhausting pursuit of progress. A mother of three children warned not to take the easy way out by blaming God for problems: 'You have to keep your own eyes open in every direction to make it in life,' she concluded. God may help people to find their ways, but as God also sends problems and sets the limits for their solutions, one copes best by using reason, by catching opportunities, and by requesting assistance from relatives, from professionals and from the saints.

Saints who Listen

The Imamzadeh – 'saints' for lack of a better word in English – by definition are paternal descendants of one of the twelve Imams in Shia history and thus of the Prophet Mohammad. Some are taken to retain or acquire extra-human powers after death which they may choose to employ occasionally to help people who petition them properly. As in most patron–client relationships, the art of dealing with patrons lies in the petitioner's fitting humility and in the ability to persuade a saint 'to listen', that is, to take an interest in the client's plight. As a descendant of the Prophet or as a Sufi mystic and thus a 'friend of

God', a saint is expected to be close enough to God to be able to intercede on behalf of the supplicant/pilgrim (Hoffman 2000).

The art of saint-petitioning includes establishing personal relationships with saints by making vows to them, promising gifts and visiting them at their shrines (mostly tombs, also called Imamzadeh). The importance of the genealogical factor in the saints' legitimacy has increased in Iran to the point where shrines are officially destroyed if they lack a 'proven' link to a descendant of the Prophet and thus likely are of pre-Islamic origin. For people less beholden to 'government Islam', though, 'saints' validate their status as healers and helpers by the degree of their (God-bestowed) efficacy even if they are not related to the Prophet, and not every buried confirmed descendant of the Prophet is a good helper. In this respect, the local aesthetic of sainthood differs from official, genealogy-based assumptions.[12]

How buildings like mosques and many big shrines get their awe-inspiring beauty and saints get powers to fill people with hope and with strong feelings that bring tears, is not much of an issue: people insist that obviously God bestows buildings and saints with aesthetic powers, and gives some people the power to heal and to help others. Critical arguments against these assumptions fall on deaf ears of pilgrims who tell of successes and miracles at shrines. But people also continue to visit purported benevolent powers at pre-Islamic tree-water 'shrines' and places where in the past a *pir*, a wise, enlightened Sufi master with spiritual authority had dispensed advice and guidance to people who consulted him. These are small, mud-brick, domed buildings without dazzling decorations, or merely a tumble of stones[13] easily destroyed, or else 'just trees and a spring'. Government agencies discourage visits to such old cult places or turn them into picnic areas. Thereby they supplant the aesthetic experiences in visits to purported powers in water and trees with those of modern aesthetics in picnic outings with enjoyable al fresco dining favoured everywhere in Iran (in practice, the two kinds of aesthetics are often combined: defying authorities, one may burn a candle or with a piece of fabric 'tie' a wish high up in a tree as a plea to the purported resident power at an officially dismantled tree-shrine while enjoying a picnic in the shade of the same tree).

Thus old traditions of support and healing have merged with the cult of saints. For local people who visit these places they are not heathen, as religious authorities and their followers claim. Rather, they have the same divine origin and aesthetic value as have the descendants of the Prophet: God existed already before Islam, people say. As the creator of everything God also must have been the creator of these powers.

The difficult theology in God's and saints' sharing of power and agency is an issue mostly for deep thinkers and for critics. Both ask if the saints' varying efficacy is due to their personal agency, that is, to a power they own and control, or due to their easy access to God? And in any case, how can saints do what God cannot? 'Why does God need saints as clerks for doing what He could do himself?' asked a disgruntled father resenting the necessity to take the whole family to a saint's shrine to plead for help for his injured son. One can hear such criticism often, but it does not hurt the popular choice of asking the saints for assistance, especially after other problem-solving attempts had failed. 'The saints are like doctors, but better,' said a pilgrim. For the pilgrims, hoped-for benefits of pilgrimages outweigh doubts and objections to the cult of saints.

Pilgrims readily comment on the enjoyment of travelling, the diversion in sightseeing and interacting with like-minded people, and on the thrills when seeing colourful, beautiful shrines.[14] People's reports of their cathartic excitement in the shrine rituals suggest that the visits induce in them an aesthetic experience, a 'bewilderment and wonder' as Ben Ami (2019) calls it, speaking of religious architecture. Pilgrims' talk about feeling something extraordinary in the dazzling colours and decorations, in the 'vibe' of the place, in everybody's expectations of a special event, a miracle even, and they use emotional responses they had learned from watching others perform rituals and prayers. 'I and my sister couldn't hold our tears when we visited Bibi Hakimeh – everybody was crying,' said an usually reserved and pragmatic young woman. Bibi Hakimeh, the sister of Imam Reza, the Eighth Imam, has a famous, impressive shrine at a cave above a big spring in southern Boir Ahmad, the place of a moving legend about her persecution and disappearance into the cave. Likely, it is built at an earlier cult place for the water-goddess Anahita (Saadi-Nejad 2021), and this is generally known, too, and easily explained: 'Anahita and Bibi Hakimeh both had power from God,' said a young man, nodding his head to strengthen his point. Another success-minded pilgrim was pragmatic: 'I'll thank whoever helps me,' he said. The Islamic government modernised the shrine lavishly, adding exhibition value to its ancient cult value. It attracts visitors from as far away as the Gulf States.[15]

Critics of what they call 'shrine-superstition' point out that the expectations, prayers and happenings around a tomb are merely a learned and shared routine that 'makes people cry together', but this explanation is irrelevant for hopeful pilgrims' experiences. 'I saw with my own eyes how a lame man from Isfahan got up from the wheelchair and walked!' was a pilgrim's put-down of a nephew's remarks about 'waste of time and money'.

Pilgrimages to purportedly efficacious saints have become the most popular reason for local people's travels inside and outside Iran. They also have become routinised commercial enterprises dominated by a growing hospitality and merchandise industry. Reportedly, virtual pilgrimages are available on the Internet.[16] The 'big saints' and their shrines' caretakers rake in donations and pilgrims' vow-payments, while inefficient, 'deaf' saints are slowly forgotten. Disappointed expectations may be explained by the saint's inability or unwillingness to help, but also may be ascribed to one's own failure to have made an adequate votive promise or to have fulfilled a vow on time, or else by one's lack of faith in the saint. Such choices for reasoning allow the disappointed to avoid shaking the aesthetic frame of pilgrimage and to keep their belief in saints' powers and pilgrim rituals. A woman doubter said she had no choice but to accompany some relatives on a pilgrimage, but that she looked forward to the diversion of the travel that would lift her spirits. 'And anyway', she said, 'if the government is arranging everything and the aunties believe that the Imamzadeh will help, who am I to say it is wrong?' A new choice to explain the increase in shrines and pilgrimages has a political twist: 'It's all government propaganda', and 'The government wants to keep people entertained in a safe way'.

Islam as Guidance

Islamic authorities and pious Muslims assert that Islam provides complete guidance for living right and well. This is based on the assumption that everything in life has an ethical–moral position, a right and wrong, allowed and forbidden dimensions, and that Islam helps people to fit into this grand aesthetic scheme. The guidance bonus is taken to be part of Islam's great beauty and comes in the form of prescriptions, proscriptions, instructions, promises and warnings that cover everything from food to financial obligations (such as tithe, *zakat* and alms, *sedāqat*); from mourning performances to prayers believed to bring health, happiness and financial benefits. Self-help prayer books for all occasions and problems promise success, peace of mind and liberation from 'superstitious beliefs'.[17]

Such self-help advice is beneficial and wise, pious people say, but difficult to follow. The suggestions and instructions are projected onto the aesthetic–ethic matrix of good–bad, beautiful–ugly, lawful–unlawful, and this means that there are right and wrong ways to deal 'with everything': with family members and authorities; with one's body 'from top to bottom', as a joker said about requested body-hair removal; with friends and enemies, all spelled out in detail. A perfect line of praying men in a mosque is called beautiful, and one who disturbs it by being late or clumsy diminishes religious merits for all who pray there. Exactly performed daily prayer rituals not only are said to please God, but are a pious pleasure to watch, and the flagellation ritual for Imam Husein, the most beloved and deeply mourned of all martyrs, has become a well-rehearsed ballet appreciated by spectators.[18]

Food, too, has a place in proscriptions and aesthetics by being either religiously lawful (*halāl*) or unlawful (*harum*), more or less healthy, more or less tasty, and more or less prestigious and expensive. Meals moved into the aesthetic realm of modernity with new lawful dishes, new paraphernalia, and popular shows on television with attractive hosts and guests who demonstrate how a modern, pious Muslim ought to cook, serve, eat and judge a meal properly (spectators watch the actors more than the food, with running commentaries on looks, kitchen utensils, social etiquette and language). Financial obligations towards the poor are turned into a quintessentially ethical matter benefiting the giver, the poor and the community. And religious ventures can turn any surplus into shiny merits for the afterlife. A wealthy benefactor building a mosque, a donor sponsoring a lunch for performers of mourning rituals and for the poor expects to earn social and eternal benefits. In Sisakht an urban entrepreneur living in town and an expatriate Iranian woman sponsored a new mosque in 2000. Proud Sisakhtis call the big, tiled building 'modern and beautiful' and remark on the merits the donors had amassed for their afterlife. 'The merits grow for them with every prayer we pray in the mosque,' said a pious man, torn between grudge and gratitude. A well-heeled businessman returning from a pilgrimage half-seriously said that every votive offering was 'a good investment for the other world and a good way to make profits lawful no matter how they were gained'.

Discussions of rules also include the popular, routine critical suggestion that only a person who has 'nothing else to do' can benefit from such detailed programmes. Although an omnipotent God's powers and orders may not be questioned, increasingly one also can hear people talk about the difficulty illiterate people and those unfamiliar with classical Arabic have with accessing scriptures containing elite religious knowledge. These arguments are weighed by the fact that God's orders reach most people in sermons and teachings by mullahs who are fallible human beings and thus may be wrong. In addition, learned theologians differ in their messages and are supposed to update interpretations and guidance to keep them meaningful for believers when times and circumstances change.[19] This means that religious proscriptions and prayers can and do change, which provoked a young doubter's tongue-in-cheek question, 'Does this mean that God is changing His mind, too?'

Critics claim that the government fails to keep religion relevant for modern life and that many of God's orders accommodate the wealthy, men, mullahs and white-collar workers better than women, the poor, labourers and farmers who have fewer means and less leisure to fulfil the commands ('One only needs a prayer rug and a prayer stone and a few minutes to do the prayers,' is the usual comeback to such objections). The argument is relevant especially during Ramadan, the month of fasting. 'It is much easier for me to fast quietly while sitting in my shop than for the workers digging up the street outside in the heat, poor guys,' said an elderly merchant, praising God for the shade in his store. And a pious doctor impatiently said that God did not make the fasting rule for pregnant women, when dehydration caused a pregnant woman's medical emergency. More women than men fasted and had problems, he said, adding, 'Women have a death-wish, very sinful!' Clerics and orthodox believers insist that sick people, pregnant women and dehydrated workers may choose – or even ought – to postpone the fasting until they are well again. For people who want to keep on good terms with authorities as well as with 'modern' ideas there is the choice to subvert the issue by declaring that fasting is good for one's health: 'I need to lose weight anyway'.

Most of the clever, pious local realists see the problems clearly but are not ruffled. They insist that God's justice will take their circumstances into account on the Last Day, and that surely God will remember that it was His own Will that made them poor farmers away in hot fields instead of rich merchants in cool shops waiting for the muezzin to call them to prayer. The choice of hope and reason douses disputes about such troublesome matters.

Men and women who choose to see religion as the path to a God-pleasing, good life link worldly success to God's approval. It is a popular choice for explaining economic standing. Although I never heard 'good' poor persons being blamed for their misery (except if an ancestor had been notoriously 'bad'), and although people are careful with calling poverty God's punishment of sins, the opposite is expressed often: wealthy, healthy, successful people have shown by their good thinking and hard work that either they deserve God's special blessing or else that God gives some people an easy life 'because he likes them better than us', as an old, tired farmer said, speaking for many. The aesthetic of poverty is negative, and so is, for many, the aesthetic of gender (in)equality. A young woman who felt cheated of the university education her two brothers got, choose to put God's preferences into a gender perspective: 'God likes men more than women. He gives men more *lotf* (generosity, kindness, grace),' she concluded. Equally popular is the choice to ascribe this inequality to people themselves when they choose to pitch men against women instead of supporting each other as God wished. 'A lot of pious words are wasted on this!' grumbled an elderly widow.

Upright citizens discussing the increasing number of 'hustlers and swindlers' who elevate lifestyle and status by questionable, 'sinful' means shake their heads in bewilderment, mutter about God's inscrutable Will and console themselves with the hope that the scoundrels will be punished eventually, if not soon here then later in the hereafter. In moments of vexation when experiencing pain or witnessing good people suffer while cads flourish, bitter feelings of cosmic injustice are ventilated in exclamations such as, 'God is not looking at us', or 'Can't God do anything about this pain?' People of all walks of life frequently lament a rapid shift in ethical norms in the aesthetic of wealth in Iran generally. Rumi's well-known poem about wealth's transience – coming in the morning and being scattered at night (Mathnawi VI, 255–260) – draws smirks: 'How come, then, that the rich get richer all the time?' asked an economically struggling government employee after quoting it. This sentiment creates new, critical choices in thinking about God's might and the workings of the world, about blind faith resting on the authority of theologians and politicians, and about nagging doubts about God's purported plans and powers.

At the heart of it all, though, is people's nearly universal insistence that God is in everybody's *del*, the seat of emotions,[20] the source and keeper of knowledge of good and bad. In this aesthetic frame, the pious who are spiritually inclined place God in the *del* as a source of strength: every person is directly linked to God. 'If there is God, He is in people's *del* and in everything that's good and beautiful,' a medical student summarised the issue. A kind of mysticism of the everyday pervades comments about God in nature, about the world being at one with God, about the value of prayer, of contemplation in quiet moments, of being content with one's lot.

Outward signs of piety, the 'loud' kind advocated by the Islamic government, are frequently put into the entertainment category with the popular epithet of 'being good for warming people's heads' in the absence of other diversions such as music and travel. 'These rituals may well please God, too, but surely God doesn't need this kind of piety,' said a young man contemplating studying theology. Even severe doubters and local critics of religion often choose the mantra that what really counts before God is how people behave towards each other. Religious proscriptions help by exhorting people to be good and kind and straight, but based on their own experiences people of all walks of life insist that the benefits of good behaviour are evident 'without anybody having to tell us'. Furthermore, proscriptions for rituals and for goodness are of limited use because to follow the first is time consuming, critics say, and, given human nature and the difficult day-to-day requirements of living, ritual and practices of 'goodness' are easily ignored.[21]

How these arguments play out on the level of behavioural choices fits into the aesthetic frame of theology. Most powerful is the assumption that God installed religion in order to assist people, especially those in a crisis. This source of assistance includes all potentially beneficial powers residing in plants, minerals and animals, in Quranic prayers and amulets, in saints and also in some ordinary people. God put this power there for people to use, and gave people a mind and limbs to find the sources of help and to benefit from them. This, locally, is the main choice to explain the popularity and longevity of traditional rituals: they are useful. However, doubters and committed Shia believers alike point out that where other help options are available, such as physicians, wage-paying jobs, diversions to 'open the spirit' and even laws such as those regulating inheritance or the treatment of women, many religious traditions fade or become a choice of last resort. An elderly farmer explained the decline in the use of amulets with images of time and culture change: 'Now we no longer have herds to protect from wolves, we have insecticides for the orchards and the wheat, we have a health clinic, we have good water and we take better care of our children. What do we need beads and amulets for? God has opened other doors for making a better life.'

Women and men say that women remain a bit more interested in old customs than men because keeping house and people safe is a woman's duty and thus women need to keep their options open to fulfil it. Furthermore, women say that a long life based on learning from their own and others' experiences taught them 'a lot about everything'. Their attention to figuring out how things work, their probing (*emtehān kardan*) and judging were their fountains of knowledge and wisdom, of self-worth and esteem. A less positive local choice to explain women's greater interest in customs is that women, especially older women, hang on to 'superstitious habits' because their reasoning power is weak. It is an unpopular choice, though, the more so as 'superstition' also is the sotto-voce verdict on new forms of 'man-made religion' and of 'blind believers' generally.

8

Shapes of Things to Come

Introduction: Choices and Consequences

To the extent that the future may be envisioned at all, feared or wished-for as it may be, it is part of the aesthetics of one's personal life, of how one is feeling right now, always at the brink of changing, of having to deal with what will come next by chance, by itself or by God's Will, or of what one will do or see or think or want. The developmental optimism of the past three generations remains popular, but the means to fully participate in 'progress' are hard to procure now and leaves few choices. This makes for anxiety, dismay and re-evaluation of ethics, and fosters disengagement with the 'Iran' presented by the Islamic government.

When local people talk about the future, three main choices emerge. In the daily give and take of life they can be mixed and used for whatever is needed at the moment.

The first choice is to say that only God knows what the future will bring, and people ought not to put certainty into their own efforts and expectations. The brand-new hotel in Sisakht which collapsed in the earthquake in 2021 is used as an example for how quickly and thoroughly one's plans and deeds can be undone. However, God's unpredictable decisions must not keep people from planning and acting either: the recent building boom in town after the earthquake is proof that the local progress spirit is alive.

The second choice for thinking about the future has people continuing to struggle to make a better life on Earth, just as they always had to do, and this needs planning. The much-quoted saying, 'God closes one door but will open five others' encourages wishful thinking and optimism in unstable circumstances. For now, in Sisakht people are rebuilding their houses and tilling fields, planning weddings and sending children to school, even if there are demonstrations against the government, a shortage of money, the spectre of Covid and a lack of the kind of luxuries that make life beautiful. One has to live, and thus one has to take care of things in the only reasonable way, by planning for tomorrow. People know how to make do, and progress is a belief in the benefits of the next day.

The third choice is to indulge in a millenarian feeling that the world, with its hostilities and unfulfilled needs and frightening global events such as wars and climate change, is in an end-stage. The eventual end is to be expected as per Islamic doctrine, but the present situation is not equally bad and compromised everywhere, and therefore young people should go wherever they find a better and more satisfying way of life. Emigration no longer is an exception but is declared an attractive or even necessary choice, especially for educated people, be it only a move to the provincial capital. Leaving Sisakht thus has entered the aesthetic frame of local life. My friends tell me that there is now somebody in every kin group who has left or is trying to leave. Reportedly, about a quarter of the families in Sisakht have a kin group member in the diaspora, from Japan to the United States, and these relatives exert a powerful pull on local young people.

For those that stay it is safe to predict that exposure to the world will go on with Internet, telephone and travel as the main conduits for information. People say that the changes they have to expect by looking at the world will have a lot more to do with regional politics, with keeping up with global trends, with *mod* (fashions), *pishraft* (progress) and *elm* (science, study) than with ancestral customs and mullahs' demands and expectations. This will multiply the criteria for evaluating lifeways and will increase the choices for how to live.

In particular, people emphasise three areas of change that 'will make everything different' within a lifespan: education and emigration; birth rate and work; marriage and staying single. To these I will add a fourth, religion, which rarely is talked about when considering the future, but some choices are gaining popularity.

Education and Emigration

Although locally the enthusiasm for university degrees has waned in favour of getting one's hands on money for business ventures that promise a better income, Iran and the town produces more university graduates than there are jobs for them.[1] This means that in order to find jobs college graduates will likely stay in the bigger cities or try to emigrate to countries that have 'opportunities and freedom' (*shans o āzādi*), as students say. This is widely seen as a loss for Sisakht, a reason for worrying about family orchards and about lack of eldercare in the future. 'Ashes on my head!' (a traditional exclamation of loss and mourning), cried a grandmother when she learned that her only grandson was leaving for college together with a paternal cousin. In her kin group eldercare was turned upside down when a cousin's son, a successful professional man in Shiraz, built a stylish Persian villa and garden in Sisakht, and in the absence of reliable servants invited (or obliged, depending on who is talking) his aging parents to live in the beautiful house. 'He comes once in a while, his wife is a city woman and doesn't come at all, and my old cousin has to take care of everything!' said a relative.

Local administrators and entrepreneurs envision Sisakht and other such places in the mountains as becoming tourist destinations with chic hotels and beautiful restaurants, built by urban developers who are buying up land from local people unwilling or unable to care for the fields. 'Our children all are doctors now', dead-panned a township clerk; and 'Look, we all have clean hands and jackets now', quipped an elderly, retired farmer, waving his white hands at me.[2] Although the job market in Iran is 'bad and uninteresting' in the opinion of an aide to the provincial governor, higher education opens a door to a good life in the diaspora, and local people and governmental authorities say that leaving will continue to be a popular choice as long as socio-economic conditions in Iran stay bleak and lifestyle aspirations stay high.

Birth Rate and Work

In Iran the birth rate has fallen steadily over the past decades, although few women participate in the labour force. 'Lack of child care' is the glib, popular, official reason given for women staying at home, yet staying at home demonstrably fails to increase the birth rate. Despite decade-long governmental attempts to raise it, at 2.103 births per woman it is below population replacement level and the rate keeps declining.[3] In Sisakht, the decline was sudden and firmly connected to the changing aesthetics of life when 'modernity' and 'progress' rapidly inflated lifestyle expectations that made increasingly expensive child-rearing an obstacle to comfortable living (A. Loeffler and Friedl 2014). This change, together with men's unemployment, low wages and salaries and the steady increase in higher education enrolment with a concomitant rise in marriage age makes people predict that the birth rate will stay low. The town has a small but steady influx of people from surrounding villages and attracts students to the local boarding high schools and a small agricultural college. People expect that for a while this pull on people in the hinterland will continue to make up for the decline in birthrate and for those who leave Sisakht.

Jobs, though, will not increase much anywhere in Iran, people say, and therefore fierce competition over resources will continue to make strategies of corruption such as nepotism and influence-peddling (*partibāzi*) seem inevitable and reasonable. There are murmurs about an increase in buying grades among college students and of local sub-contractors paying officials for government assignments. 'It's normal now!' fumed a local builder. Even if these murmurs were not true, they colour expectations and nurture feelings of injustice. The old key concepts of 'strength' (*zerengi*) and 'forced' (*majburi*) stay relevant: one has to have a good mind, few scruples, a 'quick tongue' and good contacts to be successful. There are no alternative choices for these requirements. 'The slow and the meek will fall behind, as always,' said an ambitious young engineer about the members of his cohort. Like for him and his friends, dissatisfaction with the difference between what one thinks one ought to have and one's actual choices inevitably will increase discontent in town. 'Everybody thinks so, and nobody knows what God wants of us', said a pious, *hizbollah*-oriented woman.[4] Sisakht is not hopeless, people say and show by their plans and actions, but they fear that emigration of the young as well as poverty and the lonesome aging of those who remain will continue to cause depression, to cloud future prospects and to nurture nostalgia.

Marriage and Singles

When young women talk about what they are looking for in husbands, good looks, wealth and companionship always are at the top of the 'good' qualities now, but while good looks and wealth are well-defined, shapes of a companionate marriage are vague. Young men who talk about such issues seem to want a wife who – in this order – is beautiful, will listen to her husband, is willing to take care of him without undue demands on him, and if she has a job and earns some money in addition to providing beauty and comfort, it is even better. This aesthetic model has not changed for men much in fifty years. Rarely do young women agree with this vision, though; rather, they criticise the lack of 'freedom' in the men's model and call it 'backward' or ascribe it to men's difficult character generally. But there also is the choice now to suggest that men in Iran lack role models that would show them how to be good husbands, and that this condition will change.

Until things get better on the freedom-scale, as a mother of three daughters said, a smart young woman does best by looking for a husband who is well off. After dismissing yet another suitor, a college graduate was explicit: 'If he can't be my friend and helper, at least he has to have enough money to make my life comfortable.' And a group of high school girls had fun telling me that they did not look at young men's faces openly because this was immodest, but instead studied their clothes and cars to sort the 'good' from the 'eh, not so good' ones. Given the three factors of bad economic outlook, men's fear of women's expensive demands that take caring for a family beyond many men's means, and women's disaffection with men's demands of submission and good housekeeping, the marriage market will stay problematic. Friends in Sisakht tell me that couples' demands and their expectations for marriage 'are getting better', but their optimism is short on particulars.

Urban young people model different options, though: some young people there are known to choose to skirt these cumbersome marital issues by experimenting with partnerships other than marriage. They are known to establish living arrangements such as 'white marriage' and *'boifrend–gerlfrend'* cohabitation, and even try non-monogamous arrangements between men and married women. All are illegal by law and sinful by religious standards.[5] In town they do not fit the local traditional husband–wife aesthetic that combines the signing of the contract with wedding festivities followed by cohabitation and pregnancy. Stories about extra-marital couples elsewhere are met with noises of disgust but also with pulled faces, shoulder shrugs of resignation and 'let's wait-and-see' silence.

With the widening gap between rich and poor, polygyny is increasing in Iran especially for wealthy urban men. For a man to be able to satisfy a 'love-wife' in addition to the first wife is an affirmation of his robust sex-drive and superior economic status, and for many a young second wife it promises an easy life. Legal in Iran and Islam, it does not fit local monogamy norms and marital aesthetics and is rare in Boir Ahmad. The choice prediction is that it will increase, though, and eventually may become an option in town, too, 'whether we like it or not'.

Divorce, too, is increasing in Iran, creating temporary and permanent singles, although it is not yet an issue in town either. Other factors, however, are issues: job-related emigration especially of young men that causes gender imbalance in town; spiralling costs of marriage arrangements; increasing demands of young women (and their parents) on a husband; and workers' inability to provide adequately for a family – they all weaken the assumption of the traditional husband–wife unit being a God-created cornerstone of the society. The factors are called 'true facts'. They leave few choices and point to rising numbers of singles in the future.

Men are single because they cannot afford a wife, they say; women are single because they cannot find congenial husbands, they say. Older and tradition-oriented pious people voice doubt that conditions will change fast enough to save the traditional, habituated marriage arrangement that is based on the husband as keeper of his wife and children and thus as the leader of his household and the link between his 'house' and the outside world. So-called progress and social circumstances have weakened this link, as illustrated by the example of the humdrum necessity of going shopping: when I went to the bazaar before the mid-1990s, I usually was the only woman there. In 1995, a young wife still could brag about never having to haggle with merchants 'because my husband is doing all shopping for us'; by 2006, such division of labour had lost much status-conveying impact: 'It is good that my wife doesn't mind going to the store because I don't have time for it,' said a farmer about this new choice. In 2015, a high school girl declared that if a woman cannot go shopping, 'It means that she doesn't have any money to buy things with.' And in 2020, this was followed by, 'I always go shopping – who else could I send?' said by a young, unmarried woman living with her elderly parents.

While in the past a single woman locally was referred to by her first name plus 'daughter of X' ('Maryam *duar* Ahmad'), the generic term *khānom* for any woman, married or single, followed by her paternal family name is enough to place her socially now, just as *agha* (mister) is enough for a man regardless of marital status. The derogatory term 'old maid' for single women has nearly disappeared. A single woman is more likely to be pitied for having no money, that is, no income or inheritance, than for having no husband. When recently I inquired about the marital status of a woman physician from Sisakht, her sister said, 'No, *Doktor* Maryam is not married – who cares? She is her own master!' It is a safe bet in town that this trend will continue, with mixed feelings of relief and regret.

For the time being women in town who do not want to live with the triple-burden of a job, household work and controlling husbands are looking at problematic ('no-good') choices for living arrangements, they say. Girlfriend–boyfriend cohabitation is socially impossible in town although it is known as an option in cities, and besides 'it is no better than being married, except that she can leave any time', as a student said; an unmarried woman alone in an apartment is an option but is unusual, expensive and will make her lonesome. Sharing an apartment with other women is acceptable but seen as a temporary arrangement of single nurses and women teachers from other places. For the near future the best solution for a single woman is to stay with her aging parents and to take care of them. However, this arrangement is so new that matters of financial responsibilities and of inheritance are not yet routinised and easily cause difficulties: the youngest son is responsible for the parents and is the heir to the parents' house in the tried-and-true ultimogeniture provision. 'What? I inherited my unmarried sister together with the house?' asked such an heir, who wished to sell the parental home and leave town. And the unenviable lot of one such caretaker woman, whose widowed father made her services superfluous when he remarried, was a headache-story in town: 'She has no place to go,' murmured the neighbours. When a daughter-caretaker accepted a suitor recently, she dismissed the question about her ailing parents' welfare after her move to her husband's place: 'We'll find a solution,' she said, leaving everybody a bit anxious.

Staying single also precludes having children, and this, too, changes marital aesthetics. There is no single mother or single father in town who brings up a child alone. To have a child out of wedlock never was an option locally. In the past, male relatives or the khan would have killed the woman. A widowed or divorced father will count on his mother to take care of his children until he remarries; a divorced mother's children will stay with their father's people; a widowed mother will stay in her husband's house with the children if it is convenient for her husband's people, or may marry her husband's brother. If she leaves, she will lose the children to their father's relatives. There are no good choices in place for such cases although people see a need for them in the future. 'We'll see what God wants', and 'We'll find a solution when needed', are the two standard suggestions. Nobody predicts an increase in single motherhood – it is not an acceptable choice. Adoption is not considered an option either because a child belongs to the biological father and thus will remain a stranger in any house that is not closely related to the father. There is the firm belief that in the West, where adoption is known to be practiced 'a lot', incest is likely because an adopted person may inadvertently marry a biological sibling. Adoption is called 'bad'.

Hardly anybody disputes that modern ways of life and popular new lifestyle choices combined with the bad economy are dimming the outlook for the future of conventional nuclear families based on husband, wife and children. 'This is how it goes, but it is not good,' said a disgruntled town administrator with an unmarried adult son. Popular opinion predicts that the pressure on male domestic authority and responsibilities, and the increase in single men as well as women's demands for more freedom will continue and will create problems that require rethinking of how a 'good' community works and how to judge people's living arrangements.

To these three areas where people expect changes in the future and express mixed feelings about their choices, I will add religion, where change is happening also but is less obvious and discussed rarely.

Religion (*din*)

People do not talk much about their spirituality. 'I have to make a living right here, day after day – thinking about my thoughts won't help me,' said a smallholder farmer. Most people continue to adhere to the government's calendar of mourning events as a matter of course, but civil disobedience in matters of public piety and modesty is increasing despite periodic clamp-downs by the government. 'One must act as if one agreed, even if it is a bother', in the words of a young teacher; 'One day I wear a headscarf and the next day I let it slip down', said a young woman. Occasionally, men and women will continue to regard modesty requirements and demonstrative piety also as a form of protection, as a fence against prying eyes, predatory men and scheming women in the streets, and thus as a useful choice in certain circumstances. Mothers, for example, are said 'always and everywhere' to be looking for potential wives for their sons. 'Why else is she always in the doorway when I walk by on the way to school? I always pull my scarf over my face when I see her,' complained a young woman, suspecting a neighbour woman, rightly so, it turned out, to be on the look-out for a 'bride-servant'.

Critics will continue to complain that the government uses restrictions of freedom to distract from economic problems and that therefore governmental actions and ordinances on modesty and piety have less to do with religion than with politics. Administrators know the problems when they, in turn, complain that many pious activities are 'hollow' (*pike*) for people who participate in them with misgivings or – even worse – who use them as entertainment: watching elaborate performances of mourning may be a deeply moving religious ritual but also an interesting spectacle. 'Our beautiful religion has dark clouds now,' said a pious high school student, commenting on the shift in the aesthetics of religion. Bouts of heavy-handed attempts by authorities to make people comply with demands made in the name of religion will continue and will increase tensions, but will be unlikely to reverse trends towards making religiosity more private. Voices become louder demanding that the government 'get out of religion' and instead give people freedom to think their own thoughts about God. The answer to my question about how the mosque had fared in the earthquake was a dismissive, 'I haven't looked'.

More important for shaping spirituality and piety than criticism of governmental orders is the ongoing individuation process that urges people 'to be free enough to think for yourself', as a pious engineer said, and to combine it, as a choice, with 'a natural wish for spirituality' (*ruhāniyat*). Agnosticism as well as nurturing a personal, inner relationship to God will become acceptable alternatives to 'loud' government religiosity displayed 'in the streets and in the mosques'. Yet religious authorities will continue to criticise the trend towards 'freedom' and mysticism because both challenge their authority and control.

In extreme cases the quest for spiritual fulfilment may take the form of inner emigration, people observe, of more or less tuning out of the affairs of the world. Some may make purported manifestations of God, such as in nature and in spiritual Persian poetry, 'a strong wall to lean on', in the words of a local teacher. An elderly literate man who liked to read 'the old Persian master-poets', called the poems his guides. Both men said they – and others – find Sufi-inspired practices helpful to gain inner calm.[6] Practices involving altered states of consciousness or spirit possession are known to exist, but locally are not choices for experiencing religious feelings; rather, any loss of control is likely to be treated as a form of craziness and as a matter for concern. Pious women may choose to 'carry their religion indoors again', as a farmer's wife said, with a prayer rug and the traditional rituals against dangerous forces. There are no women's prayer circles reported in Sisakht that aim to further inner peace and closeness to God by merging poetry and prayer (Haeri 2020), but new aesthetics in poetry and piety are known to exist in cities and among some women in the large provincial capital.

Critical appraisals of 'government religion', of military aspirations in the name of religion combined with disappointment over thwarted entitlement-based lifestyle expectations 'do not lift the spirit', as a pious craftsman said. It will let some people choose 'to let the world go' and find beauty and wellbeing on a private, small scale in an aesthetic of denial and retirement. A popular local choice is to expect that the necessity to find a better life in the bad economy in Iran will make it increasingly difficult to follow religious proscriptions and will widen the rift between rich and poor and between adherents to 'government Islam' and a growing number of people who form religious ideas and behaviours themselves or choose to look outside Islam for guidance. With few exceptions, people expect an ideologically and politically disquieting future.

Notes

Introduction

1. 'The things that are most important for us are hidden by their simplicity and everyday-ness.' (Wittgenstein 2022, no. 129, my translation.) Over the years some anthropologists have tried different angles to honour this insight. See Salzman 1999.
2. For the traditional ethnography of the area, see Friedl 1981; R. Loeffler 2011; R. Loeffler and K. Loeffler 2022 provide photographic documentation, as do Garthwaite and Gabbai 2021 for neighbouring Bakhtiari. Black-Michaud's 1986 descriptions of the Zagros environment and aspects of life for the Lur tribes living there around 1975 are close to those in Boir Ahmad. Feilberg 1952 provides the most comprehensive early ethnography of a people in the Zagros range, in Lurestan, in 1935.
3. Archaeological evidence from the southeastern Zagros hills of what now are Boir Ahmad territory and Fars Province suggests that the area has sustained hunter-gatherers since Upper Palaeolithic times (starting before 30,000 BC), and agro-pastoral 'mountain people' since the Neolithic period (around 8000 BC). See Ghasidian 2014; Ghasidian and Heydari-Guran 2018. Hole 2004 provides comparison with the archaeology of the central Zagros region. There is some information on Neolithic human presence immediately northwest of Boir Ahmad. Only few of many historical and archaeological traces in Boir Ahmad are documented. See Friedl and R. Loeffler 2013.
4. Schulze-Holthus was a German spy captured by the British. As a prisoner in a local khan's fort near Sisakht, he used local anecdotes as an aid to teaching the khan's son. Thirty years later the khan allowed our daughter Agnes Loeffler to copy the hand-written notebook.
5. Folkloric traditions contain hints to aesthetic norms of the past, such as in this ditty: 'Last evening I waylaid her; I raided her lips and stole her breasts' (Friedl

2018a: 83). Lyrics, proverbs and folktales from Sisakht (Friedl 2007; 2015; 2018a) stay in the ethnographic realism mode, with remarkably little symbolic content.

6. Taheri's 2009 memories of growing up in Boir Ahmad in the first part of the twentieth century provide a lively eyewitness account of 'the time of the khans'. For other examples, see R. Loeffler 1988; Friedl 1981. Feilberg 1952 describes similar conditions for Lurs in Lurestan Province, northwest of Boir Ahmad, and Baker 2015 describes them for people in the mountains of northwest Iran.

7. To assemble memories for a certain purpose is the pursuit of philosophers (Wittgenstein 2022: 86), but happens in everyday memory work as well.

8. We witnessed the severe drought of 1971. It decimated the herds of all pastoral people in southern Iran and drove many herders out of business. Locusts, too, were a threat to crops and pastures in some areas. People remember roasting and eating them during times of hunger.

9. Opium poppies were a profitable crop until outlawed, by 1960. Expensive, smuggled opium continues to be used by 'some old men' and others, as are modern illegal drugs. They are called 'not good,' and addiction is called 'very, very bad'. Reportedly, the only fatal fight in the vicinity of Sisakht within the last twenty-five years was about a drug deal. The drug trade in Iran has been a growing concern for the authorities since the 1990s. I avoided the issue and am not addressing it in the book.

10. In Iran, *kadkhodā* is commonly used for the local representative of a landlord (see, for example, Hegland 2014). Locally, it meant the head of the local group in power, implying a segmentary political structure with a khan at the top of so-called tribal and sub-tribal branches led by so-called *kadkhodā*, the 'chiefs'. During the Land Reform (1962–79) khans and chiefs tried, with more or less success, to turn their position into that of landlords, using the assignation of *kadkhodā* as an argument for land ownership.

11. Suzuki 2015 discusses local elites' options and opportunities among the Doshmanziyari in Kohgiluye, the western part of the province, who aligned themselves with the shah's government instead of fighting it like the khan and most chiefs had done in Boir Ahmad.

12. See Necipoğlu's 1993 editorial discussion of papers about shifting aesthetics in pre-modern Islamic architecture.

13. So-called corruption (such as *partibāzi*, influence-peddling; *reshve*, bribery; giving *shirini*, 'sweets') is a way of life in Iran and an ugly plague, as a government employee said, shaking his fist. On 13 June 2023 the Atlantic Council held a virtual discussion on 'The mechanisms of corruption in Iran'.

14. Lumsden 2021 discusses economic woes in Iran, and Hegland 2011, describes them in a town near the border of Boir Ahmad. Periodically, people in Iran protest loudly in the streets, as in 2022, but the 'mullah government' is resilient.
15. *Basi besāsim* (we have to submit, to agree) fits any condition to which one has to adjust. It contains submission to the Will of God, a bit of resignation and a commitment to brave the challenges of the day.
16. About various Sufi traditions, see Van den Bos 2007; Van Bruinessen 2009. Van Bruinessen 2002 describes them in Kurdistan Province in the central Zagros range.
17. For survivals of Zoroastrian cult places in Iran, see Langer 2004. Friedl 2020 discusses shrines in Boir Ahmad; Mulder 2014 discusses the meanings of shrines. Meri 1999 puts devotional propriety into a historical context.
18. See Anonymous 2021. Beeman 2017 delineates the history of religious leadership and its politics in Iran.
19. For the issue of passing over people's religious lives when focusing on Islam, see Ammerman 2006, 2021; McGuire 2008. Knibbe and Kupari 2020 discuss the concept of 'lived religion'. For lived religion in Boir Ahmad, see R. Loeffler 1988, pioneering this approach; Friedl 2020; Marsden 2005 discusses 'tribal' people's opinions about the 'new' Islam in Pakistan's northwest frontier areas.
20. R. and E. Fernea 1972 write about this pattern in Islam. It is an old, persistent problem of power: Frenkel 2008 criticises the effects of Islamic authorities' hegemony on the popular culture of ordinary people in the Mamluk Middle East, some 600 years ago, specifically on rituals and beliefs around the cycles of life and the year.
21. For financial support of several research projects over the years we are grateful to the Wenner–Gren Foundation for Anthropological Research, the University of Chicago, the Social Science Research Council, the National Endowment of the Humanities and Western Michigan University.
22. For the problem of entanglements with the people one studies, an issue Leibning calls 'the shadow side of fieldwork', see McLean and Leibning 2007.
23. Manoukian 2012 described his difficult experiences, as did participants at a Conference Roundtable on fieldwork problems, Hegland 2021. On aspects of fieldwork among pastoralists in adjacent provinces, see Beck 1991; Bradburd 1998.
24. On the shift from theory-based anthropological writing 'about' other people to writing for and with the people one studies, and the shift towards ethnography as

'history of the present', see Marcus and Fischer who first addressed these topics in 1986.

25. Dutton 2010; Prum 2017. Wragg Sykes 2021 describes Neanderthal aesthetics in mineral pigments and bone incisions. Locally, henna and an ash-based black/dark blue substance were the only pigments used for tattoos on women's skin in the past.
26. See R. Loeffler and K. Loeffler 2022 for Tang-e Servak. Henkelman 2020 addresses the aesthetics of wealth, power and deities in the Achaemenid empire close to what today is Boir Ahmad. Kaim 2016 discusses the aesthetics of royal court culture. See also Schmidt 1957.
27. A recent exception is Seremetakis 2019, an 'ethnographer of the everyday': Part Three, 'Touch and Taste', deals with this topic in modern Greece. Heider 2011 explores the cultural–cognitive moulding of emotive behaviour and vocabulary among several peoples in Indonesia on an explicitly formal, psychological basis. For the 2023 Meeting of the American Anthropological Association, R. Aras organised a workshop on 'Emotions and Affect' in Turkey (Aras 2023).
28. Wittgenstein's claim that 'aesthetics is ethics' is debated among philosophers to this day (see Archer and Ware 2017) and is obvious for me as an anthropologist. Kolb and Yildiz 2019 provide insights and a literature review for art versus aesthetics discussions. Biemel and Spiegelberg 2017 and Scruton 2011 write introductions to phenomenology.
29. There are exceptions: The photographic ethnography of R. Loeffler and K. Loeffler 2022 is a vivid illustration of aesthetic aspects of life in Boir Ahmad beyond 'Islam,' as is the local oral literature, Friedl 2015; 2018a. Betteridge 1985 reports on women pilgrims in Shiraz; R. Loeffler 1987 presents Sisakht men's interpretations of religious matters; Marsden 2005 describes a Pakistani community's discontent with the extremist Sunni suppression of local 'lived Islam'. Batmanghelichi 2020 writes about well-being among women in Iran. In 140 photographs, countless drawings and some song-lyrics, Feilberg 1952 offers insights into aesthetic aspects of the lifeways of a Lur-tribe in Lurestan Province he studied in 1935.
30. Anthropologists' problems with semiotics were discussed in a Roundtable at the 2023 Meeting of the American Anthropological Association (Cohen 2023). Cultural anthropology's recent move towards activism and advocacy necessitates taking sides in disputes. See El-Guindi 2021 on effects of this development.
31. Beck (1991: 179) includes 'aesthetics' in the index when describing Qashqa'i nomads' proper loading of belongings on pack animals. Her descriptions of life

on the migration lets one appreciate the joys and hardships of the nomadic way of life. R. Loeffler and K. Loeffler's 2022 book of photographs with explanatory text makes emotions visible.

32. For an example of 'conversation analysis' in Iran, see Rezvani and Sayyad 2023. Marcus and Fischer 1986, and articles in Panella and Little 2021, discuss 'cultural intimacy.'

33. Roy Wagner 1975 called the generalising approach to ethnography 'the invention of culture' because it leads to the construction of over-generalised coherent entities, and suggested instead paying attention to the interwoven, dialectically connected 'alterities' people manipulate and invest with meaning. These are the 'choices' people have for conducting their lives. See also the 'emotional clusters' that Heider 2011 describes for three Indonesian groups.

34. For the Middle East, such aspects appear mostly in autobiographic remarks such as in Bradburd 1998; Warnock Fernea 1969, and in ethnographic stories such as in Friedl 1981.

35. Sheehan 2003 provides a historical perspective; Jeldtoft 2011 describes such changes in religious matters of Muslims in Europe; and R. Loeffler 2022 describes them in a local man.

36. In turn, the interactions influenced us, too: our elder daughter Kati Loeffler, deeply moved by local animals' many plights while helping women with chores, became the veterinary medical director of a Humane Society Clinic in Michigan. Our younger daughter Agnes Loeffler assisted me in several projects and studied Persian and anthropology alongside medicine (A. Loeffler 2008; 2014).

Chapter 1

1. Mithen 1996 offers insights into the beginnings of 'art' and the term's problems. As to so-called popular art, only the fourth edition of a reader on art philosophy (Goldblatt, Brown and Partridge 2017) includes short pieces on everyday aesthetics.

2. This goal is still presumed in statements such as art's 'supposed function to enlighten human nature' (Darsel 2013: 167), and in the positive link teachers find between art education and pupils' developmental success.

3. Anthropologists' recent move towards social justice and the use of quantifiable data moves anthropology from practice to praxis. For epistemological problems in the social sciences, see, for example, Engel 2016; Fischer 2018; El-Guindi 2021; Whitehouse 2022. Leaf's (2022) discussion of the ill effects that the push for

'objectivity' had on the study of kinship may be extended to any topic that has a deep impact on emotional and interactive sides of people's lives.

4. The same representational bias is noticeable in the way folktales are told and in song lyrics and proverbs, and also in traditional grave-stone art: 'a man is a man, a rifle is a rifle, an ibex is an ibex, just as now a photograph of a martyr shows what he had looked like', a neighbour explained as he was walking through the old graveyard with me. (Soon after, this old graveyard was buried under a new, government sponsored 'Culture Hall'.)

5. Gruber and Haubolle 2013 discusses the 'rhetoric of the image' in the Islamic Middle East. Schienerl 1984 looks at images of animals in jewellery and amulets from various places in the region. Flaskerud 2010 describes 'religious visualizations' in Iran. For a philosophical approach to the difficulties in understanding and talking about Islamic aesthetics and art, see Leaman 2004.

6. See Leaman 2004 and Mulder 2014, with extensive bibliographies. Burckhardt 2009 and Hirsch 2020 discuss art in Islam and Arabic cultures. Potts 2019 provides an archaeologist's take on antiquities from the area.

7. Some collections of stories, songs and poems are translated into English. For the Zagros region, see Amanolahi and Thackston 1986 (Lurestan); Friedl 2007, 2015, 2017 (Boir Ahmad); Lorimer and Lorimer 1919 (Bakhtiari); Vahman and Asatrian 1995 (Bakhtiari).

8. See Marzolph 2003; R. Loeffler and K. Loeffler 2022; R. Loeffler's large collection of revolutionary political posters from Sisakht are at the University of Chicago's Hanna Holborn Gray Special Collections Research Center.

9. The first ethnologist facing this problem was Grosse 1894. Fraser 1957 provides an engaging overview of the history of scientists' approaches to 'Primitive Art'. Textbooks such as Layton 1991; Hatcher 1999; Morphy and Perkins 2006; Joyce 2020 address these thorny questions.

10. See, for example, the illustrations in Rubin 1987. *ArtfixDaily Artwire*, 1 May 2015 reported on the exhibition on this topic in New York City.

11. The nearly complete inventory of the tangible traditional culture is documented in R. Loeffler and Friedl 1967, and in R. Loeffler, Friedl and Janata 1974. A similar collection of artefacts from Lurestan that Feilberg had collected there in 1935 is in a museum in Copenhagen.

12. Examples of such art are in Wulff 1966; in the eye-popping imperial court art presented by Soudavar 1992; and in academic conferences such as the 'Persian Arts of the Book Conference', Oxford, 23–24 July 2021.

13. For an exception to this observation, see Bauer and Janata 1974 about jewellery in rural Afghanistan. It points to outside influences in tastes and adornment habits overriding local material and economic austerity. There were few such historical influences in Boir Ahmad.
14. Shells with drilled holes are the oldest 'beads' on record, likely used for their presumed apotropaic and healing powers. See El Mehdi et al. 2021 about thirty-three palaeolithic shell beads from Morocco. For the uses of beads in the Middle East, see articles in Caubet 1999; Dasen and Nagy's 2019 discussion of 'magical gems' in antiquity is illuminating for traditional Boir Ahmad, too.
15. Colloredo-Mansfeld 1999 presents an exemplary discussion of the turning of 'indigenous crafts' into tourist art in the Andes.
16. The glasses and their terms were imported from Russia together with tea. See also R. Loeffler and Friedl 1967; R. Loeffler, Friedl and Janata 1974.
17. A recent book about aesthetics (Mathiowetz and Turner 2021) deals almost exclusively with language surrounding the Flower World complex in the Americas. See also Heider 2011.
18. Some of the new forays into art and aesthetics within Western culture probe these boundaries, such as, for example, 'Pollution Art' (Leddy 2011) with junkyards, and Barker 2021 with marine plastic pollution. Philosophers, psychologists and some anthropologists argue about aesthetics as a concept and about its connection to art. See Anderson 1990, and articles on aesthetics in Zalta 2014; Seremetakis 2019.
19. On this see C. Geertz 1979, 1983; Anderson 1990; Coote and Shelton 1992. Bourdieu (1977: 2) talks of 'axes of the field of potentialities'. Wagner 1975 speaks of 'alterities'.
20. Coudenys 2015 provides an enlightening discussion of architectural choices, tastes and judgements around his 'Ugly Houses' project.
21. In alpine regions in Europe the traditional women's peasant dress, the 'dirndl', morphed into designer-branded fashion creations favoured to this day in conservative upper-class circles at festive occasions. See Bourdieu 1984 for social functions of taste.
22. Pilgrimage tourism has grown into a blooming business in Iran, accommodating pilgrim-visitors from inside and outside Iran in hotels in the cities. In Shiraz, the old district around the big shrine of Shah Ćeragh was razed for businesses catering to pilgrims. Luz 2019 discusses this big money trend in Muslim countries. Coleman 2021 discusses the opposite, that is, the emotional and aesthetic meanings of small pilgrimage places. These, too, are relevant locally.

Chapter 2

1. I am using the English term 'senses' because there is no equivalent Luri word summarising them. On the natural history of the five senses, see Ackerman 1991.
2. Locally, the so-called Dunning–Kruger effect (Dunning 2011) is in evidence mostly in the habits and utterances of a few people who are ideologically fixated on political or orthodox religious beliefs. Such firm beliefs are immune to arguments resting on scientific 'facts' and create their own irrefutable logic, a 'logic of ignorance' in epistemology.
3. This ties into local resistance to women's literacy until the 1960s. A neighbour complained that when her father caught her as a girl looking at her brother's school book, he said it was a sign that the end of the world was near. 'He didn't want me to learn to see,' she said.
4. This prejudice is fading especially in the urban middle class in Iran. Archer and Ware 2018 discuss aesthetic obligations in androcentric societies.
5. See Prum 2017 and Ryan 2018 for the evolutionary significance of beauty in mate selection. Like in many other places, in Boir Ahmad the criterion of beauty for mate selection is intersected by socio-political interests that put limitations on mate choices especially in arranged marriages.
6. For a culture history of colours see Fox 2022; for remarks on colour in the Quran see Hirsch 2020.
7. Huang 2013 discusses Qashqa'i women's self-presentation.
8. People with normal human colour perception see many colours but do not necessarily name them. Berlin and Kay 1969 provide an evolutionary model in seven stages for the acquisition of colour terms. In stage I the only named categories are 'light' and 'dark' in any colour, while in stage VII many hues have terms. People furthermore tend to name colours after objects that have them: in Sisakht, light blue is 'sky-ish (*asamuni*)', orange is '*naranji*.' The Munsell colour table is used to elicit colour terms in interviews. I used it (with everybody's permission) in 1970/71 in Sisakht and thank Paul Kay and Brent Berlin for their assistance. See Friedl 1979.
9. For the archaeology of wool and weaving, see Barber 1996; Maner 2018.
10. For information about tribal woven goods and the history of weaving, see Helfgott 1996; Opie 1998; MacDonald 2017; Mushkat et al. 2020.
11. In cities this has changed to a much more liberal use of clothes and colours especially in the middle classes, and remains a big political issue.

12. To make butter, a woman filled a bag made of a goat or sheep hide with yoghurt, firmly tied the neck-end of the sack, hung the sack on a wooden tripod and pushed and pulled it back and forth until the butter fell out. During the busy spring–summer months, women in the summer pastures found little sleep.
13. On gender issues in the Islamic Republic, see, for example, Afary 2009; Correri 2018; Kandiyoti, Al-Ali, Spellman Poots 2021; Kian 2023.
14. Schulze-Holthus (1959), who travelled widely in the Middle East and stayed in Boir Ahmad in 1944, published anecdotes common 'throughout the Middle East'. For humour among Muslims, see Marzolph 2011.
15. Locally, music was called 'oboe and drum' (*sāz o dohol*); singing (*khondan*, meaning singing as well as reading). Contemporary modern music is called *musiqi*. Our tape recordings of local music before the revolution are at the Phonogram Archive in Vienna.
16. This is in sharp contrast to what Griswold 2014 heard in Afghanistan before the Taliban takeover, where women routinely composed and sang short poems (*landay*), airing their emotional reactions to happenings in their lives. Some of them are nearly identical to the songs I heard in Sisakht fifty years ago, pointing to a shared poetic aesthetic as well as shared historical roots.
17. Gender-indexed music-making is common in Iran. In 2023, the announcer of a public concert of Persian music by the all-women expatriate orchestra 'Maryam Akhondy and Ensemble Sina' in Austria made the point that this was the only existing group of publicly performing female Iranian musicians.
18. The recent urban development of clandestine 'basement music', that is, pop and rock music performed in private venues, has not reached the province.
19. The Luri word for women's dance is '*vābāzi kardan*', from middle Persian *pā wāzīg*, foot-moving (Daryaee and Mazhjoo 2016). Lomax, Paulay and Bartieneff 1974 link this restrained posture to early humans' wood/stone technology that allowed only for up-down movements in chipping or scraping, while the later use of metal tools allowed curving motions.
20. See Friedl 2020. Mourning/funeral-dances are known from many places in the world and in some places continue to this day. The art historian Max Klimburg observed similar funeral dances in the mountains of northwest Pakistan in the 1970s (Klimburg, personal communication, February 2021).
21. The absence of private music-making is noticeable in other Zagros communities, too. The 'old' traditional instruments, flute, oboe and drums, are connected to low social status throughout the area.
22. The left hand is used for ablutions in the toilet.

23. See Wellman 2017 for food in pious post-revolutionary families in Iran; Fragner 2000 and Zubaida and Tapper 2011 for Middle Eastern areas generally; Zocchi and Fontefrancesco 2021 discuss the academic field of 'foodscapes' in the introduction to their book; and in an entertaining movie, Axel (1987) lets a French cook change a puritan community in Denmark by introducing the aesthetics of French cuisine.
24. Batmanglij's book (2020) on Persian culinary creations unite a promise of taste pleasures with sight pleasures. Bromberger (2020: 47) characterises the cuisine of Gilan in northern Iran as marked by rice, a preference for 'greens, acid, eggs and fish' and prepared by 'browning, simmering and steaming'.
25. Potts 2019 identifies the walnut tree and plantains as leitmotifs in historical Iran, cultivated first some 2,300 years ago. Apricots, apples, several kinds of prunes, walnuts, almonds are native to the area and were cultivated locally before apples became the cash crop in the 1980s.
26. The tree that produces the long acorns used for bread most often is identified as quercus Persica and quercus Brantiï.
27. Between July 2019 and July 2020, Iran imported 1,120,000 metric tons of rice (Statista Research Department, 26 August 2020).
28. The khan's families grew also, and their increasing number put great pressure on people's labour and products. Many men left to escape these pressures, poverty and discontent with elders. The large village of Konfirus in Fars Province was founded and populated by emigrants from Sisakht in the early twentieth century.
29. In fact, sexual mores in Iran are more revolutionary than just 'easing'; see Afary and Faust 2021.
30. This poetic sight brings to mind Calvino's remarks (1974: 8) about a town in Italy: 'In the square there is a wall where the old men sit and watch the young go by . . . Desires are already memories.'
31. About the local history of childhood, see Friedl 2017. The founder of the modern tribal education system, as it was called then, Mr Bahmanbeigi, told his teachers to teach by example and praise, not by corporal punishment. About this remarkable educator, see at: http://www.bahmanbeigi.ir.
32. Such self-harm is not confined to Boir Ahmad. In Kurdistan, where life conditions and misogynist practices are similar, cutting one's wrists and self-immolation are reportedly the main modes of suicide and suicide attempts among women; Sheikhouni and Sinis 2022. Report available at: https://www.bbc.com/news/av/world-middle-east-63958584. Statistical data are unreliable.

33. A. Loeffler 2015 discusses the shift of local medicine to allopathic 'modern' medicine in Iran.

Chapter 3

1. See also Archer and Ware 2018. An urban middle-class woman was explicit: it was a woman's duty to keep her home and family as attractive as possible because it made the family members content and confident, and the view of a well-kept house and children made other people happy. A. Loeffler, personal communication.
2. The energetic pursuit of beauty is ubiquitous in Iran generally and in other areas of the Middle East. A headline in *The Telegraph* reads, 'Iran may flog or jail fans of "extreme" cosmetic surgery' (Vahdat 2018). For the growing forms of beauty see McDougall 2021. Archer and Ware 2018 extend the discussion of attractiveness to power in lopsided gender relations.
3. The other public building was a small mosque, a mud-brick prayer house built by the people themselves and used occasionally for prayer, rest and mourning rituals.
4. McDougall 2021 puts this theme into a wider aesthetic and cultural context.
5. The assumption that some eyes may emit a harmful power is ancient and nearly universal. Dundes 1992.
6. The Green Movement in Iran was a political movement causing upheavals. See Karimi 2018. In Boir Ahmad it had sympathisers but little impact.
7. For the history and meaning of gardens in Iran, see Gharipour 2020; Hutter 1993.
8. Bagh-e Eram in Shiraz is a World Heritage Site built and re-built by several shahs and renovated by a Qashqa'i paramount khan in the nineteenth century.
9. Increasingly, to express gratitude local people also use imported words: Arabic *mamnun, shukr*; Turkish *teshekor*; French *merci*. The old Persian term *sepās* or *spās* for 'thanks' has all but disappeared in vernacular speech.
10. The remarkably low labour participation of women in Iran remains understudied. Golzard 2020 writes about women's new work strategies and job opportunities mostly in urban settings.
11. Shahshahani 1982 titled her ethnography of the Mamasani people neighbouring Boir Ahmad, 'The Four Seasons of the Sun', and the Tourism Agency in Boir Ahmad calls the province 'Land of Four Seasons' in its prospectus.
12. 'Circles, too, get tired', a farmer said, 'even if they have no end. I know from going around my field.' Reichenbach (1956: 8) warned that experience-based arguments about time are illogical and lead to 'a philosophy of trivialities' such as 'time flows like a river'. However pertinent this view is in formal logic, illogical trivialities structure people's lives.

13. In the Mazdaean pantheon, Zurvan ('Time') is the father of Ahura Mazda, the Zoroastrian creator deity. See Widengren (1965: 288f).
14. Only the first and last days in the week, Saturday (*shanbe*) and Friday (*jom'e*), have names; the days in between are numbered after Saturday.
15. Wednesday originally was declared to be unlucky for infidels and was later generalised, but this meaning is not popular in Sisakht.
16. For an anthropological take on time and space, see Swinehart and Brown, 2019; Cramer 1993 explores concepts and uses of time in general; Ahmad 2022 is critical of modernity's hegemonic influence on the understanding of time in Islam.
17. The Mahdi-saviour, the Twelfth Imam, expected to ring in the Day of Judgement, is also called Imam Zaman, the Imam of (the end of) Time, that is, of earth-time as people know it. Recently, new Mahdis are reportedly appearing. In Sisakht they are called 'crazy'. Their millenarianism may be attributed to stress, alienation and loss of meaning in Iran, but the regime-mullahs take it as a sign of potential revolutionary unrest and remove these prophets of doom post haste. See *The Economist* 2022.
18. See Friedl 2020 for talking with the dead.
19. These are the '*haft sin*' (the 'sevens'), all starting with an 's' and popular throughout Iran. For links to Zoroastrian cosmology, see Hutter 1993.
20. Sophiamehr 2012 calls the Islamic government a 'regime of martyrdom' that keeps the memory of Iranian fallen soldiers in the Iran–Iraq War alive as a powerful symbol of suffering for Islam and thus for its own legitimacy. See also Moaddel 2020. For aspects of the cult of soldier-martyrs in Iran, see Anonymous 2012; Wellman 2021.

Chapter 4

1. Leaf 2022 discusses history and uses of the philosophy of science that led to the near-abandonment of formal kinship studies in anthropology.
2. For effects of 'patriarchal' structures on people, see Dumont du Voitel 1994; H. Geertz's 1979 in-depth analysis of the friendship–kinship–patronage triad in Morocco is relevant for Iran, too. For Iran see, for example, Afkhami and Friedl 1994; Friedl 2017; Hegland 2014; Keddie 2006.
3. Paternal parallel cousin marriage (between children of two brothers) was declared to be the preferred choice but was not the most prevalent arrangement in a big pool of paternal second and third cousins. Health officials also warned of potential genetic problems for offspring in intra-family marriages. A father explained

his veto of his son's wish to marry his first cousin with 'children of parents who are first cousins may be crooked or dumb'.
4. For the concept of collectivism, see Talhelm 2019. A relevant study of prevarication in such groups is Triandis et al. 2001. Members of collectivist groups generally exhibit what Sigmund Freud called 'narcissism of small differences'. They are more interested in their neighbours than are people in individualistic societies where there is less pressure to conform. See Freud 2002.
5. Mousavi 2020 writes about the use of kin terms in Lurestan Province, which is culturally similar to Boir Ahmad.
6. A Seyed is taken to be a male descendant of the Prophet; a Hajji has made the pilgrimage to Mecca; a Mashhadi has visited the tomb of the Eighth Imam in Mashhad.
7. Teknonymy means to answer an address with the same term used by the speaker: a child calling 'Auntie!' may be answered by her aunt with 'Auntie, what do you want?'
8. The Luri term '*bou*' is derived from *bābā*, which in turn comes from Persian *pedar*, father, illustrating how meanings may change when cultural contexts change.
9. See relevant stories in Friedl 1981.
10. Whitehouse 2023 looks at various reasons for the endurance of polygyny, including those emerging from the point of view of the women involved.
11. In practice, the husband can force his first wife's consent by threatening to divorce her and to take the children from her.
12. For changing attitudes towards romantic love and marital expectations in Iran, see Afary and Faust 2021.
13. A girl used to be considered 'ripe' to be married when she was a reliable housekeeper, even before menarche. Birth certificates still mean little. In the Islamic Republic, the legal marriage age is thirteen lunar years for girls, but 'Islam' allows for eight-year-old girls to be married; a girl's father has final decision power. Ahmady 2017 reports that child marriages are on the rise in Iran.
14. Marriage in Islam is a contract between a man and a woman but de facto also between the two kin groups involved: should the husband die, his family would have to take care of the children and maybe also of the widow.
15. Friedl 2017 deals with the history of children, and Friedl 2021, with marriage in Boir Ahmad.
16. *Al Jazeera* 2021; Golzard and Miguel 2021 provide social background to this dating service.

17. Iranian women's labour participation is low. The country ranks No. 106 in women's education and No. 144 in economic participation, the third-lowest rate in the world, according to the Global Gender Gap Report 2022, tables 1.1, 1.2, available at: https://www.weforum.org/reports/global-gender-gap-report-2022 /in-full /1-benchmarking-gender-gaps-2022, last accessed 29 August 2022. The new trend in Iran of 'fugitive husbands' who abandon wife and children because of economic pressures but also because of disenchantment with marriage and with wives' demands and lack of support, is not an issue in Sisakht. A report is available at: hamshahrionline.ir/news/668130, 8 April 2022. I thank Amir Mirfakhraie for the information.
18. The *mehrië* is a husband's promise of money or other valuables to his wife, for her to demand any time. In practice, though, in the past a wife in Boir Ahmad was supposed to pardon this debt after the first child was born, and now it is thought of as severance pay in case of a divorce.
19. Exorbitant wedding expenses are not confined to Iran; see Rahim 2015 for the Taliban government's attempts to curb them in Afghanistan.
20. See Vatandoust and Sheipari 2021 on the increase of 'White Marriage' in Iran, that is, of cohabitation without legal and procreational consequences. On marriage issues in Iran, see Afary and Faust 2021. The officially permitted and legally valid Shia-Islamic form of temporary marriage, *muta* or *sigheh*, agreed upon by a man and a woman for a specified time, is not popular locally; most people dismiss it as 'sinful, ugly prostitution'.

Chapter 5

1. See Loeffler 1983 about game animals, hunting and the realm of fairies until the mid-twentieth century.
2. Owners of expensive, 'chic' pet dogs in the urban middle class in Iran reportedly dismiss the religious category of lawful–unlawful animals as 'superstition'.
3. Engel 2016 discusses various bases of morality.
4. Gender complementarity is a core assumption in Abrahamic traditions such as Islam. Shaw 2021 provides historical insight into how easily it is turned into a purportedly God-willed, rational order that supports so-called patriarchy.
5. In many other places in Boir Ahmad, though, it was the women's job to collect firewood: fuel, fireplace and fire were a woman's domestic core. 'The fireplace is dead' (*tash khāmush*) was any man's routine expression for the absence of his wife in Sisakht, too.

6. See Alirezanejad 2013 on how women make money decisions in 'rural Iran'.
7. Bradburd (1998: 133–5) describes 'craziness' as a strategy young Komachi people in Kerman Province cleverly acted out in order to get the spouse they wanted against the elders' will.
8. A. Loeffler and Friedl 2014. Raising many children had always been a dilemma: good in principle, but not good considering the burden of satisfying their needs and dealing with boys' purported natural tendencies towards violence and destruction (Friedl 1997).
9. Friedl and A. Loeffler 1994 describe change in housing patterns in a Sisakht neighbourhood.
10. Geologically, the Zagros range is an active seismic zone with rumbles 'all the time', as people say and we experienced.
11. Two storeys may mean two apartments. The government financially encouraged this to increase housing in Iran, but it was easy for people to take the cheap loans and leave the upper apartment empty so as 'not to be bothered by strangers inside one's own house'.
12. Pronounced *ābru* and *abru*, the much-used term deserves a note to clarify a confusion. The etymological root in *ābru* ('a' as in 'law'), is *āb*, 'water', but also power, dignity, honour. Combined with *ru*, face, to *ābru*, the closest meaning in English thus is 'dignity of the face'. But Persian folk etymology combines the primary meaning of *āb*, water, with *ru*, face, into 'water off the face', which makes no sense to them. In this case, the Farsi word *ābru* furthermore should be pronounced *ou-ri* in Luri but isn't. Pronounced *abru* ('a' as in 'sharp') the word means 'eyebrow' as well as 'face'. This 'a' precedes the old Sanskrit/Persian word '*bhru*', eyebrow (the root of English 'brow'), as an aid to speaking it. Thus, the eyebrow, a prominent, aesthetically significant beauty feature in Iran, also became a sign of 'honour'. I thank Agnes Korn for the explanations in an email, 5 January 2022. See also *āb* in Steingass 1963.
13. See Simpson-Hebert 1987. Lately, business and hospitality merged in Sisakht in summer rentals offered especially to wealthy Arabs from the Gulf who pay well to avoid male guests in hotels while enjoying the cool mountain air with their wives and children.
14. Derrida famously linked hostility to hospitality, including in the etymology of these words. See Kakoliris (2015: 145, 149).

Chapter 6

1. R. Loeffler 2006, unpublished fieldnotes.
2. Ahmad 2021 discusses the implications for taking enlightenment concepts such as 'reason' into religion. Apologetic arguments in debates over the compatibility of science with Islam are ubiquitous but are largely irrelevant in Sisakht.
3. *Tizhush* is also a family name and the name of a school in Tehran (I thank A. Loeffler for this information). Persian *tashkhis kardan*, to detect, find out, locally has become a popular term for critical evaluation.
4. For a portrait of this remarkable local leader, see R. Loeffler 1971.
5. Whitehead (1928: lecture 1) defined the principal function of reason as promoting the 'Art of Life', that is, to live, to live well, and then to live better yet. This is by far the most popular opinion about progress in Iran, too. See R. Loeffler 2011. For the shapes these aspirations may take in Iran and the lack of attention to them by social scientists, see Olszewska 2013.
6. In the United States, nearly 20 per cent of all college undergraduates were enrolled in business courses in 2020 (Hanson 2022).
7. In this context, a *darvish* is modelled after a Sufi-inspired male on the path to religious enlightenment who renounces wealth and worldly pursuits. I learned of no woman dervish in town as of 2022.
8. Men and women like this option. R. Loeffler 1987, and R. Loeffler and K. Loeffler 2022 describe this 'correct piety' in Sisakht.
9. The exceptionally astute, gifted and charismatic 'peasant' leader (see Loeffler 1971) never elevated himself above the people he represented and stayed poor all his life.
10. Personal communication from Dr Salami in 2006, and Mrs Taheri, MA in 2015.
11. R. Loeffler and K. Loeffler 2022 provide visual examples of this development.
12. Iranian Muslim feminists insist that not religion but an outdated gender-culture is to blame for misogyny. Already decades ago they encouraged Muslim women to use the Quran and Hadith to reclaim their God-willed human rights violated by Muslim people living in cultures that encourage those in power to oppress women (Afkhami 1998).
13. About performance legitimacy, see Darling 2014.
14. For 'counter-ethics' and the ambiguities of illegality that are relevant for our case, see essays in Panella and Little 2021.
15. Nineteenth-century travellers in Iran remark on the popular swearing by religious personalities to assert a truth. Bradburd (1998: 53f) quotes several

sources and discusses this truth-affirming habit among the Komachi in central Iran.

16. Bourdieu variously calls this logic 'pre-logical logic, economic logic, logic of practice', contrasting it to 'logical logic' of science and philosophers of logic. He is adamant about its importance for accessing people's world views (Bourdieu 1977: 109, 110).

17. The colour white in such context means 'weak'. Sour taste means disbalancing the Galenic warm/cold equilibrium in the body.

18. Arguing with people who fall for misinformation and demagogical statements, or calling them 'stupid' rarely convinces them to change their assumptions. In many Mullah Nasreddin stories cognitive fallacies are turned into pearls of wisdom. See, for example, Downing and Papas 1964. For 'logics of ignorance', see Hendricks 2006; Engel 2016.

Chapter 7

1. See, for example, Fischer 1990; Hegland 2014; Kalinock 2004; R. Loeffler 1988; Vivier-Muresan 2006.

2. Flaskerud 2012 observes that the state's attempts to monopolise religion led to a 'counter diskurs' in women's circles without further discussion.

3. Local variants of Sufi ideas and practices are far from what Zargar 2011 finds in Safavid writings on the subject. For a history of Sufism in Iran, see Van den Bos 2002. For a discussion of the relationships of 'popular' Islam with 'saints' and their cult, of Sufi practices within orthodox, 'authentic' Islam and modernisation, see Bekkin 2020; Van Bruinessen 2009. Gramlich's three volumes (1965–1981) on dervish orders in Iran is a standard work on the subject. Marsden 2005 describes protests against puritan Sunni Islamisation of people in Pakistan who see 'their' Islam violated. Reactions to heavy-handed ultra-orthodox Sunni groups' conduct in Afghanistan make the world news.

4. Olszewska (2013: 841) calls the 'official, canonical, orthodox' structure in the Islamic Republic 'an uneasy mix of political Islam, populism and neo-liberalism'. Van Bruinessen 2008 provides examples for the downgrading of lived religion.

5. Cuffel (2005: 401), criticising such politically motivated prejudices of medieval Mamluk theologians, asserts that 'women and men largely shared the same ideals, behaviours and rituals . . .', and that 'women's behaviour, motivations and level of involvement equalled . . . that of men'. By many accounts this also can be said about Muslims today.

6. One such women's circle in Yasuj, the provincial capital, was reportedly organised by a woman from the endogamous barber class. Kalinock 2003 describes urban practices.
7. For examples of this resilience and its deep roots in aesthetics, see Donaldson's 1938 classic book on Persian 'magic and folklore'; Einzmann 1977 describes popular 'Volksbrauchtum' (customs of the people) in Afghanistan; Poliakov 1992 discusses how popular Islam survived the Soviet purges of Islam in Central Asia; Marsden 2005 writes about religion as practiced in northwest Pakistan; R. Loeffler 1989 and Friedl 2020 write about the variety of beliefs in Boir Ahmad.
8. See Richard 1995. For implications of the various local meanings of 'religion', see Friedl (2020: 18–25).
9. For this view of religion, see Wittgenstein 1967.
10. The rift of alienation is deeper in cities than in Sisakht. For example, the recent history of the lively, yet forbidden, underground music scene in big cities in Iran described by Siamdoust 2017, hardly fits small-town aesthetics.
11. Secular trends especially in urban Iran change religious aesthetics, and are blamed for dwindling faith and attendance in rituals despite Sharia laws and intense missionary efforts by the government. See Anonymous 2021 (Gamaam).
12. See also (Friedl 2020: 66). Beranek and Tupek 2009 report this for Sunni–Salafi-dominated Muslim areas and discuss the history of religious authorities' attitudes to shrine/grave visits. The insights are relevant for the Islamic Republic, too.
13. A photograph in Feilberg (1952: 147) shows such an 'Imamzadeh' (it has a female name). In Sisakht, such stone places are a distant memory but they do appear in folktales.
14. Honarpisheh 2013 describes women's sensory experiences in pilgrimages in Shiraz and pilgrims' uses of shrines there. Davis-Floyd and Laughlin 2022 discuss social and psychological effects of rituals.
15. I visited the shrine with a group of pilgrims from Sisakht in 1975. See photographs of the new shrine at: https://www.tasnimnews.com/en/news/2019/03/20/1970892/bibi-hakime-tomb-south-of-iran, last accessed 10 July 2021.
16. Luz 2019 discusses the globalised aesthetic of pilgrimages. For the psychology of aesthetic experiences, see Marković 2012. Langer 2004 discusses the history of shrines and pilgrimages. Peleggi 2022 looks at the lifecycle of shrines and the theory behind 'devotional conservation'. Friedl 2020 discusses the lively shrine/saint-culture in Boir Ahmad.

17. A mullah in town recommended Qummi 1999, a book of many prayers, as an infallible self-help guide. Lewis' 1988 lecture on 'Limits of Obedience' is of relevance. For psychological effects of prayer in general, see Luhrmann 2020.
18. The Moharram rituals commemorate Imam Husein, a grandson of the Prophet who died defending his father Ali's political leadership. Beeman 2017 discusses the historical roots of this drama. R. Loeffler and Friedl 2022 describe what happened when this mourning ritual coincided with the completely different mood, rituals and aesthetics of the joyous, traditional New Year's celebrations in 2006.
19. The Hojjat-al-Islam has the authority to examine and proof tenets and customs, and the Mujaddiq, a 'reviver', will periodically update them to ensure that Islam stays meaningful for the faithful.
20. Usually *del* it is translated as 'heart', but local people (and others) locate the *del* in the solar plexus, not the anatomical heart, which is called *qalb*.
21. In several discussions (1998 and 2004) R. Loeffler had with a young theologian of Sisakht origin, the young scholar quoted M. Tabatabaï (1903–1981), an influential theologian and philosopher of Shia Islam, to explain the balance between observing ritual and 'doing good', adding that people in Sisakht quite generally put everyday ethics above ritual (R. Loeffler, unpublished field notes). Urban pious people often call rural people 'cows' for their purported lack of theological sophistication.

Chapter 8

1. For higher education and the brain drain in Iran, see Anonymous 2022.
2. See Hegland 2011 for the development of a former agricultural village in Fars Province into a suburb of Shiraz, and Hegland (in preparation) for how people there remember the earlier times.
3. See the UN World Population Prospects, 2022, available at: macrotrends.net/countries/IRN/Iran/fertility-rate, last accessed 4 August 2022. Bizaer 2022 provides a comprehensive, gloomy picture of the history and serious consequences of this trend.
4. Bizaer 2022 quotes a single, middle-aged childless city woman who said that her generation did not have hope in the future when she was young and still does not have hope.
5. See Afary and Faust 2021. Contractual temporary marriage is allowed in Iran, reportedly to prevent 'sinful' sexual relations among young people who are

marrying late, such as students. I learned of no such arrangement in Sisakht. There, a popular choice is to call it 'legal prostitution'. Yaghoobi 2022 provides an analysis of this law.
6. We noticed Sufi notions and practices when we first visited the area, but we know of only one attempt to create a Sufi order in Boir Ahmad, around 1960.

Bibliography

Anonymous. 2012. 'Unburied memories, the politics of bodies and the material culture of sacred defence martyrs in Iran: a collection of articles', *Visual Anthropology* 25(1/2).

Anonymous. 2021. 'Iranian attitudes toward religion: a 2020 survey report', *Gamaan*, Netherlands, available at: gamaan-iran-religion-survey-2020, last accessed 25 January 2021.

Anonymous. 2022. 'Iran's universities eyeing even brighter post-sanctions future', *Iran Digest*, American Iranian Council, 23 April 2022.

Ackerman, Diane. 1991. *A Natural History of the Senses*. New York: Vintage.

Afary, Janet. 2009. *Sexual Politics in Modern Iran*. Cambridge: Cambridge University Press.

Afary, Janet and Jesilyn Faust (eds). 2021. *Iranian Romance in the Digital Age: From Arranged Marriage to White Marriage*. London: I. B. Tauris/Bloomsbury.

Afkhami, Mahnaz. 1998. *Claiming our Rights: A Manual for Women's Human Rights Education Access in Muslim Societies*. New York: Sisterhood is Global Institute.

Afkhami, Mahnaz and Erika Friedl (eds). 1994. *In the Eye of the Storm: Women in Post-Revolutionary Iran*. Syracuse, NY: Syracuse University Press.

Ahmad, Irfan. 2021. 'Islam and the enlightenment', *Marginalia* 1(15), available at: https://marginalia.lareviewofbooks.org/islam-and-the-enlightenment.

Ahmad, Irfan. 2022. 'The time of epistemic domination: notes on modernity as an oppressive category', *ReOrient* (Pluto Journals), 6 May, available at: www.scienceopen.com/hosted-document?doi=10.13169/reorient.7.1.0072, last accessed 20 July 2022.

Ahmady, Kameel. 2017. *An Echo of Silence: A Comprehensive Research Study on Early Child Marriage in Iran*. Hauppauge, NY: Nova Publishing.

Alirezanejad, Soheila. 2013. 'Saving or spending money: women making decisions in rural Iran', *Journal of Middle East Women's Studies* 9(1): 110–25.

Al Jazeera. 2021. 'Iran unveils Islamic dating app to encourage marriage', available at: https://www.aljazeera.com/news/2021/7/12/iran-unveils-islamic-dating-app-to-encourage-marriage, last accessed 18 July 2021.

Amanolahi, Sekandar and W. M. Thackston. 1986. *Tales from Luristan: Tales, Fables and Folk Poetry from the Lur of Bala Gariva*. Cambridge, MA: Harvard University Press.

Ammerman, Nancy Tatom (ed.) 2006. *Everyday Religion: Observing Modern Religious Lives*. Oxford: Oxford University Press.

Ammerman, Nancy Tatom. 2021. *Studying Lived Religion*. New York: New York University Press.

Anderson, Richard L. 1988. *Art in Small-Scale Societies*. Englewood Cliffs, NJ: Prentice Hall.

Anderson, Richard L. 1990. *Calliope's Sisters: A Comparative Study of Philosophies of Art*. Englewood Cliffs, NJ: Prentice Hall.

Anderson, Richard L. 1992. 'Do other cultures have art?' *American Anthropologist* 94(4): 926–9.

Aras, Ramazan. 2023. 'Studying emotions and affect in Turkey', Workshop at Ibn Haldun University, Istanbul, 2023, American Anthropological Association Member Community Digest, 15 January.

Arbo, Allessandro, Michel LeDu and Sabine Plaud (eds). 2013. *Wittgenstein and Aesthetics: Perspectives and Debates*. Berlin: De Gruyter.

Archer, Alfred and Lauren Ware. 2017. 'Aesthetic supererogation', *Estetica* 54: 102–16.

Archer, Alfred and Lauren Ware. 2018. 'Beyond the call of beauty: everyday aesthetic demands under patriarchy', *The Monist* 10(1): 114–27.

ArtfixDaily Artwire. 2015. 'Exhibition focuses on the influence of primitive art on European Modernism', available at: http://artfixdaily.com/artwire/release/3376, last accessed 10 May 2021.

Axel, Gabriel. 1987. *Babette's Feast*. Nordisk Film, Denmark.

Baker, Christine D. 2015. 'The lost origins of the Daylamites', in Rebecca Futo Kennedy and Molly Jones-Lewis (eds), *The Routledge Handbook of Identity and the Environment in the Classical and Medieval Worlds*. London: Routledge, 281–95.

Barber, Elizabeth Wayland. 1996. *Women's Work, the First 20,000 Years: Women, Cloth and Society in Early Times*. New York: W. W. Norton.

Barker, Mandy. 2021. 'Plastic pollution art highlights risk to world's oceans', BBC, 26 June, available at: https://www.bbc.com/news/in-pictures-57560241, last accessed 26 June 2021.

Batmanghelichi, Kristin Soraya. 2020. *Revolutionary Bodies: Technologies of Gender, Sex and Self in Contemporary Iran*. New York: Bloomsbury.

Batmanglij, Najmieh. 2020. *Cooking in Iran, Regional Recipes and Kitchen Secrets*, 2nd edn. Washington, DC: Mage Publishers.

Bauer, Wilhelm P. and Alfred Janata. 1974. 'Kosmetik, Schmuck und Symbolik in Afghanistan', *Archiv für Völkerkunde* 28: 1–43.

Beck, Lois. 1991. *Nomad: A Year in the Life of a Qashqa'i Tribesman in Iran*. Berkeley: University of California Press.

Beeman, William O. 2017. 'Martyrdom, Shi'a Islam, Ta'ziyeh: Political symbolism in Shi'a Islam', in Meir Hatina and Meir Litvak (eds), *Martyrdom and Sacrifice in Islam: Theological, Political and Social Contexts*. London: I. B. Tauris, 224–43.

Bekkin, Renat (ed.). 2020. *The Concept of Traditional Islam in Modern Islamic Discourse in Russia*. Sarajevo: Center for Advanced Studies.

Ben Ami, Ido. 2019. 'Early modern imperial Ottoman architecture and the notion of bewilderment', 53rd Middle East Studies Association Meeting, 4–17 November 2019, New Orleans, LA.

Beranek, Ondrej and Pavel Tupek. 2009. 'From visiting graves to their destruction: the question of ziyara through the eyes of Salafis', *Crown Paper* No. 2, Center for Middle Eastern Studies, Waltham, MA: Brandeis University, available at: httpp://academia.edu 2973370, last accessed 13 May 2021.

Berlin, Brent and Paul Kay. 1969. *Basic Color Terms: Their Universality and Evolution*. Berkeley: University of California Press.

Betteridge, Anne. 1985. 'Ziarat: Pilgrimages to the Shrines of Shiraz', doctoral dissertation, Department of Anthropology, University of Chicago.

Betteridge, Anne. 2001. 'The controversial vows of urban Muslim women in Iran', in Nancy Auer Falk and Rita M. Gross (eds), *Unspoken Worlds: Women's Religious Lives*, 3rd edn. Belmont, CA: Wadsworth, 134–43.

Biemel, Walter and Herbert Spiegelberg. 2017. 'Phenomenology', *Encyclopedia Britannica*, available at: https://www.britannica.com/topic/phenomenology, last accessed 3 May 2021.

Bizaer, Maysam. 2022. 'What Iran's emerging demographic "tsunami" means for Tehran', *Middle East Institute* 8(22), available at: mei.edu/what-Irans-emerging-tsunami-means-tehran, last accessed 26 August 2022.

Black-Michaud, Jacob. 1986. *Sheep and Land: The Economics of Power in a Tribal Society*. Cambridge: Cambridge University Press.

Blair, Sheila S. 2006. *Islamic Calligraphy*. Edinburgh: Edinburgh University Press.

Blakeslee, Rosalind P. 2006. *The Arts and Crafts Movement*. New York: Phaidon.

Bourdieu, Pierre. 1977. *Outline of a Theory of Practice*. Cambridge: Cambridge University Press.

Bourdieu, Pierre. 1984. *Distinction: A Social Critique of the Judgment of Taste*. Cambridge, MA: Harvard University Press.

Bourdieu, Pierre. 1990. *The Logic of Practice*. Redwood City, CA: Stanford University Press.

Bradburd, Daniel. 1998. *Being There: The Necessity of Fieldwork*. Washington, DC: Smithsonian Institution Press.

Bromberger, Christian. 2020. 'Gilân (northern Iran) cuisine specificity', *Anthropology of the Middle East* 15(2): 47–54.

Brown, Donald E. 1991. *Human Universals*. Philadelphia, PA: Temple University Press.

Burckhardt, Titus. 2009. *Art of Islam: Language and Meaning*, Commemorative Edition (reprint of 1976 edn). Bloomington, IN: World Wisdom.

Calvino, Italo. 1974. *Invisible Cities*, trans. William Weaver. San Diego, CA: Harcourt Brace Jovanovich.

Caubet, Annie. 1999. *Cornaline et pierres précieuses: La Méditerranée de l'Antiquité à l'Islam (Cornelian and Precious Stones: The Mediterranean from Antiquity to Islam)*. Paris: Musée de Louvre.

Cohen, Adrienne. 2023. 'Affecting encounters: transcending the affect-semiotics divide', Roundtable at the 2023 Meeting of the American Anthropological Association, Toronto, Canada.

Coleman, Simon. 2021. *Powers of Pilgrimage: Religion in a World of Movement*. New York: New York University Press.

Colloredo-Mansfeld, Rudi. 1999. *Native Leisure Class: Consumption and Cultural Creativity in the Andes*. Chicago: University of Chicago Press.

Coote, Jeremy and Anthony Shelton. 1992. 'Introduction', in J. Coote and A Shelton (eds), *Anthropology, Art, and Aesthetics*. Oxford: Clarendon Press, 1–14.

Correri, Nicole. 2018. 'Reconciling Zaynab: Constructions of femininity in Shī-ī online English-Language majālis: the use of hagiography and Qur'ān to convey gender binaries', Master of Arts Thesis, Hartford Seminary, Hartford, CT, available at: academia.edu/36726533/reconciling_zaynab_constructions_of_femininity_in_shīī_online_english_language_majālis, last accessed 26 January 2023.

Coudenys, Hannes. 2015. *Ugly Belgian Houses*. Ghent: Borgerhoff & Lamberigts.

Cramer, Friedrich. 1993. *Der Zeitbaum: Grundlegung einer allgemeinen Zeittheorie (The Time-Tree: Basis of a General Theory of Time)*. Frankfurt am Main: Insel Verlag.

Cuffel, Alexandra. 2005. 'From practice to polemic: shared saints and festivals as "Women's Religion" in the medieval Mediterranean', *Bulletin of the School of Oriental and African Studies* 68(3): 401–19.

Danto, Arthur C. 1984. *The Transfiguration of the Commonplace: A Philosophy of Art*. Cambridge, MA: Harvard University Press.

Darsel, Sandrine. 2013. 'From art to ethics: exemplary nature of artworks and aspectual perception', in Alessandro Arbo, Michel LeDu and Sabine Plaud (eds), *Wittgenstein and Aesthetics: Perspectives and Debates*. Berlin: De Gruyter, 167–80.

Daryaee, Touraj and Mina Mazhjoo. 2016. 'Dancing in middle and classical Persian', *Dabir* 1(2): 10–15.

Demant-Mortensen, Inge. 2010. *Luristani Pictorial Tombstones: Studies in Nomadic Cemeteries from Northern Luristan, Iran*, Acta Iranica Ser. 47. Leuven: Peeters.

Darling, Linda T. 2014. '"The vicegerent of God, from him we expect rain": the pre-Islamic state in early Islamic political culture', *Journal of the American Oriental Society* 134(3): 407–29.

Dasen, Veronique and Arpad M. Nagy. 2019. 'Gems', in David Frankfurter (ed.), *Guide to the Study of Ancient Magic*. Leiden: Brill, 416–55.

Davis-Floyd, Robbie and Charles Laughlin. 2022. *Ritual: What It Is, How It Works and Why*. Oxford: Berghahn.

Derek, Allen. 2013. *Art and Time*. Newcastle: Cambridge Scholars Publishing.

Deter-Wolf, Aaron, Benoît Robitaille, Lars Krutak and Sébastien Galliot. 2016. 'The world's oldest tattoos', *Journal of Archaeological Science*, Reports 5: 19–24.

Donaldson, Beth Allen. 1938. *The Wild Rue: A Study of Muhammadan Magic and Folklore in Iran*. London: Luzac.

Doostdar, Alireza. 2019. 'Practice and participation in an Islamic tradition', *American Ethnologist* 46(2): 176–89.

Downing, Charles and William Papas. 1964. *Tales of the Hodja*. London: Oxford University Press.

Dundes, Alan (ed.). 1992. *The Evil Eye: A Casebook*. Madison, WI: University of Wisconsin Press.

Dunning, David. 2011. 'The Dunning–Kruger effect: on being ignorant of one's own ignorance', in Mark Zanna and James Olson (eds), *Advances in Experimental Social Psychology* 44: 247–96. Cambridge, MA: Academic Press.

Dutton, Denis. 2010. *The Art Instinct: Beauty, Pleasure and Evolution*. London: Bloomsbury.
Economist, The. 2022. 'Mahdi Mania', 21 May, 47.
Einzmann, Harald. 1977. *Religiöses Volksbrauchtum in Afghanistan: Heiligenverehrung und Wallfahrtswesen im Raum Kabul*. Wiesbaden: Südasien Institut.
El-Guindi, Fadwa. 2021. 'Has the AAA become an NGO?' *Communities* (American Anthropological Society All Member Community Digest), 23 April.
El Mehdi, Sehasseh, Philippe Fernandez, Steven Kuhn and twenty-two other authors. 2021. 'Early Middle Stone Age personal ornaments from Bizmoune Cave, Ersaouira, Morocco', *Science Advances* 7(39), available at: Science.org/toc/sciadv/7/39, last accessed 3 December 2021.
Engel, Pascal. 2016. 'The epistemology of stupidity', in Miguel Angel Fernandez Vargas (ed.), *Performance Epistemology*. Oxford: Oxford University Press, 196–223.
Feilberg, Carl G. 1952. *Les Papis*. København: Nordisk.
Fernea, Robert A. and Elizabeth Warnock. 1972. 'Religious observance among Islamic women', in Nikkie R. Keddie (ed.), *Scholars, Saints and Sufis: Muslim Religious Institutions since 1500*. Berkeley: University of California Press, 385–401.
Fischer, Michael M. J. 1990. *Debating Muslims: Cultural Dialogues in Postmodernity and Tradition*. Madison, WI: University of Wisconsin Press.
Fischer, Michael M. J. 2018. *Anthropology in the Meantime: Experimental Ethnography, Theory, and Methodology for the Twenty-First Century*. Durham, NC: Duke University Press.
Flaskerud, Ingvild. 2010. *Visualizing Belief and Piety in Iranian Shiism*. London: Continuum.
Flaskerud, Ingvild. 2012. 'Siislamske ritualer som mikro-offentligheter. Religion og samfunnsdebatt i Iran', *Din. Tidskrift for Religion og Kultur* 1: 118–42.
Fox, James. 2022. *The World According to Color: A Cultural History*. New York: Macmillan.
Fragner, Bert G. 2000. 'From the Caucasus to the roof of the world: a culinary adventure', in Sami Zubaida and Richard Tapper (eds), *A Taste of Thyme: Culinary Cultures in the Middle East*. London: Tauris Parke, 49–62.
Fraser, Douglas. 1957. 'The discovery of primitive art', in Hilton Kramer (ed.), *Arts Yearbook I: The Turn of the Century*. New York: Arts Digest, 119–33.
Fraser, Douglas. 1962. *Primitive Art*. Garden City, NY: Doubleday.
Frenkel, Yehoshua. 2008. 'Popular culture (Islam, early and middle periods)', *Religion Compass* 2(2): 195–225.
Freud, Sigmund. 2002. *Civilization and its Discontents*. London: Penguin.

Friedl, Erika. 1979. 'Colors and culture change in southwest Iran', *Language in Society* 8: 51–68.
Friedl, Erika. 1981. *Women of Deh Koh*. New York: Penguin.
Friedl, Erika. 1997. *Children of Deh Koh*. Syracuse, NY: Syracuse University Press.
Friedl, Erika. 2004. 'Stories as ethnographic dilemma in longitudinal research', *Anthropology and Humanism* 29(1): 5–21.
Friedl, Erika. 2007. *Tales From a Persian Tribe*. Dortmund: Verlag für Orientkunde.
Friedl, Erika. 2015. *Warm Hearts and Sharp Tongues: Life in 555 Proverbs from the Zagros Mountains of Iran*. Vienna: New Academic Press.
Friedl, Erika. 2017. 'A brief history of childhood in Boir Ahmad, Iran', *Anthropology of the Middle East* 12(1): 6–19.
Friedl, Erika. 2018a. *Folksongs from the Mountains of Iran: Culture, Poetics and Everyday Philosophies*. London: I. B. Tauris.
Friedl, Erika. 2018b. 'Deep Jokes from Boir Ahmad, Iran', in Regina F. Bendix and Dorothy Noyes (eds), *Terra Ridens – Terra Narrans*. Dortmund: Verlag für Orientkunde, 67–86.
Friedl, Erika. 2020. *Religion and Daily Life in the Mountains of Iran*. London: I. B. Tauris-Bloomsbury.
Friedl, Erika. 2021. 'How marriage changed in Boir Ahmad, 1900–2015', in Janet Afary and Jesilyn Faust (eds), *Iranian Romance in the Digital Age: From Arranged Marriage to White Marriage*. London: I. B. Tauris/Bloomsbury, 155–73.
Friedl, Erika and Agnes G. Loeffler. 1994. 'The ups and downs of dwellings in a village in West Iran', *Archiv für Völkerkunde* 48: 1–44.
Friedl, Erika and Reinhold Loeffler. 2013. 'Archaeology and cultural memory in Boir Ahmad, southern Zagros, Iran', *Archiv Weltmuseum Wien* 6(2): 183–231.
Friedl, Erika and Reinhold Loeffler. 2018. 'Eschatology in Boir Ahmad, Iran', *Anthropology of the Middle East* 13(1): 55–68.
Garthwaite, Emily and Arik Gabbai. 2021. 'Passage through the Zagros', *Smithsonian Magazine*, June 2021, available at: https://www.smithsonianmag.com/travel/passage-through-zagros-180977689, last accessed 29 August 2022.
Geertz, Clifford. 1983. 'Art as a cultural system', in Clifford Geertz, *Local Knowledge*. New York: Basic Books, 94–120.
Geertz, Hildred. 1979. 'The meanings of family ties', in Clifford Geertz, Hildred Geertz and Lawrence Rosen (eds), *Meaning and Order in Moroccan Society*. Cambridge: Cambridge University Press, 315–85.
Gharipour, Mohammad. 2020. *Persian Gardens and Pavilions*, 2nd edn. London: Bloomsbury.

Ghasidian, Elham. 2014. *The Early Upper Palaeolithic at Ghār-e Boof Cave: a Reconstruction of Cultural Tradition in the southern Zagros Mountains of Iran*. Tübingen: Kerns Verlag.

Ghasidian, Elham and Saman Heydari-Guran. 2018. 'Upper paleolithic raw material economy in the southern Zagros mountains of Iran', in Yoshihiro Nishiaki and Takeru Akazawa (eds), *The Middle and Upper Paleolithic Archaeology of the Levant and Beyond*. Singapore: Springer, 157–74.

Global Gender Gap Report. 2023. *World Economic Forum*, available at: https://www.weforum.org/publications/global-gender-gap-report-2023/in-full/gender-gaps-in-the-workforce#gender-gaps-in-the-workforce, last accessed 20 October 2023.

Goldblatt, David, Lee B. Brown and Stephanie Partridge (eds). 2017. *Aesthetics: A Reader in Philosophy of the Arts*, 4th edn. Boston. MA: Prentice Hall.

Golzard, Vahideh. 2020. 'Economic empowerment of Iranian women through the Internet', *Gender in Management* 35(1): 1–18.

Golzard, Vahideh and Christina Miguel. 2021. 'Negotiating intimacy through social media: challenges and opportunities for Muslim women in Iran', in Janet Afary and Jesilyn Faust (eds), *Iranian Romance in the Digital Age: From Arranged Marriage to White Marriage*. London: I. B. Tauris/Bloomsbury, 111–24.

Gramlich, Richard. 1965–1981. *Die Schiitischen Derwischorden Persiens*, 3 vols. Wiesbaden: Franz Steiner Verlag.

Griswold, Eliza. 2014. *I am the Beggar of the World: Landays from Contemporary Afghanistan*. New York: Farrar, Straus & Giroux.

Grosse, Ernst. 2012. *Die Anfänge der Kunst* (reprint of 1894 edn). Praha: Unikum (English translation 2015, *The Beginnings of Art*. London: Sagwan Press).

Grote, Simon. 2017. *The Emergence of Modern Aesthetic Theory*. Cambridge: Cambridge University Press.

Gruber, Christiane and Sune Haubolle (eds). 2013. *Visual Culture in the Modern Middle East: Rhetoric of the Image*. Bloomington, IN: University of Indiana Press.

Haeri, Niloofar. 2020. *Say What Your Longing Heart Desires: Women, Prayer and Poetry in Iran*. Stanford, CA: Stanford University Press.

Hanson, Melanie. 2022. 'College enrollment and student demographic statistics', *Education Data*, 26 July, available at: https://educationdata.org/college-enrollment-statistics, last accessed 31 July 2023.

Hatcher, Evelyn Payne (ed.). 1999. *Art as Culture: An Introduction to the Anthropology of Art*, 2nd edn. Westpoint, CT: Praeger.

Hegland, Mary Elaine. 2011. 'Aliabad of Shiraz: transformation from village to suburban town', *Anthropology of the Middle East* 6(2): 21–37.

Hegland, Mary Elaine. 2014. *Days of Revolution: Political Unrest in an Iranian Village*. Stanford, CA: Stanford University Press.

Hegland, Mary Elaine. 2021. 'Strategies to cope with fieldwork barriers and sensitive, politically fraught topics in the Islamic Republic of Iran', Roundtable at the 120th Meeting of the American Anthropological Association, Baltimore, MD, 17–21 November 2021.

Hegland, Mary, Zahra Sarraf and Mohammad Shahbazi. 2007. 'Modernisation and social change: the impact on Iranian elderly social networks and care systems', *Anthropology of the Middle East* 2(2): 55–73.

Heider, Karl G. 2011. *The Cultural Context of Emotions: Culture, Mind and Society*. New York: Palgrave Macmillan.

Helfgott, Leonard M. 1996. *Ties that Bind: A Social History of the Iranian Carpet*. Washington, DC: Smithsonian Institution Press.

Hendricks, Vincent F. 2006. *Mainstream and Formal Epistemology*. Cambridge: Cambridge University Press.

Henkelman, F. M. Wouter. 2020. 'The heartland pantheon', in Bruno Jacobs and Robert Rollinger (eds), *A Companion to the Achaemenid Persian Empire*. Hoboken, NJ: Wiley Blackwell, 1221–41.

Hirsch, Hadas. 2020. 'Clothing and colours in early Islam: Adornment (aesthetics), symbolism and differentiation', *Anthropology of the Middle East* 15(1): 99–114.

Hochschild, Arlie Russel. 2016. *Strangers in Their Own Land*. New York: New Press.

Hoffman, Valerie J. 2000. 'Muslim sainthood, women and the legend of Sayyida Nafisa', in Arvid Sharma (ed.), *Women Saints in World Religions*. Albany, NY: SUNY Press, 107–44.

Hole, Frank. 2004. 'Campsites of the seasonally mobile in western Iran', in Henrik Thrane, Ingolf Thuesen and Kjeld von Folsach (eds), *From Handaxe to Khan: Essays presented to Peder Mortensen on the Occasion of his 70th Birthday*. Aarhus: Aarhus University Press, 67–85.

Hole, Frank and Sekandar Amanolahi-Baharvand. 2021. *Tribal Pastoralists in Transition: The Baharvand of Luristan, Iran*. Ann Arbor, MI: University of Michigan Museum of Anthropological Archaeology.

Honarpisheh, Donna. 2013. 'Women in pilgrimage: senses, places, embodiment, and agency: experiencing *ziyarat* in Shiraz', *Journal of Shia Islamic Studies* 6(4): 383–410.

Huang, Julia. 2013. *Tribeswomen of Iran: Weaving Memories among Qashqa'i Nomads*. London: I. B. Tauris.

Hutter, Manfred. 1993. 'Naturvorstellungen im Zoroastrismus', *Zeitschrift für Religionswissenschaft* 1(2): 13–27.

Jeldtoft, Nadia. 2011. 'Lived Islam: religious identity with "nonorganized Muslim minorities"', *Ethnic and Racial Studies* 34(7): 1134–51, available at: http://www.tandfonline.com/loi/rers20, last accessed 29 June 2021.

Joyce, Rosemary A. 2020. 'Archaeology worlds, art worlds,' *Anthropology News Website*, November, available at: https://DOI 10.14506/AN.1542.

Kaim, Barbara. 2016. 'Women, dance and the hunt: splendour and pleasures of court life in Arsacid and early Sasanian art', in Vesta Sarkosh Curtis, Elizabeth J. Pendleton, Michael Alram and Touraj Daryaee (eds), *The Parthian and Early Sasanian Empires: Adaptation and Expansion*. Haverton, PA: Oxbow Books, 90–105.

Kalinock, Sabine. 2003. 'Between party and devotion: mowludi of Tehran women', *Critique. Critical Middle Eastern Studies* 12(2):173–87.

Kalinock, Sabine. 2004. 'Touching a sensitive topic: research on Shiite rituals of women in Tehran', *Iranian Studies* 37: 665–74.

Kakoliris, Gerasimos. 2015. 'Jaques Derrida on the ethics of hospitality', in Elvis Imafidon (ed.), *The Ethics of Subjectivity: Perspectives since the Dawn of Modernity*. London: Palgrave Macmillan, 144–56.

Kandiyoti, Denis, Nadja Al-Ali and Kathryn Spellman Poots (eds). 2021. *Gender, Governance and Islam*. Edinburgh: Edinburgh University Press.

Karimi, Maral. 2018. *The Iranian Green Movement of 2009*. Lanham, MD: Lexington Books.

Karimi, Maryam and Mary E. Hegland. *Daughter of the Iranian Revolution: A Village Widow's story*. In preparation.

Keddie, Nikki R. 2006. *Women in the Middle East: Past and Present*. Princeton, NJ: Princeton University Press.

Kemske, Bonnie. 2021. *Kintsugi: The Poetic Mend*. London: Bloomsbury.

Kian, Azadeh. 2023. *Rethinking Gender, Ethnicity and Religion in Iran*. London: I. B. Tauris/Bloomsbury.

Klimburg, Max. 2021. 'Religion in Parun', unpublished manuscript.

Knibbe, Kim and Helena Kupari. 2020. 'Theorizing lived religion'. *Journal of Contemporary Religion* 35(2): 157–76.

Koelz, Walter N. 1983. *Persian Diary, 1939–1941*. Ann Arbor, MI: University of Michigan Museum of Anthropology and Archaeology.

Kolb, Jonas and Erol Yildiz. 2019. 'Muslim everyday religious practices in Austria: from defensive to open religiosity', *Religions* 10(3): 1–15, available at: https://doi.org/10.3390/rel10030161, last accessed 5 January 2020.

Langer, Robert. 2004. 'From private shrine to pilgrimage center', in Michael Stausberg (ed.), *Zoroastrian Rituals in Context*. Leiden: Brill, 563–92.
Layton, Robert. 1991. *The Anthropology of Art*, 2nd edn. Cambridge: Cambridge University Press.
Leaman, Oliver. 2004. *Islamic Aesthetics*. Notre Dame, IN: University of Notre Dame Press.
Leaf, Murray. 2022. 'Kinship, genealogy, objectivity and ethnocentrism', *Kinship* 2(1): 28–62, available at: https://escholarship.org/uc/item/1n3646vq, last accessed 31 July 2022.
Leddy, Thomas. 2011. 'The aesthetics of junkyards', in David Goldblatt, Lee B. Brown and Stephanie Partridge (eds), *Aesthetics: A Reader in Philosophy of the Arts*, 3rd edn. Boston. MA: Prentice Hall, 345–49.
Lewis, Bernard. 1988. *The Political Language of Islam*. Chicago: University of Chicago Press, 91–116.
Loeffler, Agnes G. 2008. 'The indigenisation of allopathic medicine in Iran', *Anthropology of the Middle East* 3(1): 75–92.
Loeffler, Agnes G. 2015. *Health and Medical Practice in Iran*. London: I. B. Tauris.
Loeffler, Agnes G. and Erika Friedl. 2014. 'The birthrate drop in Iran', *Homo: Journal of Comparative Human Biology* 65: 240–55.
Loeffler, Reinhold. 1971. 'The representative mediator and the new peasant', *American Anthropologist* 73(5): 1077–91.
Loeffler, Reinhold. 1984. 'Lur hunting lore and the culture-history of the Shin', in Peter Snoy (ed.), *Ethnologie und Geschichte. Festschrift für Karl Jettmar*. Wiesbaden: Steiner, 399–409.
Loeffler, Reinhold. 1988. *Islam in Practice*. Albany, NY: State University of New York Press.
Loeffler, Reinhold. 1989. 'Boir Ahmadi I: The Tribe', in *Encyclopaedia Iranica* 4(3): 320–4.
Loeffler, Reinhold. 2002. 'The world of the people of Deh Koh', in Richard Tapper and Jon Johnson (eds), *The Nomadic Peoples of Iran*. London: Azimuth Editions, 134–43.
Loeffler, Reinhold. 2011. 'The ethos of progress in a village in Iran', *Anthropology of the Middle East* 6(2): 1–13.
Loeffler, Reinhold. 2022. 'The "Deep Believer" 30 years on, 1926–2008', *Anthropology of the Middle East* 17(1): 103–14.
Loeffler, Reinhold and Erika Friedl. 1967. 'Eine ethnographische Sammlung von den Boir Ahmad, Südiran', *Archiv für Völkerkunde* 21: 95–207.

Loeffler, Reinhold, Erika Friedl and Alfred Janata. 1974. 'Die materielle Kultur von Boir Ahmad, Südiran', *Archiv für Völkerkunde* 28: 61–142.

Loeffler, Reinhold and Erika Friedl. 2022. 'Mourning at New Year's day (nowruz): Cultural practice against ideology', *Anthropology of the Middle East* 17(1): 28–41.

Loeffler, Reinhold and Kati Loeffler. 2022. *Our Toil and God's Blessing: The Culture of Progress in an Iranian Tribal Village*. Bloomingdale, IN: Archway Publishing.

Lomax, Alan, Forrestine Paulay and Irmgard Bartieneff. 1974. *Dance and Human History: Movement, Style and Culture*, Film, University of California Extension Media Center. University Park, PA: Penn State Media Sales.

Lorimer, David L. R. and Emily O. Lorimer. 1919. *Persian Tales Written Down for the First Time in the Original Kermani and Bakhtiary*. London: Macmillan.

Luhrmann, Tanya M. 2020. *How God Becomes Real: Kindling the Presence of Invisible Others*. Princeton, NJ: Princeton University Press.

Lumsden, Andrew. 2021. 'Media Guide: Inflation in Iran', *American Iranian Council*, 2 May, available at: http://www.us-iran.org/resources/2019/1/20/media-guide-inflation-379ya, last accessed 7 May 2021.

Luz, Nimrod. 2019. 'Islamic pilgrimage observed: ruminations on an emerging field', Paper read at the Conference 'Pilgrimage Studies in the 21st Century', 12th International Colloquium Compostela, 23–24 October, Santiago de Compostela, Spain: Instituto de Estudios Gallegos Padre Sarmiento, available at: Researchgate.net/publication/336564753_Luz_N_Islamic_Pilgrimage_Observed_Ruminations_on_an_Emerging_Field_presented_at_the_12th_International_Colloquium_Compostela_Pilgrimage_Studies_in_the_21st_Century_Instituto_de_Estudios_Gallegos_Padre, last accessed 12 December 2020.

MacDonald, Brian. 2017. *Tribal Rugs: Treasures of the Black Tent*, 2nd edn. New York: ACC Art Books.

Maner, Çigdem. 2018. 'Weaving revolution in Anatolia: Historical and material value of wool from the Neolithic to the Iron Age', in Filiz Yenisehirlioglu and Gözde Ç. Yücel (eds), *Weaving the History: Mystery of a City, Sof*. Ankara: Koç University Ankara Studies Research Center, 43–63.

Manoukian, Setrag. 2012. *Shiraz: City of Knowledge*. New York: Routledge.

Marcus, George E. and Michael F. Fischer. 1986. *Anthropology as Cultural Critique*. Chicago: University of Chicago Press.

Marković, Slobodan. 2012. 'Components of aesthetic experience: aesthetic fascination, aesthetic appraisal, and aesthetic emotion', *IPerception* 3(1): 1–17, available at: https://doi.org/10.1068/i0450aap, last accessed 31 May 2020.

Marsden, Magnus. 2005. *Living Islam: Muslims Religious Experience in Pakistan's Northwest Frontier*. Cambridge: Cambridge University Press.

Marzolph, Ulrich. 2003. 'The martyr's way to paradise: Shiite mural art in the urban context', *Ethnologia Europaea* 33(2): 87–98.

Marzolph, Ulrich (ed.). 2006. *Nasreddin Hodscha. 666 Wahre Geschichten*, 3rd edn, München: C. H. Beck.

Marzolph, Ulrich. 2011. 'The Muslim sense of humour', in Hans Geybels and Walter Van Herck (eds), *Humour and Religion: Challenges and Ambiguities*. London: Continuum, 169–90.

Mashkour, Maryam. 2009. 'Faunal remains from Tol-e Nurabad and Tol-e Espid', in Daniel T. Potts, Kourosh Roustaei, Cameron A. Petrie and Lloyd R. Weeks (eds), *The Mamasani Archaeological Project: Stage I*. Oxford: Archaeopress, 135–46.

Mathiowetz, Michael D. and Andrew D. Turner (eds). 2021. *Flower Worlds: Religion, Aesthetics, and Ideology in Mesoamerica and the American Southwest*. Tucson: Arizona University Press.

McDougall, Lindy. 2021. *The Perfect Vagina: Cosmetic Surgery in the Twenty-first Century*. Bloomington, IN: Indiana University Press.

McGuire, Meredith B. 2008. *Lived Religion: Faith and Practice in Everyday Life*. Oxford: Oxford University Press.

McLean, Athena and Annette Leibing (eds). 2007. *The Shadow Side of Fieldwork: Exploring the Blurred Borders between Ethnography and Life*. Malden, MA: Blackwell.

Meri, J. W. 1999. 'The etiquette of devotion in the Islamic cult of the saints', in James Howard-Johnston and Paul A. Hayward (eds), *The Cult of the Saints in Late Antiquity and Middle Ages: Essays on the Contribution of Peter Brown*. Oxford: Oxford University Press, 263–86.

Mernissi, Fatema. 1977. 'Women, saints and sanctuaries', *Signs* 3(1): 101–12.

Mithen, Steven. 1996. *The Prehistory of the Mind: The Cognitive Origins of Art, Religion and Science*. London: Thames & Hudson.

Moaddel, Mansoor. 2020. *The Clash of Values: Islamic Fundamentalism versus Liberal Nationalism*. New YorkY: Columbia University Press.

Monsutti, Alessandro. 2020. *Homo Itinerans: Towards a Global Ethnography of Afghanistan*. Oxford: Berghahn.

Morphy, Howard and Morgan Perkins. 2006. 'Anthropology of arts: A reflection on its history and contemporary practice', in H. Morphy and M. Perkins (eds), *The Anthropology of Art: A Reader*. Hoboken, NJ: Wiley, 1–32.

Mouri, Chika, Abolfasl Aali, Xian Zhang and Richard Laurson. 2014. 'Analysis of dyes in textiles from the Chehrabad salt mine in Iran', *Heritage Science* 2014: 2–20.

Mousavi, S. Hamzeh. 2020. 'Terms of address and fictive kinship politeness in Luri', *Journal of Politeness Research* 16(2): 217–47.

Mulder, Stephennie. 2014. 'Shrines in the central Islamic lands', in Richard Etlin (ed.), *The Cambridge History of World Religious Architecture*, Cambridge: Cambridge University Press, 89–109.

Mushkat, Fred, John Wertime, Naheed Dareshuri, Lois Beck and Peter Andrews. 2020. *Weavings of Nomads in Iran: Warp-faced Bands and Related Textiles*. London: Hali Publications.

Narotzky, Susana. 2007. 'The project in the model: reciprocity, social capital, and the politics of ethnographic realism', *Current Anthropology* 48(3): 403–24.

Necipoğlu, Gülru. 1993. 'An outline of shifting paradigms in the palatial architecture of the pre-Islamic modern world', in Gülru Necipoğlu (ed.), *Pre-Modern Islamic Palaces. Ars Orientalis* 23: 3–24.

Netton, Ian Richard. 2013. *Orientalism Revisited: Art, Land and Voyage*. London: Routledge.

Opie, James. 1998. *Tribal Rugs*. London: Laurence King.

Olszewska, Zuzanna. 2013. 'Classy kids and down-at-heel intellectuals: status aspirations and blind spots in the contemporary ethnography of Iran', *Iranian Studies* 46(6): 841–62, available at: http://dx.doi.org/10.1080/00210862.2013.810078, last accessed 12 January 2022.

Özbaşaran, Mihriban and Gunes Duru. 2017. 'Asıklı Höyük', *Current Archaeology* 60: 31–5.

Panella, Christiana and Walter E. Little (eds). 2021. *Norms and Illegality: Intimate Ethnographies and Political Control*. Lanham, MD: Lexington.

Parsa, Fariba. 2021. 'Iranian women campaign to stop the rise in "honor killings"', *Middle East Institute*, 26 August, available at: https://www.mei.edu/publications/iranian-women-campaign-stop-rise-honor-killings, last accessed 28 August 2021.

Petrie, Cameron A. 2011. 'Culture, innovation and interaction across southern Iran from the Neolithic to the Bronze Age (ca. 6500–3000 BC)', in Benjamin Robert and Marc Vander Linden (eds), *Investigating Archaeological Cultures*. Berlin: Springer, 151–82.

Peleggi, Maurizio. 2022. 'When shrines and images grow tired: toward a theory of devotional conservation', *Res: Journal of Anthropology and Comparative Aesthetics* 77/78: 157–66.

Plichta, Pavel. 2023. 'The dynamics of modern pilgrimages from the inside', Panel at the 6th Conference of the European Academy of Religion, St. Andrews, Scotland, 19–23 June.

Poliakov, Sergei P. 1992. *Everyday Islam: Religion, Saints and Tradition in Rural Central Asia*. Armonk, NY: M. E. Sharpe.

Potts, Daniel T. 2019. 'Archaeology and the art of the ancient Near East', in Ann C. Gunter (ed.), *A Companion to Ancient Near Eastern Art*. Chichester: Wiley, 615–35.

Prum, Richard O. 2017. *The Evolution of Beauty*. New York: Doubleday.

Qummi, Sheykh Abbas. 1999. *Supplications, Prayers and Ziarats: Call on Me I Answer You*. Qum: Ansarian.

Rahim, Fazul. 2015. 'Afghan expensive wedding cap: lawmakers pass law limiting costs', *NBC*, 1 April 2015, available at: nbcnews.com/news/world/expensive-wedding-cap-lawmakers-pass-law-limiting-costs-n333971, last accessed 7 July 2020.

Redfield, Robert. 1941. *The Folk Culture of Yucatan*. Chicago: University of Chicago Press.

Reichenbach, Hans. 1956. *The Direction of Time*. Berkeley: University of California Press.

Rezvani, Reza and Ali Sayyadi. 2023. 'Religious Arabic exclamations in Persian talks-in-interaction: a micro-analytic approach to contexts and senses', *British Journal of Middle Eastern Studies* 50(3): 666–80, DOI: 10.1080/13530194.2021.1997713.

Richard, Yann. 1995. *Shiite Islam: Polity, Ideology, and Creed*, trans. Antonia Neville. Oxford: Blackwell.

Robbins, Joel. 2019. 'On knowing faith: theology, everyday religion, and anthropological theory', *Religion and Society: Advances in Research* 10: 14–29.

Rubin, William (ed.). 1987. *'Primitivism in 20th Century Art'*, 2 vols. New York and Boston: Museum of Modern Art/Little Brown.

Ryan, Michael J. 2018. *A Taste for the Beautiful: The Evolution of Attraction*. Princeton, NJ: Princeton University Press.

Saadi-Nejad, Manya. 2021. *Anahita: A History and Reception of the Iranian Water Goddess*. London: I. B. Tauris.

Salzman, Philip Carl. 1999. *The Anthropology of Real Life: Events in Human Experience*. Prospect Heights, IL: Waveland Press.

Schienerl, Peter W. 1984. *Tierdarstellungen im Islam* (*Animal Depictions in Islam*). Göttingen: Herodot.

Schmidt, Erich F. 1957. *Persepolis II: Contents of the Treasury and other Discoveries*. Chicago: University of Chicago Press.
Schulze-Holthus, Berthold. 1944. *Alibazer Lesebuch*. Manuscript.
Scruton, Roger. 2011. *Beauty: A Very Short Introduction*. New York: Oxford University Press.
Seremetakis, C. Nadia. 2019. *Sensing the Everyday: Dialogues from Austerity Greece*. London: Routledge.
Shahshahani, Soheila. 1982. *The Four Seasons of the Sun*. Ann Arbor, MI: University Microfilms International.
Shaw, Susan M. 2021. 'How "complementarianism" – the belief that God assigned specific gender roles – became part of evangelical doctrine', *The Conversation*, 12 April, available at: https://theconversation.com/how-complementarianism-the-belief-that-god-assigned-specific-gender-roles-became-part-of-evangelical-doctrine-158758, last accessed 14 April 2021.
Sheehan, Jonathan. 2003. 'Enlightenment, religion and the enigma of secularization: a review essay', *American Historical Review* 108(4): 1061–80, available at: https://doi.org/10.1086/ahr/108.4.1081, last accessed 26 March 2022.
Sheikhouni, Lena and Valentina Sinis. 2022. 'I wish I hadn't survived: why women are burning themselves in Iraqi Kurdistan', available at: https://www.bbc.com/news/av/world-middle-east-63958584, last accessed 18 October 2023.
Shusterman, Richard. 2011. 'In defense of popular arts', in David Goldblatt, Lee B. Brown and Stephanie Partridge (eds), *Aesthetics: A Reader in Philosophy of the Arts*, 3rd edn. Boston, MA: Prentice Hall, 327–32.
Siamdoust, Nahid. 2017. *Soundtrack of the Revolution: The Politics of Music in Iran*. Stanford, CA: Stanford University Press.
Simpson-Hebert, Mayling. 1987. 'Women, food and hospitality in Iranian society', *Canberra Anthropology* 10(1): 24–34.
Sophiamehr, Amin. 2012. 'The Regime of Martyrdom: The Mechanism of Inventing a New Shi'a Sovereignty During the Iran–Iraq War', MA Thesis, Oklahoma University.
Soudavar, Abolala. 1992. *Art of the Persian Courts*. New York: Rizzoli.
Statista Research Department. 2020. 'Volume of rice imports from Iran, 2015–2020', 26 August 2020, available at: statista.com/statistics/1035508/iran-import-volume-rice, last accessed 8 May 2021.
Steingass, Francis Joseph. 1963. *A Comprehensive Persian–English Dictionary*, 5th edn. London: Routledge & Kegan Paul.

Suzuki, Yuko. 2015. 'Between tradition and modernity: Došmanziyāri khans' adaptations to social change', in Anna Krasnowolska and Renata Rusek-Kowalska (eds), *Studies on the Iranian World II: Medieval and Modern*. Krakow: Iagiellonian University Press, 367–89.

Swinehart, Karl and Anna Brown Ribeiro. 2019. 'When time matters', *Signs and Society* 7(1): 1–5.

Ṭāheri, Ata. 2009. *Kuč, kuč: tagrobe-ye nim qarn-e zendegi dar Kohgiluye wa Boyr-Aḥmad*. (*Migration, Migration: Half a Century of Life Experiences in Kohgiluye and Boir Ahmad*). Tehrān: Soḫan.

Talhelm, Thomas. 2019. 'Why your understanding of collectivism is probably wrong', *Observer, Association for Psychological Science*, 29 October, available at: https://www.psychologicalscience.org/observer/why-your-understanding-of-collectivism-is-probably-wrong, last accessed 8 October 2021.

Triandis, Harry C. and fifteen co-authors. 2001. 'Culture and deception in business negotiations: a multilevel analysis'. *International Journal of Cross Cultural Management* 1(1): 73–90.

Tyson, Neil DeGrass. 2007. *Death by Black Hole*. New York: W. W. Norton.

Vahdat, Ahmed. 2018. 'Iran may flog or jail fans of "extreme" cosmetic surgery', *The Telegraph*, 14 November, available at: www.telegraph.co.uk/news/2018/11/14/Iran-may-flog-jail-fans-extreme-cosmetic-surgery, last accessed 10 May 2020.

Vahman, Fereydun and Garnik Asatrian. 1995. *Poetry of the Baxtiyārīs*. Copenhagen: Munksgaard.

Vali-Zade, Mahdieh. 2021. 'The aesthetic of desire and the feminine path of individuation: the case of Forough Farrokhzad', *Anthropology of the Middle East* 16(2): 110–27.

Van Bruinessen, Martin. 2002. *Mullas, Sufis and Heretics: The Role of Religion in Kurdish Society: Collected Articles*. Istanbul: Isis.

Van Bruinessen, Martin. 2008. 'Religious practices in the Turco-Iranian world: continuity and change', in Mohammad-Reza Djalili, Alessandro Monsutti and Anna Neubauer (eds), *Le Monde Turco-iranien en question*. Paris: Karthala, 123–42.

Van Bruinessen, Martin. 2009. '"Sufism", popular Islam and the encounter with modernity', in Muhammad Khalid Masud, Armando Salvatore and Martin van Bruinessen (eds), *Islam and Modernity: Key Issues and Debates*. Edinburgh: Edinburgh University Press, 125–57.

Van den Bos, Mathijs. 2002. *Mystic Regimes: Sufism and the State in Iran from the late Qajar Era to the Islamic Republic*. Leiden: Brill.

Van den Bos, Mathijs. 2007. 'Elements of neo-traditional Sufism in Iran', in Martin Van Bruinessen and Julia Day Howell (eds), *Sufism and the Modern in Islam*. London: I. B. Tauris, 61–75.

Vakirtzi, Sophia. 2018. 'The thread of life broken: spindles as funerary offerings in prehistoric Cyclades', *Arachne* 5: 100–10.

Vatandoust, Gholam Reza and Maryam Sheipari. 2021. 'Beyond the Sharia: "white marriage" in the Islamic Republic of Iran', in Janet Afary and Jesilyn Faust (eds), *Iranian Romance in the Digital Age: From Arranged Marriage to White Marriage*. London: I. B. Tauris/Bloomsbury, 55–78.

Vivier-Muresan, Anne-Sophie. 2006. *Afzād, Ethnologie d'un Village d'Iran*. Tehran: Institut Français de Recherche en Iran.

Voitel, Dumont du. 1994., *Macht und Entmachtung der Frau. Eine ethnologisch-historische Analyse*. Frankfurt am Main: Campus Verlag.

Wagner, Roy. 1985. *The Invention of Culture*. Chicago: University of Chicago Press.

Warnock Fernea, Elizabeth. 1969. *Guests of the Sheik: An Ethnography of an Iraqi Village*. New York: Doubleday.

Wellman, Rose. 2017. 'Sacralizing kinship, naturalizing the nation: blood and food in postrevolutionary Iran', *American Ethnologist* 44(2): 503–15.

Wellman, Rose. 2021. *Feeding Iran: Shi'i Families and the Making of the Islamic Republic*. Berkeley: University of California Press

Whitehead, Alfred North. 1928. *The Function of Reason*. Boston, MA: Bronson Beacon Press.

Whitehouse, Bruce. 2022. 'What Use is Cultural Relativism?' Panel at the 2022 Meeting of the American Anthropological Association, 9–13 November 2022, Seattle, WA.

Whitehouse, Bruce. 2023. *Enduring Polygamy: Plural Marriage and Social Change in an African Metropolis*. New Brunswick, NJ: Rutgers University Press.

Widengren, Geo. 1965. *Die Religionen Irans*. Stuttgart: W. Kohlhammer.

Wittgenstein, Ludwig. 1967. 'Lectures on aesthetics', in Cyril Barrett (ed.), *L. Wittgenstein Lectures and Conversations on Aesthetics, Psychology and Religious Belief*. Berkeley: University of California Press, 1–40.

Wittgenstein, Ludwig. 2022. *Philosophische Untersuchungen*. Frankfurt am Main: Suhrkamp Verlag.

Wragg Sykes, Rebecca. 2021. 'Ten things archaeology tells us about Neanderthals', *Anthropology News*, 1 March, available at: DOI: 10.14506/AN.1588, last accessed 2 March 2021.

Wright, Robin. 2015. 'The Islamist spectrum', Washington, DC: Wilson Center, 28 August, available at: wilsoncenter.org/article/the-islamist-spectrum, last accessed 18 April 2021.

Wulff, Hans E. 1966. *The Traditional Crafts of Persia*. Cambridge, MA: MIT Press.

Yaghoobi, Claudia. 2022. *Temporary Marriage in Iran*. Cambridge: Cambridge University Press.

Yavari, Neguin. 2019. 'Shifting modes of piety in early modern Iran and the Persephone zone', *Working Paper Series of the HCAS*, No. 10, Leipzig: University of Leipzig.

Zalta, Edward N. (ed.). 2014. *The Stanford Encyclopedia of Philosophy*. Stanford, CA: Stanford University Press.

Zargar, Cyrus Ali. 2011. *Sufi Aesthetics: Beauty, Love, and the Human Form in the Writings of Ibn 'Arabi and 'Iraqi*. Columbia, SC: University of South Carolina Press.

Zocchi, Dauro and Michele Fontefrancesco (eds). 2021, *The Ark of Taste in Tanzania: Food, Knowledge, and Stories of the Gastronomic Heritage*, available at: https://www.unisg.it/assets/zocchifontefrancesco_2021_ark-of-tanzania.pdf.

Zubaida, Sami and Richard Tapper (eds). 2011. *A Taste of Thyme: Culinary Cultures of the Middle East*. London: Tauris Parke.

Zulliger, Hans. 1977. *Der Zulliger Tafeln Test*, 4th edn. Bern: Huber.

Index

Abrahamic tradition, 9, 76, 90
accident, 74, 112, 159, 168, 174, 192, 193
acorn, 34, 56, 57, 58
 -bread, 56
Adam, 79
aesthetics, 1, 9, 10, 13, 15, 16, 20–1, 27, 28, 29, 31, 47, 71, 118
 appreciation of, 12, 25, 66, 70, 82
 benefits, 6, 74, 77, 107
 boundaries, 30, 54, 89, 131, 170
 and children, 160
 cluster, 39
 choices, 16, 28, 31, 33, 53, 1
 conundrum, 50, 125, 163, 187, 190
 of decay, 98
 denial, 212
 domain, 9, 10, 12, 15, 31, 36, 43, 118, 120, 124, 144, 194, 198, 201, 204
 domestic, 94, 103, 161
 of economy, 65, 166, 200
 and ethics, 34
 experience, 29, 38, 165
 family, 94, 110
 food performance, 55, 130
 gender, 39, 48, 51, 94, 117, 118, 123, 128, 145, 200

 in government, 51
 hospitality, 95, 157
 husbandry, 140, 142
 inheritance, 131, 135–6
 life, 151, 140, 204
 in logic, 175
 marital, 114, 110, 122, 124, 130–1, 150, 207–8
 modernity, 62, 207
 modesty, 47, 50, 78
 morality, 77
 in nature, 6, 74, 76, 101
 of perfectionism, 52, 55, 58
 Persian, 91
 in philosophy, 15, 28, 175
 pleasure, 22, 24
 poetry, 212
 political, 20, 28, 119
 of power, 6, 50, 119, 195
 of progress, 86
 qualities, 21, 25, 27, 29, 42, 47, 62, 153
 realism, 20
 religion, 24, 187, 191, 195, 201
 of rugs, 32
 satisfaction, 77
 scale, 30, 72, 123, 130

schema, 175
significance, 21, 23
   of skill, 27
   of small places, 168
   in social structure, 105, 136
   time and, 102
   of truth, 172
   urban, 6, 7, 1, 43
   value, 26, 27, 29, 68, 196
   vernacular, 14
   of work, 78, 81, 144, 162
afterlife, 9, 30, 36, 54, 157, 162, 168, 173, 199, 200
   aesthetics, 96
   merits, 198
   options, 96, 97
agnosticism, 10, 67, 79, 190, 211
agriculture, 2, 7, 57, 61, 73, 74, 79
   calendar, 89, 101
   fields, ix, 5, 7, 100, 102, 113, 135
   grinding stone, 57, 102
   irrigation, 116, 145
alcohol, 60, 148
alms, 8, 81, 198
amulet, 8, 24, 25, 66, 187, 202
androcentrism, 4
angel, 36, 77, 97
animals, 2, 5, 6, 9, 27, 40, 43, 46–8, 64, 73–4, 77, 80, 103–5, 113, 116, 138, 140–4, 151, 160, 162
   aesthetic value, 140, 141
   attitudes toward, 139, 141, 143
   dangerous, 140, 192
   domestic, 141–3
   health, 61, 139, 142, 142
   hungry, 90, 91, 139, 143
   killing of, 139, 141, 142

   sheep, 164, 169, 189
   wild, 140–1, 192
animism, 140
anthropocentrism, 74
anthropology, 1, 10, 16, 21, 28
antiquity, 24
apotropaic, 22, 23, 25, 28, 44, 175, 187
Arab, vii, 2, 22
   language, 174, 199
archaeology, 1–3, 12, 22, 23
architecture, 19
art, 1, 14, 18, 19, 21, 35, 139
   creations, 13, 15
   grave art, 20
   high art, 18, 19
   non-western, 21
   oral, 20
   Oriental art, 19
   permanent, 15
   photography, 20, 35
   urban, 23
assistance *see* help

bags, 26, 27
baker, 58, 63
bath house, 71
bazaar, 20, 23, 25, 44, 142, 146, 172, 208
   merchant, 39, 61, 157, 199
   shopping, 208
   urban, 27, 44
beauty, 2, 4, 10, 14, 20, 24, 32, 40, 42, 47, 68–9, 161
   bother, 70, 72–4, 85, 144, 188
   cosmetics, 37, 38, 47, 70
   danger, 41, 72, 73

beauty (*cont.*)
　as duty, 69
　ethics, 40, 43, 68, 69
　exotic, 21, 22
　and glasses, 39
　and health, 70, 176
　and religion, 187, 211
　weddings, 130
behaviour, 159, 168, 169, 201
　aesthetics, 155
　choices, 154, 184, 201
　control, 147, 159, 161
Bibi Hakimeh, 196
birth, 91, 92, 147, 204, 205
blacksmith, 24, 27, 79
blind, 39, 49, 147
blood revenge, 4
Blue Bead, 22, 25, 28, 44, 192
body language, 29
Boir Ahmad, 8, 11, 18, 19, 20, 22, 23, 32, 46, 56, 60, 79, 105, 142
　governor, 117, 205
books, 23
bread, 56, 58, 60, 82, 146
　acorn, 56, 58
　wheat, 57, 58, 91
bride, 70, 71, 123, 124, 211
　bridal gown, 35, 43, 131
　child bride, 123, 124
　consent of, 120, 123, 124, 125, 127, 129
　-groom, 63, 83, 115, 125, 151
　-price, 112, 113, 115, 124, 125, 130, 134, 151
　-wealth, 134
British Broadcasting Corporation (BBC), 180, 181, 182

calendars, 89, 91, 102
　calligraphy, 19, 20, 23
　cognitive map, 90
　New Year, 101
camel caravan, 5
carpet, 19, 22, 31, 44, 77; *see also* rug
cell phone, 92, 146
chance, 37, 86, 155, 192, 194, 203
character, 35, 153–7, 164–70
children, ix, 38, 47, 54, 61, 65, 69, 109–10, 113, 127, 160
　adoption, 210
　and animals, 142
　behaviour, 16, 93
　care of, 24, 64, 69, 77, 83, 205, 206, 209, 210
　chores, 94
　father, 82–4, 111, 119, 120
　health of, 62, 65, 169
　marriage of, 71, 123, 125
　mortality, 62, 112
　mother, 30, 156, 210
　motherless, 111, 117
　play, 64, 74, 121
　toddler, 30, 61, 63, 47, 48, 121
choices, 15, 20, 25, 29, 30, 37, 38, 68, 76, 79, 83, 84, 115
　beauty, 71
　behaviour, 184
　in beliefs, 173, 191
　change, 31, 36, 37, 66, 75
　for cohabitation, 130, 207, 208
　contradictory, 167
　critical, 201, 210
　in education, 80
　in ethics, 100–1, 139, 169, 176, 203

life, 93, 139, 146, 148, 163, 169, 191
  spouses, 117, 122
  for winner, loser, 107, 124, 133
  women's, 65, 84, 115, 128
city, 71, 127, 136, 142, 143, 208
coffee shop, 55
cognitive, 164, 175, 177
  map, 90, 174
  shortcuts, 175–84
colour, 39, 42, 46, 50
  categories
  choices, 44
  food, 54, 58, 60
  gender and, 43, 44, 46
  meanings, 41, 175
common sense, 15, 67, 77, 91, 144, 164, 167, 168, 194
  logic, 184
  religion, 170
community life, 190, 210
  collectivism, 108, 144, 168
competence, 30, 104, 159, 161–3
competition, 108, 117, 166, 206
computer, 52
corruption 8, 52, 139, 152, 155, 159, 171, 178, 206
  nepotism, 105
cosmology, 9, 98, 188, 189
crafts, 21
  craftsmen, 80, 88, 115, 145, 152, 212
creativity, 20, 21, 27
culture, 14, 22, 29, 202

daily life, 18, 164 167
dance, 38, 49, 51, 52, 130
  at grave, 51

danger, 3, 4, 12, 40, 72, 73, 74, 140, 165
daughter in law, 79, 86, 122, 126, 131, 136, 137, 149
Day of Judgement, 36, 200
death, 9, 18, 36, 43, 53, 74, 76, 96–9, 102, 103, 131, 138, 145
  commemoration, 51, 91, 100
  dead, 90, 103, 168
  elderly, 99, 191
  family members', 112, 128
  funeral 48, 162, 168
  government, 102, 148
  meaning, 95, 191
  mourning, 49, 51, 102, 210, 211
  women's, 83, 99, 117, 99
  see also suicide
demon, 151, 192
Dena Mountain, 4, 6, 60
dervish, 8, 158, 166–7
descent, x, 3, 106, 132, 133
developmental optimism, 203
devil, 48, 117
diaspora, 87, 205
divorce, 83, 119, 149, 208
doll, 21, 23
domestic, 64, 55, 75, 77, 116, 161
  decor, 20, 29
  duty 38, 76
  problems, 65, 74, 117, 120, 124
doubt, 66, 68, 104, 148, 155, 190, 191, 199, 202, 208
dream, 101
duty, 74, 81–5, 128, 189
dwellings, 26, 152; *see also* house

earthquake, ix, 6, 7, 61, 74, 87, 94, 106, 141, 152, 203, 211

economy, 7, 8, 33, 58, 60, 61, 67, 69, 87, 132, 193, 211
   bankruptcy, 130
   debts, 61, 70, 115, 130, 131
   domestic, 82, 206
   income, 8, 72, 80, 82, 83, 133, 146, 148, 165, 166
   loans, 61
   of marriage, 120, 129, 209
   modern, 146, 205
   money, 82, 112, 127, 134, 137, 146, 147, 152, 166, 167, 204
   opportunity, 205
   prices, 27, 33, 92
   property, 133, 135, 137, 153
   success, 72, 100, 166, 169, 200
   tradition, 81
   of weddings, 130, 134
   and women, 82, 84, 133
   see also work
education, 5, 6, 79, 86, 92, 99, 160
   decline of, 166
   and lifestyle, 165, 204
   literacy, 99, 103
   models, 170
   student, 75, 148, 175
   university, 79, 80, 85, 149, 152, 165, 168, 204, 205
elderly, 49, 53, 62, 64, 76, 95, 116, 137, 156, 193
   authority, 151, 205, 212
   care of, 118, 128, 131, 136, 137, 205, 209
   character of, 137, 164, 202
   death, 99, 191
   marriage, 208
electricity, 40, 77

emigration, 117, 118, 204–6, 208, 209
   inner, 211
emotions, seat of, 163, 164; *see also* feelings
empiricism, 68, 89, 97
   fact, 163, 164, 190
   observation, 91, 144, 154, 173
   see also experience
enemy, 105, 142
enlightenment, 13, 18, 165, 166
entropy, 97–9
environment, 2, 56
epistemological scepticism, 172
eschatology, 173
ethics, 5, 8, 9, 14, 18, 53, 62, 153, 185
   aesthetics and, 85, 117, 197
   alms, 198
   change in, 166, 203
   conflicts, 139, 172, 190
   food, 198
   sources of, 201
   of success, 139
   of work, 80
ethnicity, x, 2
ethnocentrism, 174
ethnography, vii, 11–13, 15, 31, 177, 186
evil eye, 22, 24, 25, 41, 73, 158, 192
evolution, 21
experience, 37, 38, 53, 89, 91, 100, 107, 147–9, 154, 165, 173, 192
   aesthetic frame of, 194
   and knowledge, 174, 201

fairy, 140, 141, 192
family, 62, 83, 105, 113, 114, 128, 129, 156, 170

aesthetics, 94
authority, 134, 138, 169, 151, 153, 156, 170
dissent, 133
duty, 73, 194
nuclear, 92, 105, 106, 210
property, 205
farmer, ix, 79, 97, 113, 141, 162, 189, 208
farming, 6, 22, 91, 143
Farsi, vii, 14, 111
fashion, 32, 42, 47, 204
fate, 189, 191
　of bride, 123, 126
　personified, 192, 193
　and wife, 192
fauna, 6
feeling, 52
　afraid, 137
　amused, 118
　anger, 85, 152, 156, 193
　anxiety, 63, 80, 83, 87, 99, 108, 109, 134, 142, 167, 203, 209
　bored, 92
　calm, 212
　cheerful, 87, 195
　comfort, 64, 79, 81, 85, 102, 128, 152
　depressed, 38, 85, 87, 206
　discontented, 87, 107, 118, 134, 135, 167, 206
　dismay, 203
　distrust, 109
　embarrassment, 52, 63, 86, 108, 109, 161
　empathy, 136, 137, 143, 155
　enmity, 133
　fear, 93, 160
　gratitude, 79, 85, 87, 101, 191, 194
　guilt, 104
　happy, unhappy, 50, 65, 85, 87, 90, 99, 116–17, 121, 124, 137
　intimacy, 63
　jealousy, 41, 72, 108, 109, 119, 193
　joy, 75–6, 80, 90, 102
　love, 120
　liking, 109
　lonely, 63, 82, 136, 137
　optimism, 203
　pleasure, 121, 135, 152, 198
　pride, 85, 101
　sad, 87, 99, 117, 137, 155, 167
　safe, 109, 162
　satisfied, 85, 116, 142
　sorry, 102, 137
　stressed, 85, 87
　tired, 81, 95
　troubled, 87, 152, 117
　vulnerable, 136
　weary, 117
　well, 64, 66, 68, 83, 102, 161
　see also women, work
felt, 26, 46
fight, 4, 6, 48, 84, 108, 141, 156, 169
five senses, 16, 30, 34, 36, 37, 101
flirt, 73, 150
folklore, 21
food, 2, 6, 8, 11, 17, 41, 53, 76, 82–3, 130, 139, 144–6, 169
　choice, 30, 53–5, 58–60, 81, 147
　drink, 60, 61
　economy, 26, 38
　ethics, 198
　game as, 2, 5, 19
　and health, 38, 62, 74, 108, 198

food (*cont.*)
  herbs, 55, 59, 65
  history, 54, 55, 108
  natural, 34, 58, 73, 75, 79
  politics of, 56
  status and, 26, 54, 198
freedom, 64, 107, 127, 151, 205, 210, 211
friendship, 36, 62, 95, 105, 108, 127, 148

garbage, 21, 27
garden, 6, 7, 26, 27, 35, 76, 147
  flowers, 46, 47
  merits of, 75, 100
gas, 6, 102
gender, 46, 77, 146
  aesthetics, 85, 94, 128, 200
  differences, 24, 67, 149, 155, 156, 200
  expectations, 116, 146
  ideology, 48, 84, 120
  imbalance, 208
  modesty, 63, 77, 102
  relations, 39, 81, 128, 145
generosity, 35, 157
girl, 41, 49, 69, 83, 118, 173
  benign neglect, 123
  dance, 50, 52
  games, 51, 52
  trauma, 124, 148
globalisation, 10
God, ix, 8, 30, 81, 82, 148, 168, 191, 211
  aesthetic structure of, 104
  before Islam, 196
  benevolent, 40, 66, 74, 79, 92, 191, 200, 202
  creator, 37, 67, 159, 188, 191, 196
  design of, 36, 38, 66, 89, 101
  doubts about, 98, 201, 202

gap-God, 98, 191
God-less, 105, 203
and hardships, 39, 104, 170, 189
must exist, 189, 191
in nature, 73, 201, 211
order of, 37, 40, 43, 53, 64, 67, 68, 78, 87–8, 170, 105, 189, 201
pleasing, 74, 77
and reason, 164–5, 194
Will of, 66–8, 72, 78, 88, 99–101, 123, 125, 139, 145, 156, 192, 194, 203, 210
work of, 154, 189
gold, 4, 23–5, 135
gossip, 73, 81, 97, 121, 134, 137–8, 149–50, 161, 171, 193
government, ix, x, 3, 6, 7, 8, 9, 10, 11, 135
  aesthetics, 20, 48, 51
  authority, 211
  Green party, 75, 77
  demonstrations, ix, 10, 151, 167
  Islamic, 101, 195, 211
  officials, 86, 167, 188
  services, 126, 58, 61
  theology of, 189, 211
  unsuccessful, 164
gratitude, 101, 191, 194
grave, 20, 40, 53, 91
  grave-house, 103
  visits, 89, 100, 101, 103
Gulf, 3, 7, 23, 24, 197
gun, 4, 5, 31, 141
gypsies, 24, 25

health, 24, 27, 61, 65, 68, 70, 71, 102, 108, 130, 206

and beauty, 37–8, 176
choices, 192
cigarettes, 62, 170
clinic, 77
diseases, 74, 100, 143, 148, 190, 192
doctors *see* physician
epidemics, 143
exercise, 75, 147
and food, 54, 56, 58, 59, 62, 108
Galen, 54, 59, 60
self-harm, 65, 81
stories, 172, 175
surgery, 37–9, 70, 71, 72
veterinarian, 142
weight, 147, 199
wellbeing, 105, 145
and women, 117, 123, 147, 149, 191
hearing, 47; *see also* sound
heathen, 196
hell, 65, 103
help, 201, 202
   options for, 202
   from people, 68, 104, 105, 108, 153, 162, 202
   from prayer books, 198
   from saints, 194–7
herding, 2, 19, 23, 26, 77, 80, 90, 133, 143–4, 117
   economy, 117, 140–3
heuristics, 164
history, x, 1, 2, 5
hizbollah, 52, 78, 85, 151, 158, 206
hospitality, 12, 59, 61, 118, 152–3, 158
   aesthetics, 95, 157
   burden, 158
   competition, 158

host/guest, 30, 35, 53, 54, 118, 130 139, 152, 158
   virtue, 167
hostility, 117, 158
house, 2, 7, 41, 62, 74, 76, 77, 90, 118, 128, 150, 152, 176
   aesthetics, 35, 103
   apartment, 119, 152, 153, 208
   chaotic, 169
   comfort, 52, 57, 117, 145, 146, 152
   courtyard, 75, 102, 124
   furniture, 77, 134
   indoor, outdoor, 102, 115, 152
   kitchen, 77, 118, 134, 137, 149
   liminal space, 74
   master of, 38, 48
   modern, 60, 61, 87, 90, 203
   mud brick, 23
   plumbing, ix, 53, 60, 71, 77, 118
   rental, 166
   stone hut, 25
human, 153, 163
   agency, 189, 190
   habits, 138
   nature, 139, 144, 154, 159, 160
   needs, 144, 145, 185
   qualities, 105, 153, 156, 159, 144
humour, 48–9, 54, 72, 92, 102, 125, 127, 145–6, 172, 198
   fate, 192
   in folklore, 158
   joke, ix, 29, 41, 52, 53, 54, 64, 70, 77, 92, 96, 102, 149, 158, 179
   leisure, 146, 147
   Nasreddin, 48
   next world, 155
   polygyny, 149, 150

humour (*cont.*)
   sex, 149
   valued, 155, 169
hunting, 5, 6, 55, 59, 79, 14, 140, 143, 192
   game, 19, 20, 141
   hunter, 55, 101, 141
   hunting-gathering, 2, 5, 41
husbandry *see* herding
husband/wife, 113, 114, 208, 170, 207
   co-wife, 207, 208
   see also gender, family

identity, x, 3, 10, 16, 23, 31, 32
   and music, 52, 85
   national, 102, 108
   Shia, 188
ideology, 120, 167
Imam Husein, 51, 198
Imamzadeh *see* shrine
immigration, 206
incest, 148, 210
individuation, 211
in-laws, 116, 122, 126, 129
Internet, 52, 82, 85, 97, 125, 126
inheritance, 7, 100, 107, 112–15, 131–2, 134–5, 137
   aesthetics, 131, 135, 136
   choices, 132
   conflicts, 120, 131–3, 156, 157, 209
   and education, 133
   equal vs equitable, 131, 133
   heir, 132–3
   ultimogeniture, 131, 208
   of widow, 135, 136
Isfahan, 55, 56
Islam, 8–10, 13, 67, 102
   beauty of, 197
   doctrine of, 204
   guidance, 197–8, 212
   hegemonic, 188
   local, 186
   pre-Islam, 196; *see also* shrine, Zoroaster
   uses of, 170
   see also mullah
Islamic
   authorities, 61
   government, 170, 203, 211, 212
   law, 118, 131, 133–6, 141
   Republic, 48, 52, 83, 92, 135, 170, 187
   theology, 144, 168

Japan, 19, 20, 98, 204
jewellery, 23, 71, 135
   beads, 66
   gold, 4, 23–5, 135
   watch, 91, 92
   see also gold
jinn, 5, 19, 22, 24, 71, 74, 141, 165, 167, 174
job, 5, 8, 53, 61, 80, 84, 127, 205
   choices, 166, 167, 169, 196, 208
joke *see* humour
Judgement, 15, 18, 27, 31, 94, 102, 106–7, 119, 144, 155, 168, 175
   Day of, 36, 200
   human, 190
justice, 72, 191, 206
   cosmic injustice, 200
justification, 167

Khan, chief, x, 3, 4, 6, 7, 10, 12, 13, 50
   dwellings, 26, 27, 32, 76

era of, 92
lifestyle, 56, 57, 86, 118–19, 121
opinion leaders, 168
oppressive, 62, 119, 160, 170, 191
order, 160, 170
status, 117, 119, 121
and women, 118, 119, 121, 126, 135
kin, 86, 106, 110, 115, 130
  aesthetics, 30, 107, 111, 116
  competition, 106
  descent, x, 3, 104, 106, 132–3
  diaspora, 204, 205
  interaction, 106, 113–16, 138, 146, 154
  obligations, 100, 101, 106–8
kin-group, 82, 83, 165
kin-terms, 105, 109–11, 114
  modern, 109
  use of, 109, 112, 113
kindness, 30, 54, 105
knowledge, 37
  religious, 199
  sources of, 144, 154, 173, 201–2
  see also experience
Kohgiluye-and-Boir-Ahmad, x, 1, 3, 33
Kuwait, 22

land, 82, 112, 146
  landscape, 2, 41, 47
  reform, 6
language, 2, 15, 28
law, 118, 131, 133–6, 141
  lawful 156
  lawyer, 84
lazy, 81, 86, 102
lie, 37, 99, 100, 169

and truth, 171, 173
uses of, 172
life, 104, 164, 190
  aesthetics, 37, 140, 155, 165–7, 204, 205
  creation of, 98
  everyday life, 14, 177
  life-soul, 140
  logic of, 139
  philosophy, 9, 166
lifecycle, 94, 137, 149
  elderly, 64, 66, 86, 94
  and gender, 95
  rituals, 94, 95
  women's, 58, 61, 62, 83, 95
life-style, 7, 8, 10, 77, 146
  aspirations, 85, 86, 92, 14, 128, 146, 167, 203, 204, 205, 212
  choices, 151, 166, 167, 204
lifeways, 1, 2, 12, 55, 101, 196
light and dark, 40
logic, 174–6
  aesthetics of, 175
  as cultural system, 175
  scientific, 174, 175
  vernacular, 174, 175
love, 49, 122, 149
  language, 121
  sick, 148–9
  songs, 121, 148
  wife, 119, 207
Lur, x, 1, 2, 5, 6, 26, 32, 48, 158, 172
  music, 52
Lurestan, 20, 22
Luri
  language, vii, 2, 4, 14, 111
  lyrics, 4, 47

magic, 125; *see also* amulet
marriage, 127, 149
   aesthetics, 114, 118, 120, 129 131, 147, 207, 209
   arranged, 122, 125, 127
   child marriage, 121, 124
   choices, 112, 113, 204, 207
   companionate, 206
   contract, 83, 116, 118, 123, 130
   costs of, 120, 129, 209
   expectations, 129, 204, 206
   levirate, 120, 210
   monogamy, 118, 122
   permit, 169
   polygyny, 118, 119, 120, 149, 150, 207
   remarriage, 136, 137, 149
   wedlock, 209
   white marriage, 207
Mathnavi, 200
memory, 1, 5, 8, 9, 20, 33, 56, 94, 95, 125, 141, 157, 174
   of dead, 100
merchant, 89, 101, 157, 172
merits, 54, 68, 157
methodology, 15, 17
migrations, 2, 26, 91, 93, 94
millenarianism, 204
modernity, 3, 13, 16, 24, 32, 47, 71, 118
   aesthetics, 195, 198
   and Islam, 186
   in kin-groups, 107, 116
   modern times, 130, 141
   post-revolutionary, 50, 54, 199
   urban, 188
modesty, 32, 33, 36, 38, 148

aesthetics, 47, 50, 151
   of women, 48–9, 161
morality, 68, 69, 140, 142, 145, 153, 157
   as burden, 87
   choices, 144, 210
   sexual, 63, 77
   useful, 210, 211
mosaic, 20, 35
mosque, 7, 35, 90, 101, 102, 180, 187, 193, 211
   beauty of, 195
   and gender, 90, 187
   sponsor, 198
mother, 109, 122, 159, 176, 192, 209
   is best, 106, 156
   of bride, 83
   capable, 161–2
   and children, 83, 91, 95, 121, 171, 190
   and daughter, 112–13, 118, 123–5, 129, 143, 149, 161, 172
   divorced, widowed, 209, 136
   and God, 194
   and son, 101, 110, 130, 132, 134, 137, 149, 154, 157, 165, 167, 211
mulla, 165
Mullah, 8, 20, 38, 49–50, 67, 69, 90, 92, 102, 153, 175, 178, 187, 199, 204
   doubted, 96, 173
   judge, 118, 119
   preacher, 8, 36, 90
   wife of, 105
   see also mosque
museum, 21, 22
music, 47, 48, 50, 52, 121
Muslim, 8, 10, 13, 19, 188

duty, 157
good, 168, 188
mysticism, 201

nature, 6, 33, 67, 74, 75, 76, 98, 101, 140
   film, 143
   and God, 73, 201
   human, 4, 34
   problems with, 33, 74, 75, 105
   useful, 76
necessity, 140, 157, 171, 192–3, 204, 206
neighbours, 104, 108–10, 116, 130, 135, 150, 155, 160, 168, 169
neolithic, 2, 27, 56, 57
nomad, 2, 19, 46
nostalgia, 8, 19, 20, 41, 58, 143, 144

oak, 2, 3, 6, 56, 74, 140
oath, 173
observation, 144, 154, 173
orchard, 4, 7, 62, 73, 74, 75, 79, 100, 102, 113
order, 53, 105, 123; *see also* God
orientalism, 29

pain, 15, 36, 64, 65, 66, 72, 104, 116
   of work, 78, 79, 86
paradise, 9, 62, 75, 76, 79, 96–7, 103, 157
parents, 79, 80, 81, 86, 106, 111, 113, 129, 156–7, 205
   authority, 129
   care of old, 128
   choices of, 164, 166, 167
   death of, 128
   discipline, 156, 162, 170
   see also children, mother

passion, 121, 148
pastures, 4, 5, 62, 71, 90, 140, 143
peace, 107, 117, 133, 167
perfectionism, 52, 58
performance, 20, 158
Persian, 41, 74, 75, 76, 90, 153, 156–7, 159, 179
pets, 141
philosophy, 15, 19, 64, 159, 188
physician, 39, 62, 66, 72, 77, 78, 99, 143, 147, 148, 172–3, 199, 208
   cosmetic surgery, 37, 38, 70
pilgrimage, 34, 101, 186, 195, 196, 197; *see also* shrine
pleasure, 54, 58, 61–2, 75, 116, 117
   of work, 78–81
poetry, 20, 211, 212
police, 11, 12, 17
population increase, 7, 143
poverty, 4, 8, 59, 62, 72, 76, 85, 92, 108, 145, 166
   aesthetics, 200
   poor–rich gap, 8, 207, 212
   see also wealth
power, 4, 6, 12, 119, 173, 177
   of elders, 121, 137
   extra-human, 192, 194
practice, 13, 18, 120
pragmatism, 99, 185, 196
prayer, 90, 92, 100, 101, 167, 198, 201
   books, 198
   circles, 187, 212
presentism, 88, 96
progress, 4, 6, 7, 20, 37, 38, 61, 66, 77, 83, 88, 91, 162, 203, 205
   aesthetics of, 86
   in culture, 165, 175, 204

progress (*cont.*)
   expensive, 142, 203
   kin, 114
   and mullah, 93
   reason, 164, 165, 188, 194
   work, 82
Prophet Muhammad, 8, 44
   and saints, 194, 196
punishment, 64, 66, 105

Qashqa'i *see* tribe
Quran, 6, 20, 25, 69, 97, 130, 173, 174

real estate, 7, 133
realism, 20, 98, 144, 200
reality, 188
reason, 3, 54, 62, 68, 101, 144, 148, 154, 162, 167, 173
   in animals, 140, 142
   as authority, 164
   explanations for, 164, 191–2
   features of, 153, 164, 200
relatives, 82, 83, 86, 92, 106, 114, 124; *see also* kin
religion, 89, 91, 104, 157, 167, 187–8
   aesthetics of, 54, 187, 191
   authority, 97, 135, 187
   benefits of, 187, 188, 196, 200, 201
   and common sense, 170, 188, 191
   future of, 212
   lived religion, 186–7
   merits, 74, 75, 78, 80
   piety, 210–12
   prescriptions and proscriptions, 199
   private, 211
   theodicy, 66, 189

resources, 132, 134
revolution, 11, 20, 101, 160
ritual, 196, 201, 211, 212
robber, 3, 4, 12, 40, 74, 165
rugs *see* weaving

Safavid, 3, 23, 26
saint, 30–1, 54, 66, 72, 195
   cult of, 195, 196
   efficacy of, 195–7
   God's clerk, 196
   patron-client, 194
   powers, 187, 194
   visits, 159, 195
   vows to, 54, 159, 195, 197
Sasanian, 3, 5
scepticism, 9, 10
science, 163, 166, 173, 190
   scholar, 13, 165
   times of, 188, 204
school, 4, 11, 38, 47, 55, 69, 70, 78, 79, 89, 91, 97, 100, 118, 122, 124
   gender, 80, 84
   student, 73, 109, 125
   see also teacher
servant, 36, 83, 205, 210
   maid, 115, 170
sex, 48, 78, 148
   as burden, 149, 150
   harassment, 63, 77
   homosexuality, 148
   incest, 148, 210
   marital, 124–5, 130, 147, 149
   men and, 77, 144–7, 210
   as need, 144, 146, 148, 207
   pornography, 125
   prostitution, 148

purpose of, 131
as sin, 150
modern, 151, 207
Seyed, 8
Shah era, 92
Shia Islam, 8, 9, 10, 186, 202
ideology, 3
theology, 101, 102
see also Islam
Shiraz, 17, 108
shrine, 5, 9, 34, 101, 187, 196
beauty of, 195–6
miracles, 195, 197
modern, 196
pre-Islamic, 195
siblings, 111–13, 126, 134, 146, 150, 158
inheritance, 132, 135
sight, 39–41
sin, 52, 66, 68, 81, 87, 92, 104, 107, 125, 141
of ancestor, 104, 200
against animals, 143
punished, 173, 191, 193
sex, 148
single women, 127, 136, 208, 210
Sisakht, 3–8, 10–13, 17, 22, 25, 29, 48, 74, 78, 81, 90, 91, 158, 188
administrator, 210
spirit of, 87, 97
town council, 108, 135
slingshot, 23, 142
smell, 53–6, 58
society
aesthetics, 153, 157, 160
class, 7, 97
social status, 24–6, 29, 33, 35, 41–2,
49–50, 53–4, 58–9, 84, 86, 72, 79, 112, 165, 168–9 173, 208
see also khan
song lyrics, 47, 49, 82, 148
soul, 36, 40, 140
sounds, 15, 27, 47, 48
laughter, 48
singing, 49–52, 63, 69
spindle, 25
spirituality, 210, 211
spouse, 13, 82, 83, 121, 129, 148
selection 122, 126, 128
stranger, 105, 113–17, 127, 136, 141, 152, 167
dangerous, 158
success, 72, 100, 166, 169, 200, 206
Sufi, 9, 187, 194, 212
suicide, 65, 83, 84, 85, 117, 118, 148
suitor, 72, 128, 137, 150, 209
qualities, 207
rejected, 124, 126, 127, 207
suspicion, 109, 168
sword, 3
symbol, 18, 20

Tang-e Servak, 1
tattoo, 71–2
taxes, 8, 57
tea, 47, 60, 77, 82
teacher, 5, 6, 14, 38, 41, 52, 58, 64, 80, 81, 84, 88, 99, 168, 208
salary, 82, 85, 118, 165
tutor, 85
Tehran, 6, 11, 12, 24, 29
telephone, 82, 204
television, 34, 47, 52, 83, 146, 187
tent, 2, 22, 25, 26, 45, 77

theodicy, 66, 189
theology, 187, 189, 194, 196
thief, 141, 165
    theft, 160, 169, 187, 189
time, 82, 88–9, 91, 100, 103
    aesthetic constant, 88
    arrow, 96, 97
    blocks of, 91, 92
    clocks, 92
    cyclical, 96, 97
    end of, 96, 97
    era, 92, 100
    festivities, 90
    and God, 88
    movement of, 88, 91, 92
    past and future, 87, 88, 89, 99, 100, 203, 204, 210
    philosophy, 88
    seasons, 4, 88, 100–2, 142
    terminology, 88
tourism, 6, 7, 12, 26, 27, 205
    pilgrimage as, 196, 197
transhumance, 1, 3, 4, 6, 12, 16, 19, 23, 27
travel, 30, 34, 61, 82, 89, 119, 129, 146, 201, 204
trees, 56, 73, 76, 79
    as claim-stakes, 56
    cult-place, 195
    merits of, 100
tribe, x, 1, 2, 3, 4, 5, 6, 26, 32, 106, 121
    Nuï, 5, 26
    Oulad Mirza Ali, 3, 42, 46
    Qashqa'i, 5, 8, 14, 41, 55, 142
    Teïbi, 46
    tribal chic, 4
    tribal emblem, 45

truth, 99, 173
    dangerous, 173
    and lies, 171

United States, 157, 204
urban, 7, 10, 35, 43, 47, 53, 205
urban models, 130, 152, 207
    cohabitation, 207, 208, 130
    fashions, 35, 69
    kin terms, 109
    marriage, 119, 131
    relatives, 146

vibe, 177, 192, 196
video recording, 20, 35, 95
violence, 4, 5, 83, 85, 142, 150, 170
    aggression, 48, 139, 153, 156
    assassination, 158
    domestic, 117, 170
    and government, 188
    and children, 64, 156, 160

war, 4, 20, 92, 102, 212
wealth, 6, 8, 12, 26, 200, 207; *see also* economy, poverty
weaving, 25, 31, 33
    aesthetics of, 162
    bags, 26, 27
    dye, 42, 45
    economy, 32, 33
    flat weave, 26, 46
    loom, 25, 31
    patterns, 25, 31, 45
    rugs, 25, 31–2, 45–6
    uses, 46
    women's work, 32, 45
wedding, 33, 49, 50, 52, 102, 120, 130

costs, 130
music, 52, 131
night, 125, 126
widow, 136–8, 149
   choices, 48, 209
   inheritance, 135–6
widower, 127, 137
wild rue, 25, 26, 72, 175, 176
women, x, 146, 147, 168
   character, 117, 120, 210
   dependent, 136, 146, 208
   expectations of, 128, 208
   inheritance, 133, 135
   pregnancy, 147, 199
   protest, 65
   rights of, 121
   rituals, 202
   safety, 75
   shortage of, 123
   work, 31, 41, 47, 53, 56–60, 81–4, 118, 128, 129, 134, 145, 162, 205, 208–9
wood carving, 22, 23, 25, 31, 82
woods, 5, 140, 141
work, 64, 78, 81–2, 84, 85, 94, 144
   as burden, 78, 86, 208
   choice, 204
   as duty, 78, 81
   as necessity, 78, 81
   as punishment, 79
   religious merits, 78, 79
   skills, 81, 94
   white collar, 79, 81, 86
   workers, 79, 81
   see also women
world, 16, 96, 188, 189
   end of, 96, 173, 190, 204

Yasuj, 92

Zagros mountains, ix, 1, 2, 3, 4, 12, 15, 16, 56, 57, 73, 155
Zoroaster, Zoroastrian, 5, 74, 157
Zulliger (Tafeln Test), 23

EU Authorised Representative:
Easy Access System Europe Mustamäe tee 50, 10621 Tallinn, Estonia
gpsr.requests@easproject.com

Printed and bound by CPI Group (UK) Ltd, Croydon, CR0 4YY
02/03/2026
02063697-0004